THE TORRES STRAIT

THE TORRES STRAIT

People and History

by John Singe

University of Queensland Press

Typeset by Press Etching Pty Ltd, Brisbane
Printed and bound by Southwood Press Pty Ltd, Sydney

Distributed in the United Kingdom, Europe, the Middle
East, Africa, and the Caribbean by Prentice Hall
International, International Book Distributors Ltd.,
66 Wood Lane End, Hemel Hempstead, Herts., England

National Library of Australia
Cataloguing-in-Publication data

Singe, John Charles, 1950—
   The Torres Strait

   Index
   Bibliography
   ISBN 0 7022 1417 5

   1. Torres Strait — History. I. Title.

994'.3[8]

Contents

Which Culture?

Illustrations

Acknowledgments

Thanks are due to the staffs of the Australian War Memorial, Canberra, the Mitchell Library, Sydney, the University of Papua New Guinea Library, the John Oxley Library, Brisbane, and, in particular, to the staff of the National Library of Australia, Canberra for their assistance in locating resource materials. Angus & Robertson Publishers kindly granted permission to reproduce some illustrations.

Thanks also to Dave Bartlett, John Manasero, Peter Berends, Tony Knight, Neal Smith and Mr Foster for allowing me access to private photographs, and to Len King of Newell Beach for assistance in the preparation of some photographs.

In particular I would like to express my appreciation of Billai Laba's assistance in those sections relating to the Western Province of Papua New Guinea.

My thanks as well to the hundreds of people — Torres Strait Islanders, Malays, Japanese, Papuans, Aborigines, Europeans and others — who, perhaps unknowingly at the time, contributed to this book.

Last, but not least, thanks to my wife for her endless patience and for her assistance, and that of her family, in putting this work together.

Preface

The Torres Strait is a beautiful but harsh environment. Nature does not give, and never has given, quarter to those who are unequal to its demands. In these challenging surroundings the Torres Strait Islanders made a home. Over the centuries they created a life style unique in the region, one totally integrated with the sea.

The arrival of other groups more than a hundred years ago forced changes upon the indigenous groups, obliterating some in the process. However the Islanders, though subdued, have clung to their traditions and their languages and were not generally dispossessed of their land. The newcomers, whether South Sea, Japanese, Malay or European, have all contributed something to the current of events since their arrival.

This is the story of all these people and the region in which they live, including the two mainlands to the north and south. The Torres Strait forms an important island bridge between Australia and its near neighbour Papua New Guinea.

Given the character of the Torres Strait and its inhabitants, it is perhaps inevitable that others may dispute my version of events. In researching oral histories especially there are always discrepancies, and I have tried to allow for this as much as possible. An informant often tells you what he thinks you want to be told or what he wants you to believe. I have heard, for example, some Islanders praise the extended family and the manner in which it is claimed to function for the benefit of all family members. Alternatively, other Islanders — mainly youngsters — feel it is more like an elaborate system of extortion. There are elements of truth in both versions but such discrepancies are difficult to reconcile.

I have deliberately not acknowledged individual Island informants. Their views were expressed to me in informal conversations over a number of years — before I had any intention of writing this book. Consequently their candid and unguarded comments reflect more accurately the reality of their situation, although I must respect their privacy here. A reliable informant was usually the source for each item relating to customary Island life, to which I added what I have observed and experienced myself.

Recent publications on the Torres Strait, some written by Islanders (Ephraim Bani's language studies of the Mabuiag dialect for example) and others direct from Island sources (Margaret Lawrie's myths and legends) have been the subject of considerable criticism by Islanders. My history must run as well the gauntlet of an ingrained prejudice in the region which rejects unpleasant details of the past, in favour of more popular, romanticized versions.

I have attempted in this book to examine the influences at work both within and outside Island society over the last few centuries and the extent to which these are responsible for the situation which exists in the Torres Strait today. I have tried to make this the Islanders' story and I hope I have succeeded. As a general rule I have included Europeans only in regard to interaction with indigenous people and the environment. This may disappoint those who expect a history of white settlement though I do not believe this book is deficient in that respect.

I have endeavoured, when discussing islands, to use the Island language name, partly for the purposes of consistency and partly because it seemed more appropriate. Thursday Island, having been continuously occupied by Europeans for a century and having been exploited and adapted to meet European demands, is the exception. Because it alone is stamped as a Westernized community, it is called by its European name.

Names of features on northern and southern mainlands are those by which they are normally addressed today.

Below is a list of islands with Island language names on the left and European names on the right.

*Boigu**	Talbot
*Saibai**	
*Dauan**	Mt Cornwallis
Buru	Turnagain*
Gebar	Two Brothers
(or Gabba)*	
*Mabuiag**	Jervis
*Badu**	Mulgrave
*Moa**	Banks
Palilug	Goode*
Keriri	*Hammond**
Waiben	*Thursday Island**
Muralug	*Prince of Wales**
Nurapai	*Horn**
Gialug	Friday*
Zuna	Entrance*
Packe*	
Tuined	Possession*
Muri	Adolphus*
Nahgi*	Mt Earnest
Mawai	Wednesday*
Waraber	Sue*
Poruma	Coconut*
Masig	Yorke*
Iama	Yam*
Ugar	Stephen*
Erub	Darnley*
Mer	Murray*
Dauar* }	
Waier* }	Murray Islands

The asterisks indicate the name in common usage today. It is no coincidence that on those six inhabited islands still popularly known by their Island name, the Western Island language is the normal language for communication. In the Central and Eastern Islands, broken English, augmented by snatches of Island language, is normally used and this tendency is reflected in the general use of the English names for islands in this area.

Those islands italicized in the left column are those occupied by predominantly traditional communities. Those italicized on the right are occupied by predominantly European, immigrant Island or mixed race communities.

This is not an anthropological work. The recommended anthropological study is the multi-volume *Reports of the Cambridge Anthropological Expedition to Torres Strait*. Those interested in legends should read *Myths and Legends of Torres Strait* by Margaret Lawrie.

Originally I intended to write language phonetically but a number of problems arose. Although Island languages are not often written there is an accepted spelling for certain words and names that is not phonetic. Badu is actually pronounced Badthoo by many Western Islanders, and I have seen Nahgi spelt Nagi, Nagir, Nagheer, and Naghir. Also the various Island dialects have varying and still evolving pronunciations of the same word. Masig for example was recorded as Masseed a century and a half ago. Mabuiag is generally pronounced "Maubiag" — except by some Western Islanders which seems to suggest that Mabuiag may be a correct phonetic version of the original pronunciation. Added to this, my knowledge of Eastern Island language is not sufficient for me to compose words on a phonetic basis. It should be noted however that in Western Island language there is rarely a "d", "t", or "th" as such. The tongue is actually placed in a position at the back of the teeth to produce a "dth" or "tth" sound. So I have written phonetically those words for which a spelling does not appear to be established.

The publications I referred to for information are listed, chapter by chapter, at the back of the book.

JOHN SINGE
Port Douglas, 1979

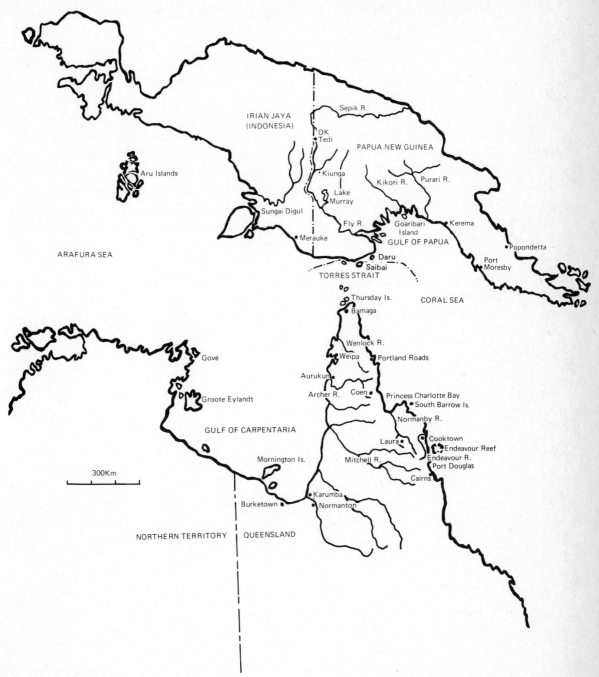

1. Map showing the vital position of the Torres Strait in relation to the Australian and New Guinean mainlands.

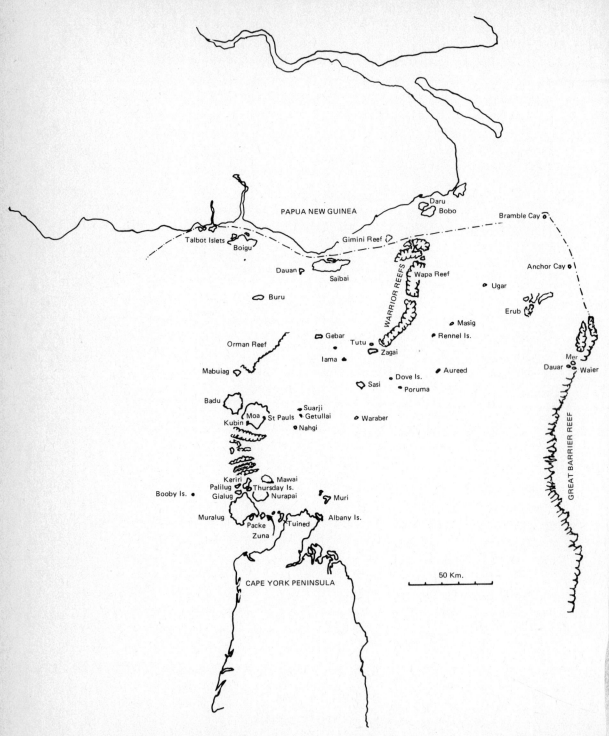

2. Map of the Torres Strait Islands. The area is a maze of reefs, many as yet uncharted.

Introduction

Between Australia and Papua New Guinea

In Papua and North Queensland there are many plants and animals which are similar if not the same — nail tail wallabies, cassowaries, sulphur crested cockatoos, black snakes, death adders, goannas, eucalyptus trees, ti trees and pitcher plants. During the last Ice Age the two mainlands were joined and the interchange of plants and animals resulted in similar environments on both sides of the Torres Strait. Today however the southern side is sandy with some raised areas, whereas the northern side is absolutely flat and composed entirely of brown alluvial soil, which turns quickly to mud with the heavier rainfall that the northern side receives. Tropical savannah is general on both sides, with pockets of rainforest, although there are more mangrove swamps in the north.

As the Ice Age gradually came to an end about 15,000 years ago so the sea once more rose, inexorably wiping away the land bridge, but here and there leaving isolated crests of the main range extending north from Cape York as islands (Muralug, Thursday Island, Moa, Badu, Gebar, Dauan...) and terminating in a low hill on the coast of Papua at the village of Mabadawan. To the east were the extinct volcanoes of Mer, Erub and Ugar. Gradually the deltaic islands formed in the north (Saibai, Boigu), and the sand cays of the central islands came into existence (Masig, Poruma, Waraber).

During the Ice Age and following the submergence of the land bridge there was constant migration and movement by different peoples. This occurred over an extended period. Some hundreds of years ago a small dark people is thought to have inhabited areas on both sides of the Torres Strait. Groups of squat, dark-skinned tribesmen are easily located amongst the wide variety of racial types in West Papua today. In the Keraki language region of West Papua, F. Williams, in his investigations between 1926 and 1932, found stories of an older race who lived in trees eating poor food and without knowledge of fire. These older races had largely succumbed before the invasion of the taller, stronger races of people. Williams was also prompted to observe that these West Papuans "recalled the Australian Aborigine". The similarity was not entirely coincidental.

At some time — probably about 2,000 years ago — migrating groups moved into the Torres Strait Islands and, of necessity, developed into a robust, seafaring people, enjoying a position of considerable importance in the region through warfare and trade.

Legends suggest that migrants moved through the Fly River area down the coast to Saibai and Dauan and thence south and east. Stories describing early arrivals at Saibai definitely indicate this course, and, with the northwest wind filling a sail, it would be difficult not to strike another island to the south of Saibai.

It is significant that the origin of fire in both Keraki and in the Western Torres Strait Islands is attributed to the lizard which in both cases brought it from the north. Yet paradoxically the Cambridge Anthropological Expedition linguist Ray in 1898 believed that the language structure of the Western Islands "has been shown to have relations in structure to the Australian".

Contact between the Western Islanders, particularly those in the south, and the Aborigines of the Australian mainland was fairly consistent, and in some cases had enormous impact. The Upanati (or Yupungatti) group of Aborigines living between the Coen and Batavia Rivers in western Cape York Peninsula told of a hardy sorcerer who left them to travel northward in his canoe. This is important because they claim that he took the first wongai seeds to the Torres Strait Islands and also because he married an Island woman from Mabuiag — the first Aborigine to do so. The Upanati called their hero Chiberie. The Djonggandji (or Tjungundji or Tchunginge) who lived around

Mapoon called their hero Siveri and associated him with the migration northward of seagulls at the beginning of the wet season.

Chiberie's son was the legendary half-Aboriginal* hero Kuiam who, armed with spears and woomera, left a trail of terror and destruction on his headhunting expeditions which extended as far afield as the coast of Papua. He was finally overcome, though not without difficulty, by three canoe-loads of Moan warriors on the south coast of Mabuiag. His son was later killed at Buzi (a Papuan village near Boigu).

The Badu legend explaining the origins of the mating turtles involves another Aboriginal hero named Bia, who journeyed north from his home at Cowal Creek eventually visiting Muralug, Badu, Moa, Gebar, Iama, Masig and Erub. He then returned to his home and traditionally the first pair of mating turtles each season should appear off Cowal Creek.

The Central Islands spoke a dialect of Western Language, though their position necessitated frequent contact with the Eastern Islands and it may be assumed that in practice many of them were bilingual.

The Eastern Islands had a very different cultural background. The Eastern Language, Meriam, is a complicated non-Austronesian language related to the Papuan Kiwai language which is spoken around the Fly River mouth and west to about the Pahoturi River. There is evidence which tends to confirm this relationship between the Kiwais and the Islanders of the east Torres Strait. Gelam the creator of dugong is closely associated with Mer. The principal feature of Mer is a hill called Gelam which is alleged to resemble a dugong. Significantly Gelam is supposed to have lived at Wabada in the Fly Delta (Kiwai language area) before his flight which took him first to Boigu, then to Mabuiag, Moa and finally Mer. Williams claims that the "horiomu" ceremony of the Kiwais, which consisted of a series of pantomines conjuring up the spirits of the recently dead and others, was centered around Daru spreading southwards to the Torres Strait.

However the Islanders, their security ensured by their

---

* This mixture of Aboriginal and Island blood seems curiously potent. Mixed race people of this extraction often have handsome and quite distinctive features. If brought up in an Island environment they frequently assume dominant roles. In some cases their wildness, attributed to their Aboriginal blood, is deprecated by full-blood Islanders.

3. The initiation ceremony of the Malo-Bomai cult on Mer. The mask is one of two used to symbolize Malo's character to the initiates. The shark head dress on the third dancer shows the importance of the shark clan which enforced Malo's doctrine. Note also the two shark-mouthed drums. The cult is usually referred to as Malo since Bomai was a secret name known only to initiated cult members. From *Reports of the Cambridge Anthropological Expedition to Torres Strait*, vol. 6, 1908.

isolation, and freed from the need to search for food by the abundance of fish in the waters around them, quickly evolved their own highly elaborate cults. Amongst the oldest and most eccentric was the cult of Waiet. Waiet came from Mabuiag, where he may be known as Naga, to the rugged island of Waier near Mer. From a cave high up among the rocks on the side of Waier this cult presided over ceremonies which included sexual excesses and perhaps ritual cannabalism.

Mer was also the centre of the tremendously important Malo cult which dominated the Straits, even claiming tribute from the Aborigines on the Australian mainland. There are indications that Malo worship actually originated on the Papuan mainland west of Saibai. Haddon, an expert on all things pertaining to the Torres Strait, noted similarities between the rain-making ceremonies of the Beizam (shark) clan on Mer and that of the Keraki rain makers. In both instances shrines consisting of heaped stones and shells representing a spirit were accompanied by several lesser shrines symbolizing young female attendants.

It is likely however that much of the ritual of the Islanders' old religion was evolved in response to their own environment. So it is that the rites for success in dugong hunting of the West Torres Strait spread to the Kiwai people east of the Binaturi River. The intricate trading system across the Strait, linking each village with other villages on the islands or mainland, meant that any social or aesthetic development in one area could be transmitted to another. The Aborigines of Cape York Peninsula are reputed to have traded turtle oil, red ochre, and strong, well made spears which were much sought after by Islanders. The Islanders in turn were in a position to dominate the shell trade up the Fly River.

When O'Malley and Jack Hides in 1935 travelled up the Strickland River to penetrate the totally unexplored area between the Fly and the Kikori, they found the many inhabitants desperate for shell — cowrie, bailer, trochus and pearl. These natives contemptuously dismissed iron and steel goods (the only trade goods carried by the patrol) in their desire for shell. Much of the shell found in the interior of New Guinea came from the Torres Strait by way of a tortuous trading network. The big, gold-lipped pearl shells were prized, as they are today, and used as currency for payment of bride price, compensation, and so on. In 1930 officers in what was then the Mandated Territory of New Guinea reported that gold-lipped pearl shell was being traded into the upper Sepik from Papua. The obvious route was up the Fly River, and the obvious source was the Torres Strait.

The Papuans in return provided sago (still an important trade item), shredded sago leaves for skirts, cassowary feathers, birds of paradise, and, above all, hulls for the sailing canoes on which the Islanders were dependent. No trees large enough for canoe construction are found on the islands. At certain times of the year, especially during the northwest season (that is, from about November to March when the wind is northwesterly), large

4. A canoe on Badu. Careful and tedious work was required to cut such a hull from a large tree trunk. Photograph by courtesy of N. Smith, Cairns.

trunks float around the northern Straits. In days gone by these trunks would have been towed ashore and, if possible, used. Generally however the Islanders must have traded with the Papuans for their hulls.

If you go to the village of Mabadawan you will see the large sailing canoes (twelve metres in length) anchored outside the village, and drawn up on the sand a row of giant trunks which the village "shipwrights" are in the process of hollowing out by fire and adze. The going price in 1975 was fifty kina for a six-metre hull and a hundred kina for a twelve-metre hull. (The kina is almost equivalent to the Australian dollar.) A century ago the hulls would have been paid for in shell and heads. Here again the Australian Aborigines may have entered the trading system as heads. As Europeans began to appear on the scene so white heads began to make the rounds.

There are indications however that the traditional island trade network was rather haphazard, involving a disjointed series of exchanges in which, for one reason or another, goods were withheld or traded at whim. The people of Moa and Badu, for instance, chose to deny coconuts, sugar cane and other cultivated crops to the people of Muralug, yet the Kulkalgal from Nahgi had no hestitation in supplying these commodities.

Similarly Saibai, several kilometres from the Papuan coast, has never grown the tree whose roots produce fish poison. Right up to the present day such poison has been traded from coastal Papuans in small quantities as needed. However Erub, much further south and more isolated, has grown the tree for a long time and been the origin of further dispersals of the poison. It is possible that the poison is a Kiwai instrument (it is well known on Daru) so that Erub, having closer ties with the Kiwais, gained possession of the trees whereas Saibai, with less direct contact, was unable to acquire more than supplies of the poison. In any case the poison is known by similar names in both places, probably indicating a common source.

It is difficult to accurately reconstruct what life in the Islands must have been like before 1871. The first and only detailed study of Island society took place nearly thirty years after the London Missionary Society had arrived. In the meantime a considerable amount of Island culture had been destroyed or forgotten with the intrusion of Europeans.

Island society was undoubtedly dominated by violence. The sacred words "Jawbones his food, Heads his food" were given as religious instructions to initiates of the Malo-Bomai cult on Mer. Heads were of immense importance both socially and religiously — the head of a woman or child being equal in value to that of a man. The legends of the islands abound with stories of raids, ambushes and massacres, for the primary tactical considerations of Island warfare were surprise and advantage. There were no set piece battles as in the Highlands of New Guinea and amongst some Aborigines of Australia.

Bows, arrows and clubs were used. The stone clubheads, in the shape of a star or disc, had a whole in the centre through which a stout wooden handle was inserted. Some clubheads may have been obtained in trade originating in the upper Fly River, though most were manufactured locally where materials were available. On Iama there remain some giant grindstones, worn and worried by centuries of patient work.

Heads were cut off with a razor-sharp bamboo knife and carried on a loop of cane passed through the mouth and out the neck. At this stage Papuans of the Transfly region would eat the cooked meat of the head — cheeks and eyeballs being especially favoured. In the story of Kuiam from *Myths and Legends of Torres Strait* it is stated that "Tomogon made an earth oven and placed the heads in it, covering them with sand. Presently he removed them and cleaned them of flesh. He placed the skulls in a heap". This could indicate a similar custom in the Torres Strait. In fact Haddon, twenty years after "the coming of the light", found elderly men in the West Torres Strait who readily admitted to this form of ritual cannibalism.

The skulls could be built up with wax and clay, decorated with shells, feathers, plaited cane and paint. Their use ranged from ancestor worship, to divination, and even to one-upmanship in arguments. Heads were also status symbols.

Although the inhabitants of different islands, and even of villages within an island, fought amongst each other, there was a general division between Eastern Islands and Western Islands on a linguistic and cultural basis, the differences often being translated into physical conflict. The Central Islanders were the meat in the sandwich between east and west on their small, sandy islands with no room to flee or manoeuvre and no natural defences. Existence for them must have been perilous indeed. Early European experiences show that the inhabitants of these small islands quickly took to their canoes when danger threatened, seeking security on the sea. The people of Masig complained that other Islanders frequently raided the island stealing the yams, bananas and coconuts which they had cultivated.

As well as having other Islanders to worry about, the more northerly islands suffered from the attacks of Papuan marauders. A Dauan legend tells the story of a murderous raid by the Kupamal (Kiwai Islanders). Men, women and children were slaughtered in a surprise assault before dawn. Only one Dauan man managed to grab his bow, in the confusion of the assault, but he killed three Kiwais with his three arrows before escaping into the rocks where other fugitives were already hiding. One Kiwai was killed by a woman after he had massacred her children with his club. She killed him with her bare hands. The Kiwai raiders took many heads, but as they tried to return back up the coast they were intercepted by the fighting men of Saibai and Maawat (on Papua) and suffered severe losses.

As the Torres Strait cultures developed, pressures in some

5. Engraving by Harden S. Melville of two men at Masseed (or Masig) in 1845. From J.B. Jukes, *Narrative of the Surveying Voyage of H.M.S. Fly*, vol. 1, 1847.

areas caused the adoption of a rather violent form of population control. Infanticide was practised on the crowded Eastern Islands before 1871 and Captain Moresby reported that it took place at Saibai also. Apparently reliable food resources had led to population growth and the need to restrict such growth.

An Islander once pointed out to me the very broad distinctions between the island groups: the Central Islanders were fishermen; the Eastern Islanders, utilizing the rich red earth of their land, were farmers; the Western Islanders were primarily hunters of turtle, dugong, geese, ducks, pigs, and fish. Of course the Westerners had gardens and the Easterners did a lot of fishing, but generally speaking their main activities followed these lines.

The most common food crop in the Torres Strait today is the sweet potato, however the sweet potato did not reach New Guinea till about 1600 and arrived in the Torres Strait by European ship. The traditional farmers in the Torres Strait were reliant on taro on Saibai and Boigu, where the marshy ground was ideal for its cultivation, and on bananas and yams on the fertile but elevated islands of the east. Where there was a shortage of arable land Islanders would plant crops on un-inhabited islands. At the western end of Buru is a raised coral bank, the only part of the island which is not a tidal swamp. In the past people from Boigu would sail fifty kilometres south to this island in order to plant taro and bananas, and perhaps to catch some crabs.

The granitic islands of the southwest, with their harsh dry seasons, obliged the inhabitants to gather and hunt to a greater extent. It is known that the Kauralgal on Muralug cultivated patches of yams on the richer alluvial flats of the island. It was slash and burn cultivation practised, not very enthusiastically, as a precaution against the failure of the natural yam crop in the higher, rocky ground. The Kauralgal, and other Islanders, also boiled turtle or dugong meat in a large shell then sun dried it, thus preserving the meat for long voyages. In spite of the close relationship between the Kauralgal and the Aborigines of the Australian mainland, the Aborigines never adopted these practices.

The abundance of fish and their acquaintance with agriculture gave the Kauralgal the facilities to live a more settled life, if they had wished. For practical purposes Muralug may be seen as the southern frontier of Melanesian, agricultural society in the region.

In order to give a clearer idea of traditional daily life and culture in the Torres Strait, the following is a brief recon-struction of some village activities which describes no particular island but rather is a generalized picture.

One Day in the life of an Island Village

An elderly man, with bamboo comb and razor-sharp bamboo knife, is trimming the close cropped hair of the young men in preparation for the feast that night, although they will actually wear carefully prepared wigs, gaudy with ochre and parrot feathers, arranged in ringlets to the shoulders. The pet cassowary stalking about the huts will shortly have its long, luxuriant, black tail plumes taken for decoration.

A party of noisy women saunters to the well, coconut shell water containers slung over their shoulders, calf-length sago leaf skirts rustling between gusts of raucous laughter. As they start along the well trodden, dusty path they meet an elderly man carrying a bunch of short, plump bananas balanced across his shoulders and steadied with one hand. In the other he has a coconut leaf basket full of tubers, the skin of which can be pulled off and made into soft, pliable strips for a skirt. Also in the basket are rough, green leaves of the "sandpaper" tree that can be used to shape and smooth softwood surfaces.

The first three women exchange flashing smiles and a "good day" with the man as they pass, but the fourth hangs back alarmed. Eyes downcast, she waits in fright as he gruffly shoulders past. He is her father-in-law and by custom she should avoid him. She knew he was going to the gardens, why didn't she anticipate that he would return by this path? Her thoughtlessness embarrasses them both.

In shallow water at the front of the village two naked young girls splash about, their heads a lather of white. A tree root they are holding, scraped down to expose creamy flesh, is being rubbed vigorously to produce this effect. Fastened to a stake nearby, a turtle surfaces momentarily to inhale then once again disappears. Its struggle will soon be ended for it is the substance of the feast tonight.

Further out, on the edge of the reef, two small fishing canoes bob in the choppy sea. A man in one of the canoes has a clutch of roots in his hand and is shaking it into the water above a coral bomby which looms to within a foot of the surface and swarms with fish. The root is a poison and, when dissolved in the water, will paralyze fish close by, forcing them to the top gasping helplessly.

In the shade of a huge wongai tree on the beach two old men are working. One repairs a coconut mat sail watched by a group of tittering children. He uses a sharpened edge of shell to hack off lengths of coconut fibre as he needs it. The other elder, who sits alone, nurses over his lap an hour-glass drum obtained in trade with the Papuans. He has stretched the black and yellow-flecked skin of a goanna across the drum's mouth and now tries to secure it in place, using a cane strap and powerful glue which has been extracted from mangrove pods. Some of the older boys in the audience climb up into the wongai tree plucking the fruit which they munch like chewing gum. Suddenly one gestures to the southeast and screams a shrill warning.

A large sailing canoe approaches slowly under a gentle breeze, the decks stacked high with skilfully made coconut mats from Masig. Also there will be pearl and bailer shells gathered on the great reefs north of Tutu. The visitors will probably want sago (obtained in trade with Papua), taro (grown locally), and bird of paradise plumes (also traded from Papua).

As the canoe grounds village men greet the sailors with wary friendship, for these sailors are from Iama and Tutu. Although few in the midst of a village, they move with a confidence and assurance that is disconcerting. Certain villagers note the daggers, ground from cassowary thigh bones, thrust through girdles at their visitors' waists. Some remember only a short time ago when the occupants of a gardening hut on the other side of the island awoke to the thuds and screams of a head-hunting raid — perhaps by these very men. . . . But the village needs the shell, which is difficult to obtain in such quantities close to the island, for their trade with coastal Papuans. And these men need the sago, so there will be trade and next time it may be a gardening party on Iama that is surprised.

HISTORY

1

The First Whitemen

In 1606 a Spanish ship, captained by Luis Vaez de Torres, sailed between Cape York and Papua. The ship was one of a fleet taken by Quiros to search for the Solomon Islands which had been discovered by Mendana. Quiros discovered the New Hebrides and the Tuamotus whilst Torres pressed westwards to the strait between Australia and Papua. During four hazardous weeks in the strait Torres was obliged to work his way to the southwest. In the Central Islands his men shot two Island men and abducted three young women. Torres probably emerged from the Endeavour Strait into the Arafura Sea. Eventually he took his men and four Islanders (one woman had given birth to a full blood child on board ship) back to Spain, but details of his discovery were not widely known. Due to intense competition in trade his reports were suppressed. The first the British knew of it was in 1762 when a British fleet occupied Manila and found an old copy of the chart. However, without question other seamen had preceded Torres and his men. Haddon claimed that the Torres Strait appears on a map as early as 1571.

On Mer a tradition persists that a village called Las (on the south side) was occupied by shipwrecked Spaniards centuries before Cook. Nobody lives in this area today but it is claimed that, even in the late nineteenth century, people from this village were characterized by a lighter skin colour (i.e. of mixed blood). It is a moot point whether these stories were prompted by Idriess's *Drums of Mer*, or whether the stories influenced the novel.

Malay traders from Makassar and other ancient Indonesian trading ports had long travelled the north Australian coast. In areas of the Northern Territory this contact had been so cordial and protracted as to produce an indigenous population with a considerable proportion of non-Aboriginal blood. In 1803 Flinders whilst circumnavigating Australia in the *Investigator* came across a fleet of six Malayan proas off Arnhem Land only a few hundred kilometres to the west of the Torres Strait.

The northern side of the Torres Strait belonged, in theory at least, to the Sultan of Tidore, King of the principal state in the Moluccas. He harvested the twin crops of birds of paradise and slaves with difficulty as the inhabitants had a reputation for ferocity. Bird of paradise hunters would have travelled as far east as the Torres Strait, though this has not been recorded and, perhaps, they would not have realised the significance of what had been done in any case. When Torres sailed through the Straits, as a navigator, he was aware of the importance of this action and so ensured that it was recorded. From that time onwards the Strait which Torres had discovered was marked on maps, though not on all maps, and it was more than a century and a half before the Strait was finally confirmed and mapped.

By the beginning of the seventeenth century the Dutch had effectively dominated both trade and government throughout the Indies. It was not long before ambitious captains were sailing further south and east searching for new lands to exploit. They were not impressed by Australia for the north coast is un-imposing and the local inhabitants had little which seemed exploitable. Nevertheless the Dutch followed their usual approach in a new land by capturing some locals, often under the guise of friendship, in order to extract the desired information and to use as pilots. In either case the results could not have proved very encouraging.

By 1606 the *Duyfken* under William Janszoon had reached the west coast of Cape York. North of the site of the present town of Weipa, in the Batavia River area near Mapoon, he sent his men ashore for water. One of the Dutch, at least, was speared to death by Aboriginal warriors. Alarmed, Janszoon pulled off the coast and, although in sailing north he sighted Muralug and adjacent islands, he never entered the Strait but continued on until he hit the swampy, malarial coast of New Guinea. Here a further eight Dutchmen were attacked and killed. Carstensz, following in

Janszoon's footsteps seventeen years later, was forced repeatedly to fire on Aboriginal spearmen on Cape York Peninsula of whom three were known to have died. He thought the Aborigines "the most wretched and poorest creatures" and reported that the country (i.e. western Cape York Peninsula) was dry and barren despite the fact that he was there in April, immediately following the end of the Wet Season, when it should have been at its best.

Voyages by Tasman in 1644 and Gonzal and Van Asschens in 1756 covered roughly the same ground and accomplished little more than that of Janszoon. The accumulation of such un-appealing reports in Batavia (Djakarta) ultimately discouraged further Dutch exploration in the Torres Strait region. As Spanish power waned so they were unable or unwilling to utilise Torres's discovery. It remained, as so many other things in the Pacific, for James Cook to properly investigate and chart.

In August 1770 Cook and the crew of the *Endeavour* passed through the Endeavour Passage into the Torres Strait. On 22 August Cook wrote that on Tuined he had seen his first "Indian" armed with a bow and a bundle of arrows, instead of the "lances" he had seen previously. Further he stated that "two or three of the men we saw yesterday had on pretty large breast plates which we supposed were made of Pearl Oyster Shells, this was as well as the bows and arrows before". These new features which Cook had not seen previously on his voyage up the east coast suggested a new race. Without a doubt they were Torres Strait Islanders, probably Kauralgal. Note also the mention of the oyster shell. It is fitting that the pearl shell should appear in this early written record of the Torres Strait Islanders, because the future of the Islanders came to be dominated by the pearling industry. Polished pearl shell is still worn, suspended about the neck, by Islanders for dancing today.

Cook saw on the nearby islands and mainland of Australia "a great number of smokes" suggesting a relatively dense population. He also saw some women with "not a single rag of any kind of clothing upon them" collecting shellfish. His observations of the inhabitants right up the east coast reveal that shellfish were a primary food source for coastal groups and that they functioned rather as nomadic food gatherers than as nomadic hunters.

Tuined was named Possession Island by Cook. This was where

he went through the motions of formally taking possession of 'New South Wales' for his king, George III. As he sailed beyond the reefs into the safe, blue waters of the Arafura Sea he took time to name an isolated, abrupt rock Booby Island for the sea birds of that name which lived there.

Cook had placed the Torres Strait on the map once and for all. It was soon to be made use of. Many British ships now showed a preference for entering the Pacific through the Torres Strait rather than going round the stormy Cape Horn. However a group of escaped convicts from Port Jackson were ironically among the first people from the infant Australian colony to use the Torres Strait.

In March 1791 eight men, a woman and two children, driven to desperation by the harsh conditions at the penal settlement, embarked in an open, six-oar boat for Timor where they hoped to masquerade as survivors of a shipwreck. Their meagre supplies obliged them to live off the turtle, birds and other wild food along the eastern Australian coast. They found that unfriendly Aborigines were easily dispersed by discharging a musket over their heads.

However among some small islands just inside the Gulf of Carpentaria they encountered a number of canoes. The natives were described as "very stout and fat and blacker than they were in other parts". The escapees saw one man with shells around his shoulders and took him to be the chief. Blithely they approached the canoes and fired a musket over the natives' heads, but their confidence turned to consternation when, instead of scattering, the natives stood their ground and launched a barrage of arrows. It was the Europeans' turn to flee and in great haste.

A little further into the gulf the convicts were compelled to visit a river to obtain fresh water and found an apparently deserted village of twenty large, well-made huts. The following day, when they attempted to revisit the site, two huge canoes sallied out to meet them. Each contained thirty to forty men and was fitted out with matting sails. The Europeans turned directly west across the gulf and were pursued for some time before they escaped. Eventually they reached Timor only to be imprisoned in any case for their trouble.

Some important points emerge from this narrative. The Islanders encountered were certainly a separate race easily distinguishable from the mainland Aborigines by even an inexpert observer. More surprisingly the Islanders had confidently and aggressively exerted control over what they considered to be their sea space. It also shows that seafaring Islanders apparently frequented and even established settlements on the northwest coast of Cape York Peninsula.

This phase of the Strait's history is tied up with another interesting incident in Pacific history — the mutiny on the ship *Bounty*.

In 1788 Captain W. Bligh, on his way out from England and having battled west to round the Horn, eventually turned the *Bounty* east instead and entered the Pacific via Tasmania. Bligh, who had been an officer with Cook in Hawaii in 1779, had taken part in the scattered fighting during which Cook had been killed. Now he had been ordered by the British Government to Tahiti (mapped by Wallis in 1767) seeking breadfruit seedlings. It was hoped that breadfruit, when introduced into the West Indies, would prove a reliable staple food for the plantation slaves. Bligh took his job seriously — his sailors thought too seriously — and on 28 April 1789 he was set adrift with 18 companions in a small boat. Before them lay a 6,000 kilometre voyage with inadequate provisions to Timor. Now Bligh's severe discipline was to save all but one of them. They trailed a line and caught a dolphin. They killed seabirds and ate eggs they found on cays of the Barrier Reef. When they reached the Torres Strait they sailed straight through north of Mawai, opening a new route. As they entered the Arafura Bligh saw a high, rocky island and called it Booby Island, after the birds which haunted it, only to find that, by a coincidence, Cook had given it the same name. After a voyage lasting forty-one days Bligh and his loyal sailors arrived at Timor and safety. But it still remained for the Royal Navy to track down the mutineers.

Captain E. Edwards was despatched in the H.M.S. *Pandora* to Tahiti where fourteen mutineers, who had unwisely remained on the island, were soon captured. With these locked in a grill cage on the deck, Edward then set out to retrace Blighs steps through the Torres Strait. Having sighted and named the Murray Islands (Mer, Dauar, Waier) from the eastern side of the reef, Edwards sought an entrance through the coral barrier.

On the evening of 28 August 1791 Lieutenant Comer had a cutter out in front examining an opening when, at twenty past

6. H.M.S. *Pandora* going down south of Mer in 1791. Thirty-five lives were lost in the wreck. Photograph by courtesy of the Dixson Galleries, Sydney, from a drawing by Robert Batty.

seven, while the lead still read fifty fathoms, the *Pandora* struck. The coral wall rose hundreds of feet, almost vertically, from the seabed, rendering sounding (throwing a lead-weighted line) unreliable. Edwards released three prisoners to work the pumps but resisted suggestions that he release the others. The *Pandora* went down suddenly the next morning with Edwards being amongst the first to leave the ship. As she went the boatswain's mate risked his life, and charges of insubordination, to release another seven prisoners. Four went down with the ship, still in their chains. Thirty-one other seamen perished. The *Pandora* was a total loss, the first recorded wreck of the hundreds which have littered the Strait with their bones. In apprehension, Edwards set sail for the Indies.

Before entering the Arafura the party camped on the north coast of Muralug where the men were upset at night by the howling of "wolves" — possibly dingoes. Edwards named the bay Wolf's Bay. He and his men took note of the manner in which a gravesite at Wolf's Bay had been decorated with dugong and turtle bones, two human skulls and a long wooden paddle. There was no trouble with Islanders, probably because there were over ninety men in the group. Edwards continued his barbarous treatment of the prisoners, having two, including a James Morrison (who was subsequently acquitted of all charges), bound in the boat bottom. When Morrison protested Edwards abused him as a "piratical dog" and threatened to shoot him. Eventually the unhappy party reached safety in the East Indies.

Yet this was not the end of the Tahitian breadfruit story for Bligh was given another chance to complete his original mission. He was given two ships, the *Providence* and the *Assistant*, departing England on 3 August 1791. On board the *Providence* was a young midshipman named Matthew Flinders.

With over 2,000 breadfruit seedlings successfully loaded at Tahiti, Bligh elected to take his two ships through the now familiar Torres Strait. Bligh was determined to accurately map the Strait for shipping. In the nineteen days which he spent in the area during September 1792, Bligh discovered a new opening in the Great Barrier Reef, named the Bligh Entrance, and a new passage passing through near Erub. Bligh's crew, in fact, are thought to be the first Europeans to see Erub, and it was Bligh who gave it the name Darnley Island. Further south Mer (named Murray by Edwards) came into view.

On the morning of 2 September the cutter, under Lieutenant Tobin, was despatched to examine what appeared to be a passage to the south of Erub. Spectators on the *Assistant* noted four large canoes sailing to intercept the cutter. Tobin meanwhile had also noticed the canoes and, not wishing to be caught in a situation where he was outnumbered and isolated from his main force, sought to rejoin the *Assistant* almost ten kilometres distant. A grim race developed which the Englishmen seemed certain to lose. Flinders wrote that: "No boats could have been manoeuvred better in working to windward than these long canoes by the naked savages."

One canoe even lowered its sail and, driven by paddles, gained appreciably on the cutter. On approaching Tobin's boat, where the seamen were armed and ready, the Islanders gestured for Tobin to stop. One Erubian held up a coconut as if to trade, but when Tobin pointed, directing him to the *Assistant*, the Islander reached below the cane enclosure that lined the canoe's sides and brought out a bow and arrows. Suddenly other men, who had been concealed behind the enclosure, rose, stringing arrows to bows. With the other three canoes closing fast, Tobin gave the command to his men to fire.

7. Seamen in a cutter, under the command of Lieutenant George Tobin, firing on Islanders near Erub in 1792. Tobin, who painted this watercolour, was careful to emphasize the distinctive aquiline noses of the three Islanders at the right. Photograph by courtesy of the Mitchell Library, Sydney.

At least one of the bowmen was mortally wounded and the others dived behind the enclosure for cover. Gradually the cutter drew away to safety as the dazed warriors tried to work out what had happened. They had never before seen firearms.

Tobin reported that "self preservation prompted me to fire a volley of musketry among them", but Bligh was upset: "This was the most melancholy account I have received. All my hopes to have a friendly intercourse with the natives were now lost."

Nonetheless fleets of canoes trailed the ships as they threaded their way amid the banks and reefs, some coming close enough to receive presents thrown from the ships. Three courageous men even came abroad but were dismayed at nothing (which dismayed the Europeans), asking only for iron. The men were naked but for shell jewellery and cane wristlets. It was observed that all the Islanders were covered with oil, so that they emerged from the water perfectly dry.

The canoes were fifteen metres long carved from a single trunk with an outrigger on each side. Over the middle section a platform was built with a hut of thatched palm leaves on top. The sails were flimsy-looking but effective coconut mats a metre and a half wide and more than two metres high raised between two poles.

Flinders examined an Islander's bamboo bow and found that no European on the ship could bend it, let alone shoot it. Stout clubs made from casuarina wood were seen but, curiously, no stone-headed clubs were reported. However, the two vessels were nearing Iama and Tutu, and the Englishmen were to have the opportunity of observing the primitive weapons in action at first hand.

Nine canoes carrying about one hundred men sallied out from the islands, some clustering around the *Providence* and others around the *Assistant*. On the *Providence* Bligh cautiously invited the men aboard but they declined, intimating that food and water were available on Tutu and urging Bligh to take his men ashore. Bligh's suspicions were confirmed when a battle suddenly erupted around the *Assistant*. A barrage of missiles wounded three sailors and in the ensuing hail of musketry a number of Islanders were killed. The large canoe that had initiated the attack drifted, apparently empty, but with the survivors actually sheltering in the water behind its hull.

Meanwhile, warriors in another large canoe under the *Providence*'s bow had commenced firing arrows at Bligh's crew, who responded with small arms fire. Bligh had a four pounder cannon turned on the canoe and at almost point blank range knocked down the crew and shot holes in its hull. Soon it was floating about with a cargo of dead and wounded, while others sought refuge in the water.

As the English vessels sailed on, tending the injured, the officers examined the arrows which littered the *Providence*'s deck and riddled the cutter. They were impressed by the force with which the arrows had been driven into the wood. The surviving canoes returned for the two that had been disabled, and towed them to shore.

Because the encounter occurred near Tutu, Bligh named this small sand cay Warrior Island, and the extensive reefs stretching away to the north, almost to the coast of Papua, he named the Warrior Reefs. It is on this basis that some people claim that Tutu supported a heavy population of warlike warriors. Probably the canoes and warriors came from elsewhere, probably Iama, and they sought to have the Englishmen land on Tutu merely because it was convenient, being close, and well known to them, at times supporting a fishing village.

During a touchy passage between Badu and Mabuiag, so dangerous that Bligh called it "Bligh's Farewell", muskets and cannon were again fired to frighten off canoes from Badu, though without causing casualties.

It is probable that Tobin's shootout at Erub prompted the massacre of passengers and crew from two visiting ships the following year.

In March 1793 Governor Grose chartered the South Sea

whaler *Chesterfield*, and the ship *Shah Hormuzear*, to take supplies from the young settlement at Port Jackson to Norfolk Island and, on 10 April, he entered into an agreement with William Bampton, master and owner of the *Shah Hormuzear*, to ship further supplies from ports in India. Bampton, as other captains sailing to or from southeast Australia, had a choice of three routes. The stormy passage around Tasmania was not a real alternative for a ship sailing to India. The route east of New Guinea would lose time and would be at least as dangerous as a voyage through the Torres Strait which had been partially mapped by both Bligh and Cook and which, therefore, was the third and most likely alternative. Bampton selected the Torres Strait as did an increasing number of masters after him.

It was twelve months before the first reports reached Sydney of a tragic incident in the Torres Strait culminating in another memorable small boat exploit.

The *Chesterfield* and *Shah Hormuzear* had anchored off Erub on 9 July 1793. A party sent ashore for water met Islanders who appeared friendly and agreed to barter for "emu" (cassowary) feathers. Consequently a group consisting of Captain Hill (New South Wales Corps), Shaw (first mate of the *Shah Hormuzear*). Carter (a friend of Bamptons), Ascott (an ex-convict from Norfolk Island) and four Lascars, went ashore to barter for feathers and look around.

While Hill and the Lascars remained with the boat on the beach, Carter, Shaw and Ascott, who carried a musket, climbed a hill. As they pushed up through the thick scrub Carter, who was ahead,was suddenly attacked and struck down. Ascott hearing his screams fired into the scrub and the attackers fled. Carter's skull had been shattered by stone clubs and he was barely conscious. Supporting the injured man between them, Ascott and Shaw struggled down the hill. On approaching the beach however they found that their five companions had already been killed and dragged some distance away to where a fire was blazing. On the beach, unguarded, sat their boat. Somehow the three managed to launch the boat but, strangely, decided to run for Timor instead of making for the two ships in the vicinity.

Bampton, anxious when the boat failed to return in the morning, sent a search party ashore. On the beach were found blood stained clothing, a lantern, a tinder box and three badly

8. Another watercolour by Tobin showing H.M.S. *Providence* and *Assistant* under attack near Tutu in 1792. Photograph by courtesy of the Mitchell Library, Sydney.

burned human hands. Grimly now the searchers descended on the villages, where they found a tomahawk and some greatcoats. In the corners of some huts were wooden images daubed with red ochre and adorned with feathers, resembling men and birds. Over these images were suspended strings of human hands, five or six to a string.* In some huts were heaps of skulls and in one a larger pile before a wooden statue. Concluding there were no survivors the seamen burned the village. One hundred and thirty-five huts were destroyed and sixteen large canoes measuring from fifteen to more than twenty metres were broken up. The bay was named Treacherous Bay. Next Bampton sailed to Ugar which lay twenty-five kilometres to leeward of Erub, searching for the missing boat. The Islanders attempted a stand, firing arrows at the landing party but, after several had been shot, the whole population decamped by canoe. This village also was burned.

Meanwhile the missing boat was sailing westwards and after an eventful journey lasting some months finally reached safety. Carter had died from his terrible wounds, but it is worth noting that the two survivors owed their lives to the hospitality of the natives of Sarreet in Indonesia, who recalled Bligh's similar visit some years earlier, and arranged the pair's transport to Timor.

The passage of the *Chesterfield* and *Shah Hormuzear* is significant for another reason. In between watching reefs and burning

---

* It was the custom of bereaved relatives in the Eastern Islands to take off and dry the soles of the corpse's feet and the skin of the hands, including fingernails. The hands were usually strung up in huts, but the soles were sometimes worn strapped to the back in remembrance of the loved one.

villages Bampton found time to take possession of the south coast of New Guinea for the British government, an action taken without authority and which remained unrecognized. However the events surrounding this voyage were dwarfed by a notorious incident which took place forty years later.

In July 1834 the barque *Charles Eaton* sailed from Sydney bound for Canton in China. On board were twenty-nine people including Captain and Mrs D'Oyley and their two children. The *Charles Eaton* never reached Canton. About a year later, in September 1835, the *Mangles* anchored near Mer. In the forty or more years since Bligh's visits, the Islanders had seen an increasing number of ships scudding east and west through the blue waters surrounding their islands. They had acquired a taste for the more utilitarian benefits of European contact. Iron and glass, in any form, were tradeable commodities for which the Islanders would barter feathers, turtle shell, mats, shells or food (including yams and bananas). Although trouble did frequently occur between Islanders and passing ships' crews, if precautions were taken contact could be cordial if not relaxed. So it was that as *Mangles* lay at rest off Mer a number of canoes came out to trade. In one of the canoes was a white man as naked as any of the Islanders. The master of the *Mangles* shouted across to the white man, asking who he was. The man claimed he was an Englishman from the ship *Charles Eaton* which has been wrecked but, when given an opportunity of boarding the *Mangles*, he refused to do so, saying that other white men were being held ashore.

The master manned and armed a boat and took her across to the beach. The natives were anxious for him to land but, as there were several hundred people gathered on the sand, he declined to take the risk. Next the Islanders brought down a little white boy of two or three to the waterline but they were unwilling to take him out and the whites were still unwilling to land.

So the *Mangles* sailed west to Koepang in Timor and it was some months before there was any definite news of the *Charles Eaton*. Then the ship's carpenter and four seamen turned up in Amboyna in the East Indies. They stated that the ship had sunk at the entrance to the Torres Strait, that they had taken the only boat and considered themselves the sole survivors. Later they admitted that as they bore away through the surf, which was pounding the ship, they saw the ship's captain, D'Oyley, his wife and children about the main chain. In other words there was every indication that other survivors of the wreck could still be living on islands in the Torres Strait. Fortunately the D'Oyleys had influential relatives in London who were able to bring some pressure to bear on the authorities. Largely as a result of their efforts the colonial schooner *Isabella*, under Charles Lewis, sailed from Sydney on 3 June 1836.

Sixteen days later the *Isabella* arrived at Mer where Lewis found the Islanders not "ferocious and mischievous" as he has been led to believe in Sydney, but very helpful. Two survivors were in fact found — William D'Oyley, by then four years old, and John Ireland, ship's boy.

Ireland explained that after the ship struck a reef the carpenter and four crew escaped in the only remaining boat. The twenty-four people left constructed two rafts from the wreck and floated northwestwards till they reached an island, known to the Islanders as Boydang, near Aureed Island. Nobody lived on Boydang but a number of men from Aureed had come across to fish. The ragged band of European castaways was set upon and massacred, only young William and Ireland surviving. Some accounts claim that another child, spared in the initial massacre, was killed three months later.

The savage treatment of the Europeans by the men of Aureed can be explained, as can the sparing of the two boys. In Island language the word for ghost and European was the same (western — *markai*, eastern — *lamar*). It was logical then to destroy these "ghosts", although the Islanders also had a healthy respect for their power. The sparing of the two boys may have been an act of compassion by an individual who wanted a boy, for Islanders love children, and even today, will adopt a succession of children from other families. As well there may have been a resemblance between the boys and some recently deceased children, the Islanders thinking that they had assumed the spirit of the dead children.

The two boys and the heads of the other Europeans — these heads constituting another important reason for the massacre — were bundled into canoes and taken to Aureed. Some time later visitors from Mer bought the boys for a bunch of bananas each. On Mer the two were treated with the greatest consideration. The Islanders gave up the boys reluctantly and remained on the best of terms with Lewis during his stay.

Lewis determined to go to Aureed to attempt to recover the skulls. The inhabitants of the island fled in canoes at the *Isabella*'s approach. Forty-five skulls were found under a shed, arranged into the figure of a man and painted with ochre. Lewis also believed this was the site of cannibal feasts. Every house on the island was burned and every coconut tree cut down.

Seventeen of the skulls were identified as European, including one which still had long strands of blond hair clinging to it. Subsequently all forty-five were buried in the cemetery at Bunnerong near Botany Bay, the inscription indicating that among these skulls were those of the passengers and crew of the *Charles Eaton*.

Another comment made by Lewis on the people of Mer is revealing. He said that they were "very much afraid of a gun, or small arms". No doubt they had good reason. It can be assumed that most of the violent exchanges between whites and Islanders went unrecorded by ships' masters reluctant to publicly expose their conduct, or who simply saw no point in putting them down on paper.

One example of the many disputes that may have occurred took place in May 1814. The *Frederick* during a visit to Mer put off a boat to pick up coconuts offered for trade. However, men in six canoes (twelve to fifteen metres long) tried to cajole the boat crew into landing at a place where the Europeans felt an ambuscade was being prepared. Accordingly the boat put about to return to the *Frederick*. The canoemen in agitation pursued it to the ship and seemed to be working themselves up to an attack when two cannons were fired over their heads, at which they quickly withdrew.

McFarlane in 1888 heard, from the people of Erub, a version of a second massacre on the island, which took place when sailors came ashore to obtain water and wash in the well there. The Islanders objected because, McFarlane said, the sailors were lathering up in the only drinking water remaining on the island. In spite of the seamen's firearms the Islanders attacked, killing the captain of the ship and some crew. Retribution was inevitable and heavy. Once again, the villages scattered around the little coves and sandy beaches were burned. Islanders were shot and some girls abducted. Gardens were ruined. If the people of Erub had not been gun-shy before then they may, with justification, have been after this time. This is believed to have occurred about 1840 so that at least twice within fifty years Erub had been devastated.

The sixteen canoes lost in 1793 would have been difficult, almost impossible, to replace. They were indispensable for trade, warfare and food gathering. The destruction of the huts with all the odds and ends essential for life in the very demanding circumstances on Erub (which was a small area with a large population), would have been disastrous. What could be done without fishing spears and with the gardens ruined and the water in the well spoiled? Certainly these things could be eventually repaired, but the psychological effects must have been more lasting.

The warriors on Erub had been swept away by musket fire on these occasions and chased into the hills — helpless even to prevent the abduction of their sisters and daughters. The shrines which they held sacred had been reviled and hopelessly compromised by the white sailors. Consequently the old men and leaders, who drew much of their power and authority from these shrines and the rites connected with them, had been revealed as impotent. Thus the basis of Island society was being eroded away. Through lack of direction it began to falter and the Islanders began to die. In 1848 the population of Erub was still between four and five hundred. By 1871, just twenty-three years later, only a hundred and twenty remained alive.

In 1845 Jukes, naturalist on H.M.S. *Fly*, visited Erub. He described the Islanders as follows: "The men were fine, active, well-made fellows, rather above middle height, of a dark brown or chocolate colour. They had frequently almost handsome faces, aquiline noses rather broad about the nostril, well-shaped heads, and many had a singularly Jewish cast of features." The people of Erub do not look like this today due to the infusion of South Sea blood, however Jukes's note and the illustrations accompanying his narrative portray vividly the "aquiline nose" and "Jewish cast of features" so common among the Kiwais of Papua today (see figure 5). Originally the Islanders of the Eastern Islands must have been of similar racial stock to the Kiwais.

The women wore skirts made of pandanus (available on Erub) or sago (traded from the coastal Kiwais), had tattoes about the arms and chest and wore their hair close cropped. The men's long hair was arranged in ringlets down to their shoulders, sometimes smeared with red ochre and decorated with brightly coloured feathers. The men of Erub, like those of Mer, wore no clothing. Both men and women hung pearl shells around their necks, and perforated their ears to such an extent that in some cases the distended skin of the lobe had torn away and dangled down onto the shoulder.

Jukes was astonished to discover that the men smoked, a habit he found difficult to explain, and he concluded that the Torres Strait Islanders had come from New Ireland or New Caledonia. This would have been possible in their fifteen metre canoes but is rather unlikely. A later visitor to "Torotoram" (Tureture), a Kiwai village on the Binaturi, commented on the "formidable papuan pipe". It was almost a metre in length consisting of a wide bamboo cut off above and below the knuckles, so as to be sealed. A hole was made in one end through which to draw and another hole in the top accommodated a tobacco bowl. The smoke was drawn in till the pipe was full, whereupon the bowl was removed and the hole covered with the palm of the hand. The strong, green-leafed tobacco smoked then still grows wild along this coast though modern tastes in Papua have turned to Muruk (a popular black twist tobacco) and the Islanders now smoke tailor-mades.

Another distinctive feature was the rounded beehive hut with the centre pole protruding some feet above the roof and festooned with human skulls. These huts were common to the Eastern and Central Islands though those of Masig were thought to be of a more sophisticated style employing intricate weaving of coconut fronds for parts of the walls. The Kauralgal of Muralug merely threw up bush lean-tos as they moved from place to place but on the far northern islands (Saibai, Boigu and Dauan) Papuan-style stilt houses, with the floor elevated off the ground, were erected.

Another point emphasized by Jukes was the Islanders' dependence on the "coconut" tree as a food source although the degree of dependence varied from island to island. Neither Jukes, Cook, Flinders, King, Wickham nor Stokes, all of whom had explored the northeast Australian coast, had found a coconut tree on the mainland. Jukes picked up a few coconuts from beaches down the coast but no coconut tree was seen. He was surprised then to discover Mer "absolutely within the Great Barrier Reef, covered with them". The coconut had travelled

9. Islanders at Erub in 1845. The man standing has an unstrung bow and wears a shell decoration round his neck. From Harden S. Melville, *Sketches in Australia and the Adjacent Islands*, 1848.

along the southern coast of Papua with migrating groups and had been taken into the Torres Strait with the Islanders.

Whilst the story of the *Charles Eaton* may have enhanced the reputation enjoyed by the Islanders on Mer, it did nothing for the advancement of the Torres Strait as a whole. In fact the period 1840 to 1870 was perhaps the grimmest in the Strait's history. Islanders were frequently shot on sight whilst any boat crew less than well armed would be risking massacre.

In 1846 a schooner off Badu sent six men ashore to barter for "tortoise shell". Although they took the precaution of camping on a sandbar four of the six were killed in a surprise attack launched by the crafty Badulgal (Badu men) that night. The schooner captain did not feel he had sufficient forces to retaliate on this occasion.

As elsewhere in the Pacific lawless Europeans raided the islands for women and Islanders slaughtered Europeans for their iron. Records of early travellers and traders emphasize the desperate hunger of Islanders for iron. "Tooree" or "toolick" were demanded of Lewis at Mer in 1837. In return Islanders

10. Meriams almost swamping a boat from H.M.S. *Fly* in their eagerness to trade. Iron, glass and tobacco were traded for their coconuts, turtle shell and other goods. From J.B. Jukes, *Narrative of the Surveying Voyage of H.M.S. Fly*, 1847.

traded turtle shell and a stick of tobacco could buy a kilogram or more of it.

Some ambitious traders supplied the Islanders with guns and ammunition (something commented on by Haddon). The men of Poruma are reputed to have ambushed and shot up one of Kebisu's war canoes with their newly acquired firearms, a rebuke felt all the keener because the people of the sandy Central Islands had been very much ill treated and despised by the haughty warriors from Tutu and Iama.

As the years passed it became obvious that the Islanders were losing in the battle of European encroachment. Wini, "the wild whiteman of Badu", encouraged resistance to any form of civilized white penetration in the Western Islands, but against firearms the Islanders could not win. Wini is supposed to have died when a naval party landed on Badu about 1860. Screaming and ranting he urged his warriors to attack the whites. The warriors sensibly refused to face musket fire and fled. Wini went berserk, attacking the sailors single-handed before being shot dead. From his gibberings a naval officer deduced that he was a Frenchman not, as has been suggested elsewhere, an English convict.

All of these incidents, however violent and tragic, set the stage for the final act of European intervention — the lucrative exploitation of pearl shell.

Cook in 1770 noted the presence of pearl shell in the Strait and since that time the abundance of shell in northern Australia and particularly in the Torres Strait had been commented on repeatedly. It was not till 1868 that a Captain Banner sailed his brig the *Julia Percy* from Sydney, with the express purpose of spending a season exploiting the pearl beds of the Torres Strait, the first to do so. Banner though was no pioneer. Bêche-de-mer fishing for the Chinese market had taken place for years. The preparation of bêche-de-mer required drying or smoking so that shore stations were needed. The station at Albany Island had been functioning intermittently since the 1840s and captains had ensconced themselves on various other islands at times, with the Islanders often not having a great deal of say in the matter. Labour was conscripted at gun point — it being necessary to walk over the reefs and sand flats at low tide to collect the slugs for drying and bagging. But whatever profit these men made on sea slugs was miniscule compared to the incredible profits awaiting the early pearl shellers.

Popular legend in the Torres Strait, supported by Ian Idriess's powerful narrative, has Banner sailing by luck or design directly to the person who would be most disposed, and who had the power, to help him. This was supposedly Kebisu of Tutu. His strength and the consequent well-being of his people depended on his ability to dominate affairs in the Strait — trade, warfare, seamanship — but the increasing intrusion of the white man was undermining his control. Kebisu had many canoes and warriors but Banner had cannon on board the *Julia Percy*. Banner wished to harvest the shells which were common around the island but Kebisu wanted steel knives, axes, cloth, canvas and firearms. In those days shell could be collected by wandering over the reefs at low tide, and there was so much that tons could be gathered in a few days.

Kebisu's men assisted Banner and were subsequently rewarded in those commodities which Kebisu regarded so highly. In this respect Kebisu's strategy was successful, but the consequences of his collaboration were so far outside the field of his experience, that it would have been impossible for him to have foreseen the ultimate result.

Although it is certainly true that Banner collected a valuable cargo of pearl shell in the vicinity of Tutu, it is less certain that the Tutu community alone was ever a significant force in the region or that the Chief Kebisu of Tutu ever existed.

Evidence suggests that Tutu was just a poor outpost of the Iama community. Early captains found Tutu covered with low scrub, with no trees for shade. At one end was a collection of mean huts where up to fifty men and their families lived according to season — perhaps a hundred and fifty people in all. As there were only shallow pools of brackish, dirty water on Tutu, drinking water was brought in lengths of bamboo from Iama, twenty kilometres away. Significantly Kebisu's name rarely appears in historical accounts yet the name Maino of Iama appears frequently, and it is known that he guided early missionaries along the Papuan coast where he had considerable influence. It has been claimed that Kebisu planned the attack on Bligh, also it has been said that he was Maino's father, but all that can definitely be said is that Maino was probably a leader among the Iama/Tutu community in the early 1870s and that this community did exert some control over trade between Papua and the islands further south. Yet whatever the truth, the hour of change was upon them, and the Europeans' greed for shell was to throw the Islanders into a period of confusion and despair.

Banner returned to Sydney where the arrival of tons of good shell at three to four hundred pounds a ton caused a stir in the bustling *entrepôt* port. In the next few years swashbucklers from all over the Pacific flocked to the Torres Strait.

Banner established a permanent station on Tutu, and other adventurers quickly set up stations on other islands.

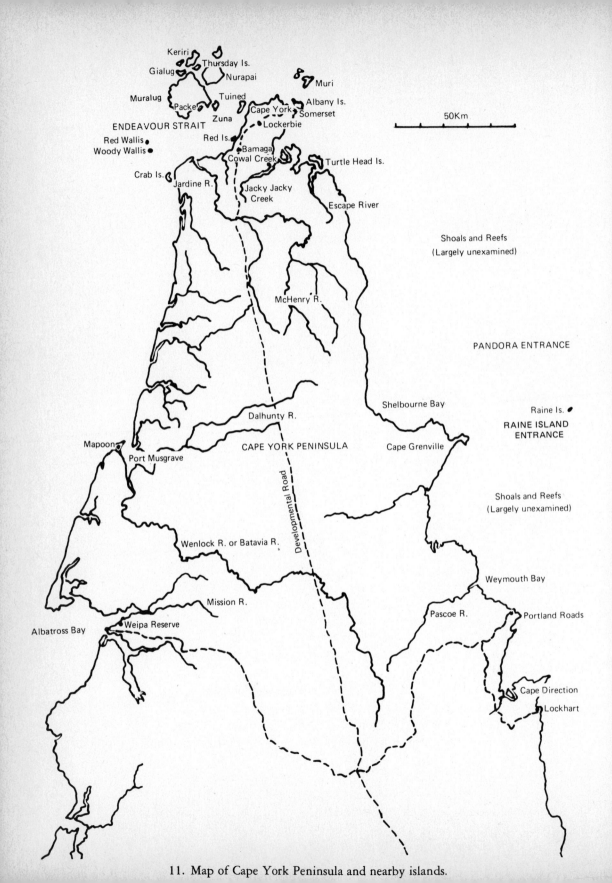

11. Map of Cape York Peninsula and nearby islands.

2

Cape York Peninsula: Explorers and Developers

On 11 June 1770 the *Endeavour*, with James Cook as master, struck a reef about thirty kilometres off the north Queensland coast. At one time the ship seemed likely to sink but running repairs enabled it to limp in towards the coast where, three days after first striking the reef, Cook was fortunate to discover an excellent anchorage and laying-up place within a river mouth. Here the ship was unloaded and careened. A small tent colony and piles of the *Endeavour*'s stores and equipment marked the first European settlement on Cape York Peninsula.

Cook was the first European to maintain friendly contact with the indigenous Australians over an extended period. They visited his camp in groups of up to eighteen, though they never brought women any closer than two hundred metres. None was taller than about a metre and a half and all were slender with close cropped hair. No clothing was worn at any time but some men were found to decorate their bodies with red and white ochre, and ornaments of twisted hair and shell. Some wore bones through their noses. They speared turtle, kangaroos, fish and birds, cooking them over fires before eating. A species of taro grows about the area, the roots providing a starch food base and the tops a green vegetable. Shellfish could be easily obtained by coasting over the shallow sandbanks about the mouth of the river.

Cook's men in fact spent much of their visit exploiting the natural food resources. Each day parties went out netting fish, shooting kangaroos and birds, collecting shellfish and spearing turtle. At one time twelve turtles lay upturned on the deck of the *Endeavour* waiting for use. Fresh food was a welcome change from the severe biscuit and salt meat diet necessary on a long voyage; however it also brought about a dispute with the Aborigines.

On 19th July eleven Aboriginal men on board the *Endeavour* attempted to carry off two of the turtles lying on the deck. Sailors intervened and, after an argument, evicted the Aborigines who tried to throw overboard everything they could lay hands on. On reaching shore the Aborigines, thoroughly aroused, set fire to grass about the camp so that the European sailors were fortunate to lose only a pig. Cook felt obliged to fire a musket, hitting one man who fled leaving a trail of blood. Yet an hour later the British sailors and Aboriginal warriors were again reconciled and friendly. Four days later an unarmed white straggler sat down to a kangaroo and fowl lunch with some Aboriginal men in the bush, who then directed the muddled sailor back to his ship.

On 4 August the *Endeavour* sailed out into the maze of reefs once more. Cook and his men left Cape York Peninsula with a mixed impression of its inhabitants. They could certainly be friendly and Cook felt that "in reality they are far more happier than we Europeans", noting that they declined to accept any of the trinkets he pressed upon them and refused to part with any of their own meagre possessions. They could also however show great truculence in relation to the exploitation of their land by Europeans, particularly when in the case of the turtles they had wanted only two of the twelve the whites had taken. It would have been more diplomatic and fairer to have let them go.

The Aborigines of Cape York Peninsula were divided into a multiplicity of different tribes, each living a nomadic existence in its own circumstances. Some groups dwelt on the rocky east coast and visited the reefs and cays in outrigger canoes. Others paddled bark canoes around swampy river estuaries. Others lived on the flat plains of the west coast — with clearly distinct dry and wet seasons. Others lived about the rainforest running down the skeleton of the Great Dividing Range. Each environment demanded different customs, priorities and foods.

A feature of northern Cape York Peninsula Aboriginal society was its contact with Papuan society via the Torres Strait. Two significant Papuan importations were the dug-out canoe and the wooden drum using a reptilian skin. At first the canoes were traded across by Islanders in the Torres Strait but eventually Australian craftsmen began constructing their own, employing fire and an adze with a hard shell as a cutting edge. Dug-out canoes with outriggers were found as far south as the Endeavour River where, during Cook's visit, the group apparently possessed only one, a little over four metres long and able to seat four people. Cook also discovered that every island within the Great Barrier Reef on which he landed, had been visited by Aborigines on a regular basis.

It is known that seventy-three different fruits, forty-six different roots, nineteen different seeds and eleven types of green leaves were eaten by Aboriginal food gatherers on Cape York Peninsula. This region compares favourably with other areas of Australia (such as Arnhem Land) and, with other food sources available, provided for the dense coastal population commented upon by Cook. Along the coasts shellfish were of great importance. At Weipa great shell mounds nine metres high mark traditional camping grounds used over eight centuries.

The Wik Monkan group on the west coast stored nonda plums in deep holes dug in the sand, whilst on the east coast other fruits were sun dried, treated with red ochre and carried in ti tree bark containers. However, while these efforts at preservation show foresight, they were in a sense luxuries because natural foods were so abundant as to make such pre-cautions unnecessary. This abundance probably explains why the Aborigines of the peninsula, though in contact with agricultural practice through the Islanders of the Muralug group, Badu, Moa and Nahgi, did not take it up. But whilst they may have enjoyed a more varied diet than their northern neighbours, their wandering, nomadic life retarded other features by which sophistication is sometimes measured. Elaborate housing, clothing, art or utensils could play no great part in a life dependent on facility of movement. In the absence of material items the whole society resided in the people of the society and the land in which they lived. As the land was lost and the people died, there was little for the survivors to cling to, and so they too would die.

In the years that followed Cook's visit, with the establishment and expansion of Australian colonies, ships sailed north and south, mostly outside the reef till they reached Raine Island which designated the entrance to the Torres Strait. There was little need for ships to visit the coast of far north Queensland and little inclination in view of the reefs that enveloped it.

King in 1818, with the *Mermaid*, explored and surveyed the east coast, inaccurately as it turned out, and for one reason or another fired on the Aborigines on several occasions. On 24 June 1843 the *Bramble*, whilst engaged in charting the coast with the *Fly*, was sent ashore to measure a meridian bearing near Cape Direction. The landing party was attacked and a man hit in the back by a barbed spear, which proved impossible to remove. He died three days later.

This documented history of hostility which began with the visits of Janzoon (*Duyfken* 1606) and Cook, and continued with King and Yule (master of the *Bramble*), augured ill for the plans of Edmund Kennedy when in 1848 he decided to trek up through the interior of Cape York Peninsula from base to tip — an area completely unknown to Europeans. Calling on eight years' experience in surveying and exploration throughout southern and eastern Australia with Sir Thomas Mitchell, he intended to take a heavily equipped party from Rockingham Bay (well south of Cairns) overland to Albany Island, where the *Rattlesnake* would replenish their supplies. From there the party would pass down the west coast of the Peninsula to the Barcoo River in Central Queensland.

This hopelessly ambitious project was further hampered by other factors which, though not known, should have been anticipated. The first was that the country through which Kennedy now sought to push thirteen men, twenty-eight horses, a hundred sheep, four dogs and three carts, was not the rolling plains, desert and woodland he was accustomed to. Kennedy would encounter rugged mountains, mist, dense rainforest and leeches; ti tree plains with scorching baked mud underfoot and vision restricted to a few feet; impassable mangrove swamps swarming with mosquitoes and crocodiles; stoney ridges where only the anthills rose from the rocks and rubble.

Via the traditional trade routes Aboriginal groups had knowledge of white men, with their wealth of goods and behaviour which often seemed selfish and intractable. In no way could the European motive for exploration be understood or appreciated by the locals, who were consequently uncertain in their dealings with whites. It is probable that had they appreciated the motive they would have resisted even more strongly. The poor mobility of Kennedy's column left it vulnerable to the Aboriginal harassing tactics.

On 21 May 1848 the *Rattlesnake* landed the adventurers, their stores and animals, on the beach at Rockingham Bay. Two weeks later they were still there, as the rainforest prevented them travelling west or north. Fortunately the *Rattlesnake* was able to ferry them over the Tully River to the south but it was not till 27 June that the expedition finally was able to move off the beach. Almost immediately they met large groups of Aborigines who casually picked up and carried off anything they fancied, Kennedy generally not wishing to press the point until one, who appeared a group leader, snatched a pistol. The party's blacksmith forcibly removed the gun from the man's hand hoping to mollify him with the gift of a handkerchief.

In early July came the first fight. Jacky, the only Aborigine with Kennedy's party, was alone some distance from the main group when he was threatened by excited warriors with spears poised. Kennedy with armed men in support came to his assistance and, ignoring Jacky's warning, walked towards the spearmen motioning them to lay down their weapons. A spear was thrown, narrowly missing Kennedy, followed by a roll of musketry. When the smoke cleared one Aborigine was dead on the ground and at least three others had been dragged away by their comrades. Kennedy was upset, knowing that news of the encounter would spread far and wide across his intended route, alerting groups he had yet to meet and disposing them to hostility.

A week later the carts were left bogged to the axles in a swamp and the party set out again — more mobile but with insufficient supplies. In the rainforest-clad ranges around the present site of Cairns the first horses began to drop. The exhausted men now had their food rationed so that energy expended could not be replaced. In twelve days to 8 August the party travelled only a few kilometres.

Finally free of the ranges, they still had almost a thousand kilometres of scrub and rough country to struggle through. Dying horses were shot for meat and the hungry men resorted to theft from the dwindling stores. Kennedy felt he could trust only two of the twelve men in the camp so that one of these had constantly to guard the rations. The sheep were bone and wool and the burly kangaroo dog Kennedy had brought with him died of exhaustion. Only the sick now rode the stumbling horses but salvation lay in reaching Albany Island, so Kennedy pressed them northwards.

Ever present were the people of the swamp, bush and forest — following behind, hemming them in. As the party tried to pull their horses across a dry gully near the Mitchell River Aborigines again disputed their passage, throwing spears till five shots were fired and some tribesmen wounded. On two occasions on the dry plains Aborigines started grassfires to chase the whites along.

Every weary night each man in the party stood a one-hour watch. Sometimes, as the Irishman or Englishman stood in the red glow of the fire peering into the implacable blackness of the Australian night, spears hissed into the camp. Shots were fired off blindly into the dark.

By the time the exhausted party reached Weymouth Bay eight men could go no further. Leaving these men what scanty provisions he could spare and two horses for meat, on November 13 Kennedy, Jacky and three others continued north. The only men with any strength left were the wiry, young Aborigine and Kennedy who drove himself on. Six days later another man dropped in his tracks and the blacksmith accidentally shot himself in the chest. Kennedy left them with the other European in an inland camp amongst thick scrub near a low hill. The two sick men were near death and the third could not live alone in this land without food.

A hundred kilometres north was Albany Island, the *Rattlesnake* and safety. Kennedy was months late but he still hoped the ship would be there — it was the only hope for any of them. But now Kennedy and Jacky were entering the grounds of the Jadhaiganas. Tempered by contact and friction with the Islanders of the Torres Strait and Europeans they presented a formidable obstacle for the two intruders, one white, one black, who blundered into their domain.

Kennedy and Jacky came across one group of men who called "*Powdah, powdah*" and rubbed their abdomens. Kennedy interpreted this as a sign of peace.* In any case he thought the

---

* This is a direct link with the Torres Strait confirming the cultural exchange that had taken place. Lewis landing at Mer in 1836 was greeted by Islanders calling "*Poud, poud*" and similarly rubbing their stomachs. Like Kennedy, Lewis interpreted this as a peaceful greeting.

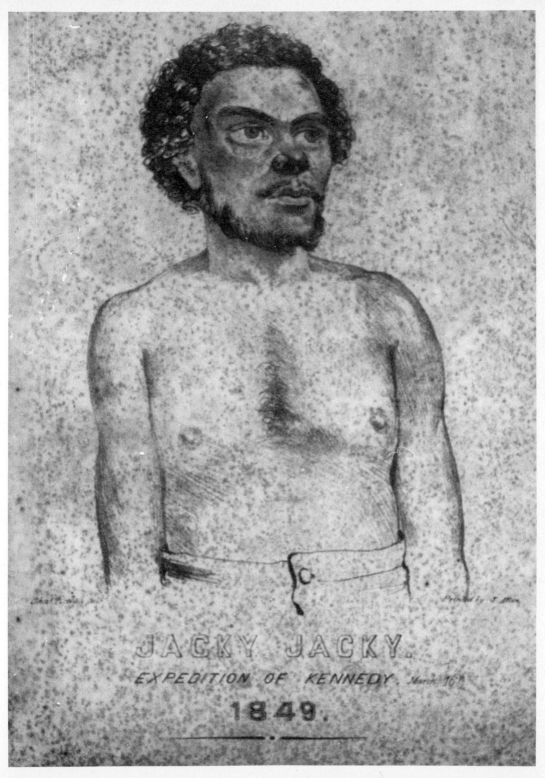

12. Jacky, the hero of the ill-fated Kennedy expedition, on his return to Sydney in 1849. Photograph by courtesy of the Mitchell Library, Sydney, from a lithograph by Charles Rodius.

men friendly and gave them fish hooks and ordered Jacky to give them his knife. But Jacky did so reluctantly, as he did not trust them.

Here the inaccurate observations of King were to contribute to the tragedy. King had compiled a detailed but totally misleading report on the Escape River area, which Kennedy and Jacky were now entering. He wrote that the Escape River turned northwards from its mouth and that the land to its south was "woods" with "an inviting aspect". In reality the Escape flowed from the south and the country was a vast flood plain. It was by then early December and the wet season was upon them so that, unbeknown to Kennedy, they were heading into a swampy cul-de-sac. It was here that the Jadhaiganas caught them.

On December 13 the two men plodded amongst the scrub and anthills, leading their horses through the streaming rain. Behind and to the sides armed warriors flitted between the trees. Kennedy forbade Jacky to shoot at them, even when spears started flying and both horses were wounded. Then Jacky's horse went down and Kennedy was hit in the back. Jacky pulled him behind some anthills and, as the attackers closed in, shot one in the face at close range knocking him back into the grass to be pulled away by other tribesmen.

In the lull which followed Jacky examined Kennedy's wound to find the barbed spear head protruding from Kennedy's abdomen. He knew it was fatal and told Kennedy so. Soon spears began to fly again, striking Kennedy in the side and the leg. Jacky was wounded in the head, and blood streaming down prevented him from aiming his musket accurately. After it seemed that the warriors had again withdrawn, Jacky dashed out to recover saddlebags from the fallen horses. While he was away Aborigines stripped Kennedy's body. He buried Kennedy and hid the expedition logs nearby.

Two weeks later Jacky finally emerged from the crocodile infested swamps onto the beach opposite Albany Island to be picked up by the *Ariel* which was still there, in spite of the expiration of its charter and the departure of the *Rattlesnake*.

The *Ariel* quickly returned to Shelbourne Bay where a party was sent ashore. No trace was found of the three men, however a canoe came out to the ship and in it was discovered clothing belonging to the missing men. One of the Aborigines in the canoe was captured, others were shot as they tried to reach shore.

During the night the prisoner escaped overboard and there was nothing to do but go to Weymouth Bay where the eight men had been left some eight weeks before. Here they were just in time to avert the massacre of the two men still alive. The bush swarmed with Aborigines and the landing party was obliged to retreat hurriedly, half carrying the scarecrows they had rescued, whilst the camp was ransacked by triumphant warriors. Of the six men in the camp who had died of hunger and exhaustion the remains of only two were recovered. They were later buried on Albany Island.

On his return to Sydney in 1849 Jacky was a hero. A portrait of him was painted within a week of his arrival, showing the spear wound in his forehead received in the Kennedy fight.

The annihilation of the expedition profoundly shocked the colony and was to discourage any further land exploration in Cape York Peninsula for another fifteen years. An outraged white in 1888 wrote: "As cowardly as cruel, the blacks had never dared to face them whilst in an attitude of watchfulness and defence. They were simply harassing them to death — watching and waiting, night and day, for a chance to steal on them unperceived, and slaughter them at no risk to themselves". This of course was the rather jaundiced view of the losing side. The Aborigines, on the other hand, could regard their tactics as both sensible and effective. Any parties venturing into the area in future would know what to expect.

Jacky, confused and scarred by his experiences, went droving in western New South Wales. One night in 1854 near Albury he fell into a campfire whilst in a drunken stupor and was burned to death.

The future of the northern Peninsula was, to a large extent, to be determined by events in the Torres Strait, for the Strait had become an important shipping route. From 1791, when Edwards lost the *Pandora*, to 1864 more than thirty ships had been completely wrecked, with the loss of hundreds of lives. Fifty-six lives were lost in the wreck of the *Mersey* alone in 1805.

1829 was a bad year with at least three total wrecks in the Torres Strait and others off the east coast of Cape York Peninsula illustrating just how treacherous the coral barrier could be.

In May 1829 the *Comet* went down on Boot Reef, apparently

without loss of life.* In the same month the *Governor Ready* was wrecked on reefs near Aureed Island with the crew subsequently making a safe passage in small boats to Timor. In June the *Mermaid* was lost among reefs near Cairns. The crew, after eleven days in the boats, were rescued by the *Admiral Gifford* and shortly afterwards were taken aboard the *Swiftsure* bound for Africa. Within eighteen hours of boarding the *Swiftsure*, the *Mermaid*'s unfortunate crew were again shipwrecked when their host vessel sank somewhere in the Torres Strait. The *Resource* picked up both crews and transported them to Port Raffles (in the Northern Territory).

Bligh was the first to officially suggest a refuge for seamen in distress in the Torres Strait. It was not till 1824, however, that a depot was actually established on Booby Island as it had been found that Islanders rarely visited the rock. Another famous function of the Booby Island Depot was that of a post office. Passing ships would leave mail, which they were unable to deliver, in a steel box in the "Post Office Cave" and pick up that which they could convey to the correct destination. The system apparently worked.

In 1844 H.M.S. *Fly* and *Bramble* constructed a beacon and shelter on Raine Island marking the eastern entrance to the Torres Strait. Beams salvaged from the *Marthe Ridgeway* (wrecked 1842) and local stone and lime were employed. The building took the form of a circular tower nine metres in diameter at the base and about twenty metres high. It took Lieutenant Ince and his forty-man working party — including twenty convict volunteers from New South Wales — four months to complete the task. The beacon was painted with alternate red and white vertical stripes and, standing twenty-three metres above sea level, was visible from the masthead of a ship up to twenty kilometres distant. The shelter is thought to have been first used by the survivors of the *Enchantress* in 1850.

In 1848 thirty-two vessels from Sydney alone passed through the Torres Strait so that the total could well have exceeded one hundred. In 1861, by which time from fifty to eighty ships

* The master of the *Comet* on this occasion was James Fraser. Fraser was involved in another, more notorious, shipwreck in 1836 when the *Stirling Castle*, of which he was master, went aground near Cook's "Great Sandy Island". The entire crew excepting Fraser's wife Eliza were killed by Aborigines. She was subsequently rescued by a Brisbane convict and the island became known as Fraser Island.

annually passed through the Torres Strait heading south, Governor Bowen wrote to the British government proposing a settlement in the north: "In a naval and military point of view a post at or near Cape York would be most valuable, and its importance is daily increasing with the augmentation of the commerce passing by this route, especially since the establishment of a French colony and naval station at New Caledonia."

The Imperial government agreed to contribute £7,000, twenty-five marines, under a Lieutenant Pascoe, and a Dr Haran as medical officer. Mr John Jardine (police magistrate, Rockhampton) was appointed government resident to the new station, named Somerset (after the Duke of Somerset), on the mainland opposite Albany Island.

On 29 July 1864 the party arrived on the H.M.S. *Salamander* in the Albany Passage. They found that a Captain Edwards had been living on Albany Island for some time, having erected a store and a curing house for bêche-de-mer out of local stone. By 1 August four ships were anchored off Somerset, the marines were ashore throwing up the prefabricated housing the expedition had brought, and the horses and some wretched sheep had been put onto Albany Island to graze.

Jardine's two sons Frank, aged twenty-two, and Alexander, twenty, decided to use the settlement as the nucleus of a cattle run. They resolved to take a mob overland, through unmapped country, from a station at the head of the Gilbert River to Somerset. They planned to avoid the country that had defeated Kennedy by keeping west on the more open country round the Gulf. A government offer to promote the party was refused on the grounds that it was a private business venture. With the Jardines went four Aboriginal stockmen and four Europeans, all armed with powerful, breech-loading rifles. Forty-one horses and a mule were taken for packing and riding.

As anticipated the ten-month trip (from Rockhampton to Somerset) developed into a struggle against hunger, the country and the people who lived there. At an early stage grassfires destroyed most of the Jardines' camp and provisions, restricting the travellers to a predominantly beef diet. Twice Aborigines offered battle — the second being the notorious "Battle of the Mitchell".

At the Mitchell River eighty determined spearmen attacked the ten intruders with vigour and courage. One of the whites to

13. Albany Pass was found to be a useful passage but an uncomfortable anchorage. Somerset is on the right. From the *Picturesque Atlas of Australasia*, vol. 2, 1886.

have a narrow escape that day was Alexander Jardine; a barbed spear lodged in the ground between his legs. Using the superior mobility of horses, and their superior weapons the Jardines forced the Aborigines to retreat, caught them against a swamp and shot them to pieces. The ten cattlemen fired fifty-nine shots killing thirty Aborigines, yet not one of their own party was injured.

The encounter merely emphasized the futility of frontal assaults on well-armed whites. The blacks fell back on their guerilla tactics, worrying the expedition to within sight of the Somerset settlement which was reached on 2 March 1865. The overlanders had lost fifty of their two hundred and fifty cattle and nearly all their horses, walking the last five hundred kilometres, but they had not lost a man and they had shown that it could be done.

Near the top of Cape York Peninsula Frank followed a river which he believed was the Escape, however it flowed towards the west coast rather than the east. Frank named it the Deception River — later changed to the Jardine River.

Somerset soon justified its existence when it gave succour to the crews of three wrecked ships, however it remained a besieged fort on a hostile coast. Few ships in fact bothered to call there as it lay to the south of the shipping passage. Unscrupulous bêche-de-mer captains frequently had every reason to avoid the law and resent its intrusion into the area.

John Jardine returned to Rockhampton before the end of 1865. The next appointee, Captain Simpson R.N., left after completing little more than a year at this lonely post despite the fact that he had been appointed for three years. In desperation the Queensland government appointed Frank Jardine who was young, but tough and experienced. Jardine in fact spent much of his time battling Aborigines. Fortunately for Somerset, the Gudangs of the extreme north of Cape York Peninsula had received rough treatment from their neighbours to the south, including the Jadhaigainas who had killed Kennedy. In the past these Gudangs had often allied themselves with the Islanders of

14. Somerset near Cape York. Following the transfer of the administration to Thursday Island, Jardine purchased the comfortable residency on the hill, from where he supervised the operations of his pearling fleet. From the *Picturesque Atlas of Australasia*, vol. 2, 1886.

the southern Torres Strait and now they were prepared to assist the whites in return for protection, or perhaps merely to see their old enemies discomforted.

The Royal Marines clumped about the bush for a while in their heavy boots and red coats but, proving completely useless, were withdrawn. In their place came a small party of Aboriginal policemen belonging to the Queensland Native Mounted Police. This organization was an extremely effective instrument from the white point of view. The black policemen, working far from their own tribal grounds, under the loose control of white officers, became the scourge of the bush Aborigines. The whites armed them, mounted them, and more or less pointed them in the right direction. In the hands of a man such as Jardine they became a terrible weapon.

Jagg and Kennet who tried to conduct an Aboriginal mission at Somerset, beginning in February 1867, wrote of the impossible situation prevailing at the time. On one occasion an Irish policeman ordered an Aborigine to make him a spear. When the Aborigine refused he was threatened with imprisonment and as a result the whole tribe took fright and disappeared. Later an Aboriginal policeman shot a Gudang woman, cut out her liver and ate it. On another occasion two of the Aboriginal police, named Sambo and Barnie, deserted to the Aborigines in the bush, whom they encouraged to attack the outstation which lay five kilometres inland from Somerset. The man in charge of the station was killed in the attack. However the local Aborigines were not happy with these developments and allowed the Jardines to persuade them to capture the deserters. When word was received that the two had been caught and lay bound in the bush, Frank and Alexander rode out and shot them in the back of the head. It was Sunday 20 June 1867. Twelve months later the mission, unable to prosper under these conditions, was closed.

In 1869 Frank Jardine was given leave of absence and Henry Majoribanks Chester was appointed in his place. Chester was thirty-seven years of age, with experience in the Indian Navy and throughout southern and central Queensland. He must have been appalled at the appearance of the settlement. There were five European police and five native troopers with seventeen horses. Many of Jardine's cattle had been speared or chased into the bush so that only a hundred remained. The nearest town was Cardwell a thousand kilometres to the south.

Jardine's instructions could not have encouraged Chester: "He impressed on me never on any account to leave the house without carrying a revolver even if only going as far as the stock-yard and cautioned me, in the event of a night attack by the Aborigines, never to stand upright on the verandah where the Aborigines could see me but to go on my hands and knees, the better to see them." As late as December 1873 local Aborigines killed a pearler at his camp almost within sight of Somerset.

Despite difficulties Chester made an effort to institute justice, rough though it necessarily was. He also became involved with events in the Torres Strait when he investigated the massacre of the crew of the *Speerweer* in 1869 at Gialug. He took fair and decisive measures when, in April 1870, he had the three alleged ring leaders shot on the beach at Nahgi. However his tenancy on this occasion was of brief duration for Frank Jardine returned in 1871. In May 1873 D'Oyley Aplin was appointed resident magistrate but he died shortly afterwards and was buried on Albany Island. Jardine was appointed again, and then in 1875 Chester once more took over. There were also at times several temporary or extremely brief tenants such as Dalrymple and Beddome. This confusing merry-go-round reflected the futility of the Somerset post. Pearling was by 1875 well established with permanent stations on several islands of the Torres Strait. The tempestuous Italian, D'Albertis, pushed up the Fly River and the L.M.S. had teachers on many islands and even scattered along the coast of Papua. Yet in spite of this activity the "New Singapore", as Somerset had been termed, did not grow. There were the same ramshackle huts, the wild Aboriginal troopers, the crocodiles and the trackless bush. It was not until 1877 that the Somerset station was closed and Chester was appointed as the first police magistrate at Thursday Island. Most government buildings at Somerset were dismantled and removed to the new post.

In 1873 the interior of Cape York Peninsula was still largely unknown to the Europeans. Kennedy and the Jardines had passed through with their small groups of desperate men, but the work of a prospector named Mulligan unleashed a flood of miners into the area. In September 1873 Mulligan and his party emerged from the bush of southern Cape York Peninsula with a valuable weight of fine alluvial gold. The rush was on. Eighteen months later 35,000 miners were in the Cooktown-Palmer River region, more than half of them Chinese.

Naturally this enormous concentration of diggers quickly exhausted available alluvial deposits on the Palmer. Enterprising men fanned north and west searching for similar strikes. Gold was soon discovered on the Laura and Normanby Rivers and later on the Coen and Wenlock further north. These smaller successive rushes were rough affairs with hundreds of tough, heavily armed diggers forcing themselves into the traditional lands of an Aboriginal people determined to resist them at every step.

Around Cooktown hundreds of whites and Chinese died by spear or club. The Aborigines, deprived of their hunting grounds, are alleged to have resorted to large scale cannibalism. For their part the whites and Chinese resorted to a barbarous war of extermination. Warden Hill, a government officer, summed up the general policy: ". . . the only wise thing to do on seeing a black was to shoot, and shoot straight".

Sub Inspector O'Connor established a Native Mounted Police post at Laura with twenty-four Aboriginal troopers — mostly from Fraser Island. The white officers led their troopers from the rear, often becoming mere horse holders as their men stripped down to cartridge belts and caps and wriggled into the scrub to shoot wild tribesmen — men, women and children.

One such punitive raid followed the wounding of the Cooktown harbour master and a merchant, on a beach not far north of Cooktown. O'Connor, now based in Cooktown, and his black police, a week after the incident, came across thirty-one Aborigines bathing at a beach near where the attack had taken place. The N.M.P. efficiently killed twenty-eight of them. One wonders what the Fraser Island men thought at the sight of the broken bodies on the bloody sand and the corpses bobbing in the shallows on a beach so much like the beaches of their own beautiful island so far to the south.

This butchery so close to Cooktown by members of the colony's police force received official sanction. The situation in the recesses of forest clad mountains and on the endless plains can only be imagined.

Lawes of the L.M.S. who had visited both Cooktown and Somerset before entering New Guinea wrote in 1883: "Nowhere in the world have aborigines been so basely and cruelly treated as in Queensland — the half has never been told...". A comparison of the fortunes of indigenous people on either side of the Torres Strait is illuminating.

Sir William MacGregor, administrator of British New Guinea, later served as governor of Queensland (1909-14) and, though successful, he confessed in confidential despatches to the Colonial Office that he was troubled by the attitude and methods adopted by white Queenslanders towards their black minority. Sir Hubert Murray of Papua conceived a rational "catch the guilty" policy and prided in it. In 1904 he wrote: "However there is one thing of which the New Guinea Administration can not be proud enough, and that is their treatment of the natives; it is a great contrast to the way we dealt with them in Australia. There have been no 'dispersals' as in Queensland...". A select committee on the Queensland Native Police had already established that "dispersing" meant "shooting at them".

The gold miners explored every possible area of Cape York Peninsula where gold might be found. Robert Logan Jack, a government geologist, went on two expeditions during 1879 and 1880 with two other Europeans and two Aborigines. He commented on the vast areas which had been swept by grassfires begun by Aborigines. He supposed this was to produce green shoots for kangaroos and wallabies, though a more reasonable explanation is that it was employed as a hunting method, as it still is today at times by semi-tribalized Aborigines on the Peninsula. A further explanation lies in the fact that unburnt grass, over three or four seasons, often becomes long, tangled, and matted — the refuge of snakes and difficult to walk through. Regular burning keeps the country open for ease of movement and denies game thick cover. Fires were not used as a battle tactic against Jack's party, but he was left in no doubt as to the Aborigines' attitude. He was ambushed, and wounded in the neck by an iron-tipped spear.

In the hundred years since Cook's visit Aborigines had gradually started to use metals in the construction of their few utensils — old tins, bolts, door hinges, telegraph wire, pickheads — and so even away from the shootings and the police, Aboriginal society was changing, however imperceptibly, and would never again be the same.

No other gold field such as the Palmer was ever found but the miners had opened up the region and were soon followed by cattlemen. The gold miners had come and gone but the cattle-men and their coastal counterparts, the copra producers, were there to stay. Soon the coast would be dotted with coconut plantations and the near-empty bush would ring to the stock whip and bellows of thousands of cattle.

The commencement of the direct steamship service from England via the Torres Strait in 1880 prompted construction of a telegraph line from Cooktown to Cape York. Telegraphic communication between the Strait and Brisbane was a matter of great concern particularly with regard to German interest in New Guinea.

In 1883 John Bradford, Queensland's Post and Telegraph Department inspector of lines and mail route services, was detailed to lead a four-man party from Cooktown to Somerset in order to survey a route for the telegraph line that would follow. During a brief stop at Townsville on the voyage north Bradford visited R.L. Jack, the ex-government geologist who had been speared whilst exploring the Peninsula four years previously. Jack's maps were to prove extremely useful.

On arrival at Cooktown Bradford was advised by the police to increase the size of the expedition by at least another two men. When finally the party left Cooktown on 6 June 1883 Bradford had four Europeans with him, Jimmy Sam Goon (a Chinese cook) and Jacky (an Aborigine). Each man was armed with a Martini carbine and heavy revolver and had been led to anticipate trouble with the blacks.

Bradford was required to traverse fairly difficult country along the east coast where it was expected that settlement would take place and where telegraphic services would be demanded. For one section of the journey they followed the track blazed by Jack.

Aborigines again confirmed their mastery of the environment by being an ever present threat without revealing themselves to be shot. Their fires constantly hounded the expedition, obliging it to alter course to the west and depriving the horses of feed. Eventually twenty-three of the party's thirty-six horses died, and the others survived by eating the men's flour ration and were reserved for carrying equipment.

By early August the men were starving. No game was seen.

Plodding along over the sand ridges and breaking through almost impenetrable belts of scrub had taxed their strength to the limit and the party covered only six or seven kilometres a day, but fortunately the end of the journey was in sight. On 12 August they stumbled across the Jardine River, though they did not realize it at the time. Several good-sized fish were caught and devoured. The expedition wandered about for another twelve days before finally emerging onto the shores of the Gulf of Carpentaria between the Jardine River mouth and Cowal Creek. Bradford's task now was to examine the area about Cape York and find Somerset which lay on the east coast.

The pack horses were so weak at this stage that equipment was buried at locations along the beach where it could be easily retrieved by boat. But as the whites straggled east towards Cape York the Aborigines followed digging up the equipment. None of it was ever recovered. On Wednesday 29 August the expedition followed a horse track into Somerset where Frank Jardine welcomed them.

During his eighty-five days in the bush, despite difficulties, Bradford had compiled a satisfactory account of terrain over the projected route and the local resources (such as bloodwood, ironbark) which were available. His report provided the basis for the subsequent construction of the line which began in late 1885 and was completed on 25 August 1887, terminating at Cape York where it was connected to a submarine cable from Thursday Island laid the previous year. Five relay stations had been built (McDonnell, Moreton, Mein, Coen and Musgrave). The Cape York Telegraph Office was a large wooden, verandahed building with loopholes cut in the rear walls for the operators to shoot through in the event of Aboriginal attack. Only two and a half years after its construction a breathless Aborigine galloped up the dusty track from Somerset with probably the most important message the office was ever to transmit. The steamship *Quetta* had foundered in the Adolphus Passage and three hundred people were missing.

An industry which flared briefly then died was sandal-wooding. By 1900 sandalwood was difficult to find on the islands of the Pacific, following a century of exploitation with much of the produce passing through Sydney, however it was still much in demand. The wood gives off a strange, aromatic, sweet acrid smoke when burning and had from time immemorial been used for making joss sticks to be burned in Chinese temples. It was also used to construct luxury items. Sandalwood is the term applied generally to varieties of trees of the genus *Santalum* and some of the *Fusanus*. In Australia it is found in Western Australia and Cape York Peninsula. The sandalwood once found heaped on the wharves at Thursday Island was spindly and twisted and of poor quality compared with that of Fiji or Hawaii. Yet Australian sandalwood shipped from Perth and Thursday Island was sold to Singapore, Hong Kong and ports in China and was to continue to be exported till shortly before World War II.

Luggers working the Gulf of Carpentaria anchored at one of the muddy estuaries of that coast, sending teams into the dry woodland searching for the trees, or perhaps meeting a gaunt, sunburned bushman with his black helpers, horses and a ton of sandalwood they had packed to the coast from the interior. Paid in food, tobacco and ammunition they would disappear into the bush to emerge again with another haul of sandalwood when the lugger called again in eight weeks time.

Among those Europeans who settled on the peninsula was Jack McLaren. In 1911 he took up a lease on 120 hectares and over the following years developed a coconut plantation. Subsequently he wrote a book, *My Crowded Solitude* (1926), describing his own experiences and recording those of the Aborigines who lived around him. Nevertheless despite the sympathetic attitude of many Europeans, the Aboriginal population of Cape York Peninsula was in a period of decline. Whilst many died of bullet wounds, the fact was that disease was the real enemy. It stalked unseen among them killing, crippling, and sapping the energy of a society in confusion. Those tribes who had befriended the whiteman now found that their tribes were dying anyway. Leprosy was thought to have been introduced by the Chinese at Cooktown and spread throughout Cape York to the Torres Strait Islands where isolated cases may be found to this day.

A report by the H.M.S. *Beagle* as early as 1879 stated that "the chief sickness amongst the (pearl) shellers is, I believe, venereal, which they pick up from the native women, there being camps of natives along the Australian coast where regular prostitutes are kept who are badly diseased". Thus the entrance of some Aborigines into a European exchange economy was not a happy one. In order to obtain goods which they desired they sometimes traded one of the few commodities they had which outsiders were interested in — women. Untreated, venereal disease resulted in sterility, fear and death. Birth rates fell and death rates rose.

Ion Idriess, in two separate books, described an occasion on the east coast of Cape York Peninsula when he came upon rows of dark shapes washing in the tide. An influenza epidemic had fatally infected whole tribes who sought relief from their fever on the cool beaches of the Cape. High temperatures forced them into the shallows where they died, and the tide washed them up. The Spanish Influenza epidemics which swept the world after the Great War had an especially disastrous effect on the Aborigines of Cape York Peninsula. Some groups were completely wiped out, others decimated and broken.

The Jardine name continued to be linked with the area although Alexander Jardine was long gone from the cape. He worked as an engineer building roads in central Queensland after 1874 and died in London in 1920. His brother Frank however lived on Cape York Peninsula for the rest of his life and was buried there.

When the administration was transferred to Thursday Island Frank bought the residency on the hill overlooking the Albany Passage. His brother Charles joined him in establishing a copra plantation and pearling fleet based on Somerset. Following the H.M.S. *Basilisk*'s stay in 1873, the irascible Captain Moresby had complained that Frank was using his position and government employees to assist in these private projects. A board of inquiry subsequently exonerated Jardine. In 1880, by which time Frank was thirty-seven years old and no longer occupied a government position, the brothers owned four apparatus boats, three swimming boats and a tender, and employed two Europeans, fifteen Malays and Manilamen, sixteen Polynesians, two Chinese and thirty-two Aborigines.

Jardine came to rely heavily upon Manilamen, Malays and Samoans in his pearling and copra operations, and even married a Samoan girl. Yet there was another, more violent side to him. Dan de Busch, a half-caste Samoan who was reared at Somerset told of a time when Jardine, looking across Albany Passage with a telescope, saw an Aboriginal man fishing from the rocks. Without saying a word he took his rifle and with great deliberation placed a bullet in the man's chest, shattering a shell he wore suspended from the neck. Jardine then blew his whistle and when his retainers ran up, told them to go across to Albany Island in the whaleboat to pick up a crocodile he had just shot. After rowing through a stiff current to the spot indicated by Jardine, they discovered the dead man with the broken shell ornament around nis neck. The wanton killing put a chill of fear through the whole Somerset community, such intimidation probably being Jardine's intention.

Inland, Jardine had another station constructed to serve as head station for his cattle run. The new station, called "Lockerbie", continued to suffer attacks from neighbouring Aboriginal tribes — the contest becoming a vicious battle for survival. Aboriginal oral tradition gives accounts of the fighting which subsequently degenerated into a massacre. On one occasion the Aborigines, in an effort to escape their relentless pursuers, climbed trees, but were shot out of the branches like parrots. Around Cowal Creek it is said Jardine killed black babies by striking their heads against trees. Jardine could not be speared, it is claimed by many Aborigines today, because he used to wear armour so that spears recoiled or broke. Whatever the truth of these stories they convey graphically the merciless nature of the struggle. It could have only one end. The area north of the Dulcie River was cleared of indigenous peoples, except for demoralized survivors gathered about Lockerbie and Somerset. These Gudangs were a classic example of how friendly Aboriginal tribes were doomed, just as their fierce cousins south of the Dulcie were also doomed.

The Gudangs had cooperated with both Jardine and Chester, yet they lost their land, which was now part of Jardine's cattle run, and their society disintegrated. In 1874 an officer on the H.M.S. *Challenger* wrote of the sorry, derelict Aborigines seen about Somerset: "a few more cases of gin and a few more years will see the last of them". He was not far wrong. In 1898 Haddon asked Jardine if it would be possible to include a study of the Gudang language in his general study of the Torres Strait. Jardine replied that whereas he could round up a few persons of Gudang descent, a language study was impossible since the language was to all purposes extinct. Yet this was only thirty three years since Jardine had first stumbled into Somerset after his epic trip up the peninsula.

When Frank Jardine died in 1919 he was buried on the hill at Somerset. His wife Sania died four years later and was buried next to him.

Among Europeans Jardine's passing was mourned, for he had contributed to development and progress. During his life he had generally been accorded great respect. In his later years ships passing the old residency frequently fired a salute.

Amongst elderly Aborigines today however Jardine's memory invokes a bitter hatred for it was their grandparents, uncles, aunts and parents who suffered. Tradition has it that after Jardine's burial tribesmen secretly visited the grave and through desecration committed a final act of vengeance.

3

The Coming of the Light

On 30 May 1871 the *Surprise* hove to off Erub in the eastern Torres Strait. The London Missionary Society leaders, Rev. S. MacFarlane and Rev. A. Murray, were beginning the slow conquest of southwest New Guinea for Christianity using the Torres Strait Islands as stepping stones. The station at Somerset had been functioning since 1864 and Jardine encouraged the L.M.S. to enter the islands as "The natives in the islands northwards and eastwards are said to be of milder dispositions especially islanders of Darnley . . . being of friendly dispositions and displaying considerable intelligence". He was also aware that South Sea and European boat crews were creating havoc around the islands. First bêche-de-mer, then pearling, had lured all types of men from all parts of the Pacific to the Torres Strait, and Jardine knew that it was beyond his capacity to regulate interaction between the indigenous people and avaricious newcomers. Permanent missions on the islands would provide a medium of local order and stability which could later be expanded.

Responsible pearlers realized that such a development was inevitable and advantageous in the long run. So it was that Banner, who now had a permanent station on Tutu, provided every assistance to the missionaries.

MacFarlane and Murray were guided about the strait by John Joseph, Banner's right-hand man. Joseph was a Tongan but had served in the British Navy in Crimea before coming to the

Torres Strait where he had quickly earned the friendship of several group leaders and become competent in the different Island languages. He was to prove invaluable.

For the Islanders too, the arrival of the missionaries was providential. Many islands were already being deserted by Islanders moving to larger groups for protection, yet even numbers could not prevent well-armed boat crews doing almost as they wished. Only the year before Mer had been the victim of a particularly vicious raid by crew from the *Woodlark*.

The Woodlark was a three-masted ship under a Captain Bruce who, seeking bêche-de-mer, had used Dauar (near Mer) as a base for two years in succession. The crew, who were mainly from the New Hebrides, amused themselves when not working by chasing girls.

On one occasion a party led by Jack Maori came across to Mer. Most people had fled into the forested hillsides of Gelam or the valley of Deaudupat. Some men however, incited by visitors from Masig, armed themselves and met the raiders on a path which runs east along the northern base of Gelam. A dispute followed and Jack Maori shot a Meriam with his pistol. In the confusion that ensued four Meriams isolated Jack, speared him in the back and cut off his head. The surviving boat crew retreated hurriedly to Dauar where Bruce grimly gathered his men together and armed them with cutlasses and firearms for a retaliatory raid. The following morning he led his men ashore on Mer. An old man came forward through the deserted village making signs of peace, indicating that he was not connected with the trouble. The excited South Sea men literally cut him to pieces with their cutlasses. Another man and woman were killed before Jack's headless corpse was found where it had fallen, and buried.

That night the entire population of Mer — which was probably greater than eight hundred — fled to traditional refuges in the interior, so that when Bruce's avengers landed next morning they were able to rummage through the empty huts and gardens, shooting any fragmented, fleeing groups they came across. Ten Meriams died that day, only three of whom were men. One of these men, after watching the cold-blooded shooting of a woman and her child, had launched a desperate attack on the heavily armed party. His knife was useless and he was gunned down without difficulty. The following day no

15. The Anglican Church on Erub. In 1971 ceremonies were conducted here to celebrate the centenary of the landing on the island by L.M.S. missionaries. This first major landing by missionaries on the Torres Strait Islands is commonly referred to as "the coming of the light". Photograph by courtesy of J. Manasero, Cairns.

raids were made but the South Sea men intercepted a canoe, kidnapped a girl and boy, and callously shot a number of men with them.

Haddon noted that "although they were great braggarts, the natives [of Mer] were unskilled at fighting, probably owing to lack of practice on account of their isolation".

Some days later the children were returned and relations restored. Bruce continued to use his station on Dauar and came into partnership with Douglas Pitt, a West Indian negro of similar character to himself. John Douglas writing in 1900 remembered how "our old friend Douglas Pitt was quoted to me . . . as an instance of how there were some of our people who had got beyond the jurisdiction, and were living on the islands without the benefit of judge or jury".

One might imagine with what disillusionment the Meriams regarded their future. Consequently they were susceptible to a missionary organization expressing sympathy and a real commitment to their interests; and if Christian teachings went against traditional beliefs then Christianity would triumph eventually for European incursions had already undermined the foundations of Meriam society.

On Erub a Captain Edwards had conducted a permanent bêche-de-mer station as early as 1865, commenting favourably on the people of Erub. When the L.M.S. landed there in May 1871, a European named Thorngreen was living there as were dozens of South Sea Islanders. The indigenous population had dwindled to 120 people, harassed and bullied by the South Sea migrants. Although Thorngreen offered the mission every assistance, many of the South Sea Islanders were opposed to it, as they realized that it represented a first step towards an ordered community.

During the night following their arrival a Rotuma man spread rumours attacking the missionaries. He claimed to have seen missionaries at work in his own islands but was also probably worried about his four wives, since he knew better than the Islanders that Christianity tolerated only monogamy. When two teachers, Gucheng and Tepeso and their wives and families, were put ashore they met strong opposition from the Rotuma man who tried to frighten them with talk of centipedes, snakes and other dangerous animals which infested the island. Tepeso is supposed to have replied "Yes! These things there well may be, but there are also men, and men have souls that need to be saved — so we stay." Brave words, for within a year Tepeso, his wife and child were dead, killed by an unknown disease.

Nevertheless the mission was established and the following year (1872) Murray and Rev. Gill brought a further thirteen South Sea workers and their families to be scattered about the other islands. In all its activities the L.M.S. was looking through and beyond the Torres Strait to the untouched island of New Guinea. This function of the Torres Strait as a marshalling area and base for the assault on New Guinea explains the L.M.S. invasion of some fifty South Sea Islanders into the Torres Strait mission in a little over one year.

On Mer a Papuan Institute was begun with a joint theological and manual curriculum. Buildings were constructed of local wood and coral-lime cement, and suitable students were selected from islands of the Torres Strait. One of the earliest was Aet Passi, previously a leader in the Malo cult, who under L.M.S. tutelage contributed to the development and use of Meriam as a

16. Celebrations marking the "coming of the light" on Thursday Island. The procession is passing in front of the Federal Hotel, with Muralug in the background. Most Islanders belong to the Church of England, though other denominations are represented in the procession. The Anglican Church is now conducted largely by the Islanders themselves and is a source of considerable pride. Photograph by courtesy of D. Bartlett.

written language. He recorded many ancient stories before their obliteration by the "light". However by 1887 only fourteen students had graduated from the institute. MacFarlane retired in the same year and the institute was closed in 1888 by Rev. A. Hunt who later moved to Papua.

The effect of the massive influx of South Sea Islanders was dramatic. In spite of the liberal attitudes of most European missionaries, the South Sea people often took a definite, unambiguous stand against local customs they felt were objectionable. Clothing soon became the rule. The ridiculous neck to toe mother-hubbards imposed on Island women must have been uncomfortable and hot, yet to expose more could mean punishment at the hands of a mission court.

Captain C. Pennefather of the Q.G.S. *Pearl* reported after a visit to Mer in 1880 "the teacher Josiah is most arbitrary and despotic in his rule on the island: men, women and children are flogged severely for the most trivial offences". The victims were tied to a fence and whipped with a stingray tail. Pennefather saw with his own eyes unhealed cuts on the backs of two women and four men who had recently been punished. Josiah and other South Sea hangers-on (Pennefather called them the "loafers") kept all young women in the mission away from their families. During the day they did mission work and at night they were locked up and guarded. Josiah when he went fishing took a crew of these girls to row his boat for him. Naturally this provoked the inevitable comments, but three young men were unfortunate enough to have their remarks reported to Josiah who flew into a rage and had the three savagely flogged. Another youth was punished for pulling a woman's hair and two women for quarreling with their husbands.

The chief of Mer, Harry, and the "policemen" had obeyed Josiah as they were frightened of him. They were also under the impression that the *Pearl* and the government supported the missionaries. Pennefather commented: "The Chief is a helpless poor fellow, completely under the thumb of the missionary teacher, who is supported by a staff of idle, loafing, South Sea Islanders located around the mission station. The natives of the island told me before the teacher that the chief was not to blame, as he (the Chief) was merely a tool in his hands".

Pennefather warned Josiah against such actions in future and made plain to the Meriams that no one, let alone the L.M.S. teacher, had the power to have them flogged, and that the police magistrate on Thursday Island would settle any disputes they might have. Under Josiah no young men could take a wife from the internment camp without the teacher's permission. This notion too Pennefather firmly quashed before leaving.

Pennefather concluded his report on the matter to Chester: "It appears to me that these native teachers require a great deal more looking after by the gentlemen at the head of the London M.S. in these waters. These 'Native Evangelists' are very fond of a little power, and from what I have seen of them up here, are rarely the men to use it wisely. They are left for months without any supervision from the heads of the mission."

A serious case, not in the Torres Strait but in nearby Papua, shows the fanaticism of these imported teachers. Chalmers complained in a letter to a fellow missionary in 1885 of "bouncing" — a euphemism devised by Chalmers in referring to his teacher's excesses. Some Tahitian teachers had shot a woman for working on the Sabbath. She was seriously wounded and three shotgun slugs were subsequently removed from her back.

On most islands the teachers, with such widespread power over communal life, suppressed traditional songs and dances, since many of these related to the old ways of the heathen. The traditional dancing of the Torres Strait was a vibrant, springing step with performers leaping from side to side and into the air, while singers lifted their voices gradually to a crescendo then back again. This dancing and singing was a reflection of the virile, energetic people from which it came but, like everything else, it too changed. Dances in the heavy footed South Sea fashion began, and gentle melodies in South Sea language came to be used. Later when the Islanders composed lyrics in their own language, they used mostly the new melodies.

Some traditional artifacts were destroyed by enthusiastic teachers, and others sold by dispirited Islanders to passing ships. Most artifacts today were taken in this way. The more prudent cult leaders buried relics of the old religion in isolated spots known only to themselves, but though the material effects of the old religions were no longer seen, they lived on in the hearts of some men becoming *pouri pouri* (magic), which dominates Island society to this day.

Not least of the problems with which an Islander, whether indigenous or a South Sea migrant, had to cope was the need to acquire a second name where previously he or she had possessed only one. Some adopted common European names as surnames, such as Joe (Badu), Tom (Boigu), Billy (Poruma), Charlie (Mer) and Harry (Iama). Others, perhaps through their association with a particular form of employment, used Bosun (Mer), Pilot (Erub), Cook (Erub) and Captain (Erub). Others turned to the Bible for surnames such as Levi (St Pauls), David (Iama), Jacob (Saibai), Reuben (Erub) and Matthews (Mabuiag). On Ugar, named Stephen Island by Bligh, an Island family appropriately adopted Stephen as their surname. Other Islanders still devised Island surnames. In many cases this was obtained in a logical fashion by adopting their father's name as a surname.* Yet, despite these efforts and, no doubt, despite European pressure, a century after the coming of the light "one name" people could still be found.

* Adoption of surnames continues on a wide scale so that each of three brothers might have a different surname and may actually change the surname from time to time during childhood and youth depending on family circumstances. Some children remain totally alienated from their real parents, others may rejoin their real parents at some later stage.

So the Torres Strait Islanders laboured on towards "the light", though increasingly it must have seemed the light at the end of the tunnel. However teachers of the L.M.S. were not the sole catalysts of radical change, for the marine industries brought hundreds of other outsiders to live among the Islanders and it is possible that the L.M.S. helped save the Islanders from extinction at this crucial time. The alternative to mission control was heavy protectionist government and this was not to occur for some years.

When the settlement at Somerset had begun in 1864, the agreement between the Queensland and Imperial governments had provided for the visit of an Imperial man-of-war three times annually, yet the agreement seemed to neglect the fact that the Torres Strait was a part of the region covered by the China Station, and that ships based in Australia had no specific authority in the area.

By 1871 the Queensland premier, Palmer, prompted by increasing lawlessness in the straits, proposed that the Queensland area of responsibility be pushed a hundred kilometres north of Cape York. The Imperial government approved and the change was passed by the Queensland government on 24 August 1872, though it could have brought scant relief to the overworked ships' masters of the China Station.

On 27 June 1872 the "Kidnapping Act" passed by the British Parliament sought to regulate the controversial labour trade in the Pacific — not a small part of which was related to North Queensland and the Torres Strait. It stipulated that all British labour vessels apply for licences and that they enter into a bond of five hundred pounds for the prevention of kidnapping and mistreatment of indigenous labour.

Six months later Captain Moresby in the H.M.S. *Basilisk* detained two schooners, the *Melanie* and *Challenge*, in Papuan waters east of the Torres Strait. On board were eighty-eight South Sea Islanders (or Kanakas as they were called). Many claimed to have been kidnapped. Two, whilst fishing in a canoe, had been run down by a whaleboat and pulled from the water by the hair. Others had boarded the *Melanie* in Sydney under the impression that the master was taking them back to their home islands. Instead he had taken them to the Torres Strait forcing them to dive for pearl shell. A dozen more had been working for three years with no pay besides clothing, tobacco and food. It is little wonder then that these desperate, ill-treated men, when they came into contact with the Torres Strait Islanders, often ill treated them in turn.

Three days later Moresby boarded the *Woodbine*, finding twenty tons of pearl shell, three South Sea Islanders and no licence. A week later the *Crishna* with thirty-five Kanakas on board was apprehended.

All four ships seized were sent to Sydney or Brisbane where the supreme courts, under the act, had the power to try the cases. Three masters were released since they had committed the assaults, kidnapping and abduction before 27 June. The *Crishna* alone was condemned and sold. Nevertheless it was apparent to freebooters that the long arm of Imperial law was descending on the Strait.

The transfer of Chester, the police magistrate, from Somerset to Thursday Island in 1877 was a step in the right direction, and the Imperial government contributed £600 annually to the maintenance of the "Humane Establishment at Torres Straits". But the northern strait still came under another authority, this time the British Western Pacific Commission in Fiji, and Chester was able to exert any authority at all in the area only because he had been made a deputy commissioner. He was still dissatisfied. Partly in response to Chester's urging, John Douglas, the Premier of Queensland, proposed a change in the colony's border to bring all Torres Strait Islands including Saibai, Boigu and Dauan, under Queensland authority. However it was not till 24 June 1879, the following year, that the act was passed under a new premier, Thomas MacIllwraith.

The system of administration which evolved under the Queensland government on the Torres Strait Islands involved the appointment of a Mamoose, or chief, who, with the assistance of policemen, would maintain order on an island. As Pennefather had discovered the Mamooses were often in-effectual or subservient to outside parties. On Mer at this time, apart from the L.M.S. mission, there were three permanent bêche-de-mer stations staffed by fifty Europeans, South Sea Islanders and Aborigines, over whom no indigenous leader could reasonably hope to assert authority. As well Captain Bruce, in partnership with Pitt and operating two boats, was still in residence and had gone completely unpunished for the massacre of twenty or more Islanders on Mer ten years earlier.

On Masig Yankee Ned Mosby, an American whaler who hailed from Boston, had taken several wives and made himself comfortable. Ninety years later one of his descendants was the island's chairman.

In fact the influx of outsiders, even when taken independently of the L.M.S. activities, was significant. There was a tendency among discharged crews to simply take land and a wife on an island where none dared gainsay them. The situation was exaggerated by the large numbers of young men and women from the islands who now worked full time on the luggers.

Lieutenant De Hoghton commanding the H.M.S. *Beagle* during a visit to the islands in 1879 was alarmed by this situation: "From what I have seen at Jervis Island there can be no doubt that a watchful eye should be kept on the more remote islands (Darnley, Murray, and others), to prevent their being infested by a lot of discharged South Sea Islanders and others, who take up their abode there with no employment or visible means of support, and if not looked after might be a cause of disturbances and trouble, and even a danger to small craft landing there; this duty seems to require some such vessel as the *Pearl*, whose captain is a magistrate and has powers accordingly." The following year Pennefather visited Jervis Island (Mabuiag) in the Pearl and found that South Sea men had been openly abducting girls despite the protests of the L.M.S. teacher. The government was in a quandary for it had sought vigorously to stop mistreatment of the Islanders by whites and it could be reasonably satisfied on this score. De Hoghton had written: "I do not believe that any cases of oppression of the blacks by the whites do occur". Yet the South Sea Islanders were committing outrages almost at will. It was a situation that Pennefather, Chester, Douglas, Millman (an acting resident magistrate at Thursday Island) and a dozen others fought to resolve, but which was not finally ended till the inflow of South Sea migrants tapered off decades later.

Those South Sea Islanders who remained, and there were many, built their homes and gardens following practices in their own islands. Torres Strait Islanders imitated them, abandoning their round, grounded huts in the east and their rough lean-tos in the southwest for angular, stilted buildings similar to those which had been standing on Saibai, Dauan, Boigu and Daru all along. Improved gardens using the newly arrived sweet potato, corn, new banana types and other fruits, revolutionized some societies which had previously been semi-nomadic.

Within a generation most South Sea Island families, usually Torres Strait Islander on the maternal side, had been accepted into the local communities, though they tended to gravitate towards positions of leadership (where many are still found today) and retained considerable prestige.

4

The New Guinea Coast

In the early nineteenth century a hundred ships annually were passing through the Torres Strait. Maps by Cook and Bligh had been added to by later navigators so that voyagers in the Cape York and southern Torres Strait region had a reasonable idea of the area's geography and the problems it represented. In the northern Torres Strait it was a different matter altogether.

The approximate dimensions of the Papuan mainland adjacent to the Torres Strait were known. Bligh had sailed south of Saibai in 1792 and named the elevation on Dauan Mt Cornwallis. Bampton and Alt, in the following year, passed within a few kilometres of Bobo but were forced off the coast and to the south by the Warrior Reefs. After negotiating a passage near Tutu they again were able to move north sighting Boigu and smaller islands to its northwest. They named the group the Talbot Islands.

For the next fifty years, despite the busy seaway only a hundred and sixty kilometres to the south, little additional information was gained of the Papuan coast. In 1848 the *Illustrated London News*, when describing the explorations of the H.M.S. *Fly* and *Bramble*, stated that the southern coast of Papua "had hitherto only been seen from a distance, and not visited by navigators, on account of the dangers with which it is beset". The *Fly* and *Bramble* in fact undertook the first deliberate survey of the west Papuan coast and Gulf of Papua.

In March 1845, having completed a series of surveys off the

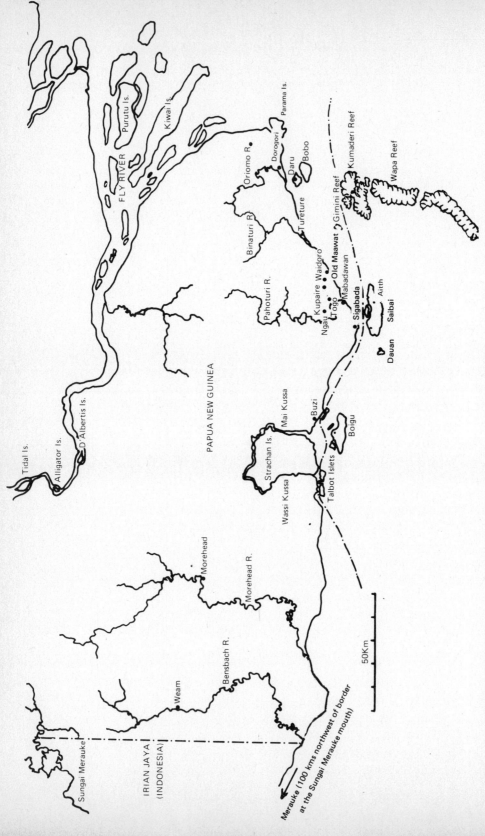

17. Map of the southwestern coast of Papua New Guinea. The settlement sites of Old Maawat and Aith are no longer occupied. Saibai's close proximity to the Pahoturi River mouth has meant that the Gizra people of Togo, Kupaire and Waidoro prefer to identify with the Torres Strait Islanders on Saibai rather than with the Kiwais to the east.

AFFRAY WITH THE NATIVES ON THE COAST OF NEW GUINEA.

18. Lieutenant Yule and his party from H.M.S. *Bramble* in trouble following a ceremony which formally took possession of Papua for Queen Victoria in 1846. None of the Englishmen was seriously injured and the action was never officially recognized by the British government. From the *Illustrated London News*, 5 August 1848.

coast of Queensland, Captain Blackwood, the expedition commander, took the ships to the Torres Strait. Excitement ran high on board the vessels as they sailed north from Erub towards the unknown coast inhabited by an unknown people. The most significant of their discoveries was made quickly when in early June the mouth of a huge river was explored and charted. It was named the Fly. At the time Jukes on the H.M.S. *Fly* fully realized the river's potential: "A small light steamer, drawing six feet of water, might probably penetrate for a couple of hundred miles, or into the very heart of the country".

As Jukes suspected the discovery was of monumental importance, but this was the H.M.S. *Fly's* last survey voyage in Australian waters and it returned to England shortly afterwards to be paid off in June 1846. In the meantime however the *Bramble*, under Lieutenant Yule, continued to be employed on a survey of southwest Papua.

In April 1846, whilst in the eastern Gulf of Papua, almost five hundred kilometres east of Erub and Mer, a large sailing canoe was encountered. It was double hulled, fifteen to eighteen metres in length, constructed of enormous, hollowed tree trunks. Except for the second hull it was very similar to canoes of the Eastern Torres Strait (in size and the shape of its rigging) and strongly suggests a link between the two areas, since Papuans to the west of the Torres Strait and Aborigines to the south had nothing resembling these vessels. In fact observers on the *Bramble* remarked on apparent similarities between the Central Papuans and Islanders of the Eastern Torres Strait for whom they had a high regard.

On 16 April Lieutenant Yule conducted a ceremony to take possession of Papua for Queen Victoria (although Bampton and Alt had conducted a similar ceremony in 1793). The union jack was hoisted and three cheers rattled through the bush, but as the party prepared to re-embark disaster occurred. First one boat, then another, was swamped in the surf, leaving fifteen unarmed men, including Yule, stranded on the beach. A body of Papuans one hundred strong descended upon them and violently stripped them of all their possessions so that they had to be dragged naked into rescue boats. It had been a hair-raising episode for as Yule confessed "I fully expected death would be my fate in a few minutes".

Yule's possession ceremony was not, of course, binding on the British government which had no intention of adding Papua to

19. A large Papuan canoe, which resembles those of the Islanders in the eastern Torres Strait. From the *Illustrated London News*, 5 August 1848.

its already considerable administrative responsibilities. In its un-developed state Papua could only be an economic liability: its rugged topography and the ferocity of its inhabitants meant that administration would be more strenuous with fewer returns than could be expected elsewhere. It was to be thirty years before a European exploited the discovery by the H.M.S. *Fly* of the river Fly, and a further ten years before Britain finally annexed Papua. Annexation finally took place at Queensland's behest for reasons which Queensland felt to be compelling.

Somerset on Cape York Peninsula was originally established in 1864 as a refuge for shipwrecked seamen, a customs post and the magisterial seat. The station was shifted to Thursday Island in 1877 to bring administration closer to the Torres Strait Islands which had already been badly affected by the first rapacious decade of pearling.

Queensland was intensely interested in the south coast of New Guinea — especially in view of the German thrust into the Pacific. The reasons were best stated later in a letter from the agents general of Victoria, Queensland, New South Wales and New Zealand to Lord Derby in 1883: "New Guinea is in such close proximity to Queensland, that whatever is done there must affect Queensland more than anything that is done in the other islands could affect the rest of Australia or New Zealand. All the trade of Queensland with England and India by steam, passes through Torres Strait, regular steam communication is now established there; it is really indispensable not only that the Straits should be free to navigation but that there should be no risk of a Foreign power establishing a naval station there. Adventurous men are occupying portions of the New Guinea coastline, and irregular settlement is sure to take place more and more . . . . . and Queensland of all the Australias, will suffer from them [the adventurers] most." Actually these reasons had been felt just as strongly five years previously. In that year a minor goldrush occurred on the Goldie River near Port Moresby. The Queensland government, headed by Premier Sir Thomas McIllwraith, seizing upon the fact that most of the diggers had come from Queensland, took the totally unauthorized step of appointing Q.B. Ingham as Queensland government agent in Port Moresby. Whilst legally dubious, perhaps the Queensland government's action can be interpreted in a sympathetic light. Hundreds of white battlers, toughened by years on the track and often embittered by lack of success, had descended on an area with a large indigenous population where no administration or law (apart from native law which they would not have respected anyway) was functioning. Ingham as Q.G.A. held courts, registered land titles and sent reports to the colonial secretary in Brisbane — the first vestige of European administration in southeastern New Guinea. Unfortunately it did not last long. Before the year 1878 was out Ingham, whilst investigating murders of Europeans east of Port Moresby, was himself killed.

Not daunted, McIllwraith in 1879 arranged for the Queensland border to be placed so that it included Saibai, Dauan and Boigu — a border which stood for a century. The move had been pushed by Premier John Douglas in 1878 but was not confirmed by an act of parliament till 24 June 1879, by which time McIllwraith was premier. The immediate reasons were based on bringing all pearling grounds, shipping channels and adjacent islands within Queensland, these being the colony's main interests in the area.

Still unsatisfied, McIllwraith in February 1883, through the Queensland agent general in London, asked the British government directly to annex eastern New Guinea to Queensland. Sir William Macgregor wrote later that "the desire for the annexation of British New Guinea . . . arose simply for the purpose of preventing undesirable neighbours from coming near them [i.e. the Queenslanders]".

Lord Derby failed to respond so Chester, police magistrate at Thursday Island, was instructed to annex southeastern New Guinea. He sailed immediately in the Queensland government vessel *Pearl*. On 3 April 1883 at Port Moresby Chester met his friends Lawes and Chalmers of the L.M.S. who assisted him by explaining to the local natives what was happening, though they were more than a little bewildered themselves. How was a cutter with two small guns and a half a dozen ragged police representing a colony of less than 300,000 Europeans entitled to take such a step? The fact was, of course, that it was not entitled to. It required further effort by Queensland, with the support of the other colonies, including the letter of July 1883 already quoted, before Britain finally agreed to annex southeastern New Guinea in 1884.

Two flag raisings and ceremonies occurred. The first by Romilly on 23 October 1884 was a mistake. The second by

ANNEXATION CARRYING THE BLESSINGS OF CIVILIZATION INTO NEW GUINEA.

20. Cartoon in the *Bulletin*, 9 June 1883, reveals the scepticism felt by many Australians concerning Queensland's motives for wanting to annex Papua. Even this early Queensland had a reputation for the mistreatment of Aborigines and for allowing the continuation of the Pacific Island labour trade.

Commodore Erskine ten days later on 4 November was the first and only legal ceremony. Lawes was bemused at the farcical aspect of the situation but relieved that the initial ceremony — which was Queensland's — had been superseded. McIllwraith also could have reason for satisfaction, for if Papua was a British colony then it served his purpose just as well as if Queensland ruled Papua. Queensland, New South Wales and Victoria had agreed jointly to pay £15,000 annually for the administration of the new colony. The Imperial government provided £18,000 and a ship, but facilities in British New Guinea were so primitive and Europeans so few at that time, that the administration in Port Moresby simply could not operate independently.

At the Colonial Conference of 1887 a bill was drafted to account for the difficulties being experienced by the administration of British New Guinea. Thereafter the administration would be guided by the Queensland governor (in council), who also could disallow proposed expenditures. In both civil and criminal cases provision was made for appeal to the Supreme Court of Queensland. To many people British New Guinea now appeared to be a colony of Queensland and, because of Queensland's notorious reputation for its treatment of Aborigines, many were opposed to these new arrangements.

The first special commissioner Scratchely was in Papua only twelve weeks when he died of malaria. John Douglas (ex-premier of Queensland) was the third special commissioner from early 1886 till 1888. He divided the colony into "three centres of action", an Eastern Division, a Central Division and a Western Division which was to be administered from Thursday Island for many years. This would have been nothing new, for Chester and others at Thursday Island had been exploring the coast of Papua opposite Cape York for a decade or more.

The first outsiders to live along the Torres Strait part of the Papuan coast were teachers from the Loyalty Islands working for the L.M.S. In 1871 teachers and their wives were placed at Dauan and others at Mabadawan village which is further east on the mainland of Papua. The coast had been previously visited by Europeans but little exploration had taken place till 1875 when the Chevert expedition from Sydney examined the Katau River east of Boigu.

In the same year the L.M.S. steamer *Ellengowan* penetrated the Mai Kussa (opposite Boigu and forming the eastern channel around Strachan Island). The Rev. Samuel McFarlane, the L.M.S. expedition leader, was disappointed as he had been led to believe by his South Sea teachers that the Mai Kussa ("Kussa" is Western Island language for river) cut New Guinea in two. However perhaps it was only a case of misunderstanding, for two months later he took the *Ellengowan* into the Fly River, which does not divide the island but is nevertheless a thousand kilometres long. With him on this trip was an Italian named D'Albertis. Also aboard were Chester and six of his ubiquitous Aboriginal policemen.

At a point on the lower Fly, where the channel passed near an island, six large canoes and two smaller ones crammed with armed men were observed racing for the island. It seemed their intention to land and, using the dense foliage as cover, to ambush the steamer. As the canoes crossed in front of the *Ellengowan* at about two hundred metres, some warning shots were fired. These went unheeded so Chester and his men opened up with their Sniders. The would-be ambushers with no experience of firearms, quickly turned and fled back to the river bank, where canoes and weapons were abandoned. Chester and his men enthusiastically followed them and towed an eighteen metre canoe back to be broken up for firewood. That night D'Albertis fired one of his rockets into the village suspected of launching the enterprise. The whole affair had been conducted along the lines of the "dispersals" carried out in Queensland, with which Sir Hubert Murray was to disagree so strongly later.

This expedition penetrated 240 kilometres into the interior. For McFarlane the results were negligible since the L.M.S. had its hands full on the coast. Chester had to get back to his work at Somerset, which was soon to be transferred to Thursday Island. It was in D'Albertis that the giant, mysterious river sparked a flame. D'Albertis was an adventurer who had fought with Garibaldi for Italian independence, and the big river presented him with an irresistible challenge.

Somehow D'Albertis was able to persuade the government of New South Wales to supply him with a nine tonne steam launch, the *Neva.* In May 1876 once again, using Somerset as his base, he crossed the Torres Strait and pushed up the Fly at the rate of almost fifty kilometres a day, his boisterous enthusiasm stirring up a hornet's nest everywhere he went. Rockets and rifle fire rattled for the 930 kilometres that the *Neva* ascended the river and all the way back again. At a point 800 kilometres from the sea D'Albertis named a river the Alice, in honour of the wife of Sir John Robertson, the premier of New South Wales.

Triumphantly D'Albertis returned to Somerset in November by sail. The small ungainly riverboat must have sailed badly but the engine had broken down. Those on board were fortunate that the wind had already changed to the northwest, thus blowing them south to Somerset.

Shortly afterwards Chester as police magistrate moved to Thursday Island but he had not heard the last of the volatile Italian explorer. In 1877 D'Albertis tried again to ascend the river. Remembering him from his previous voyage, the river people greeted him with implacable hostility. The *Neva* plunged through barrages of arrows and dozens of Papuans were shot. A Fijian member of the crew cut off one Papuan's head which D'Albertis preserved in a bottle. However he probably had more trouble with his own crew than with the locals. One Chinese had been wounded in the buttock by an arrow, another had died after receiving a beating from the fiery Italian, and still another became lost in the bush and was never seen again. While still 800 kilometres inland the three remaining Chinese (including the wounded one) deserted in a dinghy and are believed to have been killed by Papuans further down the river.

During the *Neva*'s descent of the Fly, Bob and Jack, two Fijians, also deserted using a stolen canoe and, surprisingly, were able to reach Thursday Island, where they complained to Chester that D'Albertis had killed the first two Chinese. With only two of his original crew of nine aboard, D'Albertis staggered into Thursday Island and found himself fighting charges of assault and even murder. Fortunately for him the expedition's only other European named Preston had survived, though seriously ill from malaria, and was able to speak in D'Albertis's defence.

Chester, conscious of the delicacy of the case in an area where usually no more than two or three of a boat's crew were European, turned the tables on the unfortunate Fijians. Bob and Jack found themselves sentenced to four months' imprisonment for mutiny. There were in fact grounds for such a charge, however compassion and justice may well have taken second place to practical expediency. It is an illuminating case and emphasizes that whereas Chester now had effective control of the Torres Strait, his control was intended more to regulate white exploitation than to assist the indigenous or imported coloured people. Moreover, D'Albertis had alienated the inhabitants of the Fly for a generation or more to come. Haddon wrote later that his methods involved "frightening people away from their villages, then going into their houses and ransacking them" and blamed D'Albertis for later attacks on the river. It was perhaps no coincidence that D'Albertis's marauding in 1877 was followed in 1878 by Queensland's sending poor Ingham to Port Moresby and by the 1879 act pushing the Queensland border to the Papuan coastline. In the vacuum of power Queensland was constrained to act and to continue to urge Britain to act.

However intrusion by Europeans from the south was not the only pressure to which local Papuans were being subjected. Fleets of Tugeri raiders paddled eastwards, from what is now Irian Jaya, seeking heads. The northern Torres Strait Islands, and any coastal or river villages as far east as the Fly River, suffered from their raids, mainly over the northwest season.

Tugeri (or Sugeri) is actually only the name of one of their villages. In practice any peoples living on the coast between the Bensback and Digul Rivers may be referred to as Tugeri. Their attacks during the nineteenth century probably influenced the Papuans on the coast adjoining the Torres Strait to a greater extent than did European incursions at the time.

The Tugeri placed great emphasis on a man's ability to procure heads. In this region of Irian Jaya today skulls still swing from ridge poles and are placed under the head to be used as pillows for sleep. It was important for the skull to have a name. After painting themselves with white chalk, the raiders would surround a hut in the hush of the predawn dark. When escape was impossible for the inhabitants a Tugeri called out "What is your name?". The first intelligible word uttered by the unfortunate occupant was taken and remembered. This was the skull's name henceforth.

Haddon whilst visiting the Torres Strait in 1888 noted the effect of Tugeri raids on the far Western Islands. He found Dauan packed with Boigu refugees who had forsaken their own island on account of their terror of these pirates, and who paid brief visits to Boigu in order to tend their gardens. On Saibai nearby he saw houses raised on poles where the lower portions had been roughly closed in with coconut leaves, providing shelter for more fugitives from Boigu. In fact it was necessary at times to evacuate Saibai also, so that Dauan was crowded with the people of Boigu and Saibai. The Tugeri, using small canoes without outriggers or sails, could not negotiate the rough passage between Dauan and the mainland.

If this was the result on islands 130 kilometres from the Dutch border, which had been part of Queensland for nine years, under mission influence for seventeen years and administered closely from Thursday Island, then the result in unmapped areas further west, under no effective government control, was far worse. Villages along the coast moved inland or were devastated, and those close to river mouths moved upstream. This effect of coastal depopulation and dispersal marks the region to this day and most villages are still found at secure inland sites. The social dislocation caused by the raids is claimed by some to have retarded the progress of the indigenous Papuans west of the Fly. In fact, the area of Tugeri raids was expanding during the second half of the nineteenth century, moving steadily east. British administration in Papua was moving westwards about the same time, and sooner or later the two would meet.

In 1883 a Captain Strachan during an expedition for the Melbourne *Age* discovered and named Strachan Island near Boigu. He also came into conflict with Tugeri who were to regret this, perhaps their earliest contact with a European force. Strachan sent a raft packed with explosives into the midst of their war fleet and blew it apart.

Sir William MacGregor, administrator of British New Guinea 1889-99, was an energetic and resourceful man. He formed the first permanent police unit in Papua, recruiting men from the South Sea boat crews. He also regarded it as part of his administrative duties to fight the Tugeri. On one occasion his party intercepted a fleet of canoes with more than six hundred warriors in the estuary of the Fly River. In a one-sided sea battle the Tugeri were routed. MacGregor thought that perhaps twenty were shot. The canoes streamed back along the coast to their sanctuaries around the Digul River over the border.

The Western Division had previously been administered from Thursday Island but MacGregor, in view of his own experiences, considered a closer administration to be necessary. In 1889 an administration post was established on the east bank of the Pahoturi river opposite Mabadawan village. In 1893 this post was moved to Daru. Daru was selected because it was close to the mouth of the Fly River, the gateway to the major part of the Western Division. Also it was close to Thursday Island which would alleviate the problems of supply across the Gulf of Papua on the colony's slender resources.

21. Papuan policemen at Daru employed by the administration of British New Guinea before the turn of the century (both with and without their uniforms). They proved to be tough, loyal and courageous. From John Douglas, *Past and Present of Thursday Island and Torres Straits*, 1900.

As a port Daru was as good as anything else on the coast. The long, flat coast on the north partially protected the anchorage during the northwest season, while Daru and Bobo islands protected it in the southeast. Best of all there was an elevation on the northern end so that the houses would not go under water when it rained.

When the Europeans landed on Daru they found the people of Tureture laid claim to the island, although they only visited for a few days at a time to look after their gardens there. There had however been earlier inhabitants. These original people, the Hiamu, seem to have been a guileless, inoffensive group and were repeatedly attacked by the Kiwais who were moving westward from the Fly mouth. On at least one occasion, visiting Islanders from Iama were also killed. Under this pressure the surviving Hiamu fled to their friends in the western Torres Strait — some, it is claimed traditionally, settling as far south as Muralug.

The post at Daru more or less confined the Tugeri to areas west of the Oriomo River but could not prevent raids. In 1898 the Austrian explorer Dammkohler shot five Tugeri with the six bullets in his revolver, when surprised in thick bush on the bank of the Morehead River. He escaped to Daru with an arrow in the shoulder.

Meanwhile the Dutch were bombarded with complaints by the British government. In response to these complaints the Dutch finally admitted responsibility for the southern coast of West New Guinea, paying the Sultan of Tidore 6,000 guilders for certain rights he had previously exercised over it. In 1902 an administrative post was established among the Tugeri at Merauke and the severity of the raids was gradually reduced.

Despite the establishment of the post at Daru the administration had neither the manpower nor the resources to extend control to the west of the Port Moresby area till early in the twentieth century. The one whiteman who explored more of the Papuan coast and developed friendly, working relationships with more Papuans up to the turn of the century was the Rev. J. Chalmers of the L.M.S. He travelled the coastal waters between Port Moresby and Thursday Island constantly, visiting villages, poking into creeks and rivers and supporting South Sea teachers scattered along the low, swampy coast.

Using the Torres Strait missions as a base the L.M.S. had been able to consolidate in Daru among the Kiwai people, who were closely related to Islanders of the eastern strait. The Kiwais themselves then became the mission storm troopers who were to carry "the light" up the Fly to the north and east in the Gulf of Papua.

On 7 April 1901 the L.M.S. schooner *Niue* arrived off Goaribari Island, which lies some two hundred kilometres northeast of Daru. The 3,000 inhabitants had a very bad reputation as evidenced by Sir George LeHunte's reports and as was known by Chalmers. Soon after anchoring the *Nuie* was surrounded by natives clamouring for Chalmers, or "Tamate" as he was called, to come ashore. He promised to do so in the morning.

It must be remembered that Chalmers was no beginner. He had been on the coast for twenty-five years. Also he was no stranger to trouble, as he had personally investigated the shooting and spearing near Port Moresby in which "Chinese" Morrison of the Melbourne *Age* was badly injured. He could not have trusted these Goaribaris. Why then did he behave so irrationally next morning?

In fact Chalmers was quite depressed at this time. The previous year his second wife had died on Daru after only two years of marriage, his own health was failing and his diary reflected his despondency.

Without waiting for breakfast Chalmers, Rev. O. Tomkins, Navagi (a Kiwai Island leader) and nine Kiwai mission students went ashore in a whaleboat, followed by half of the native canoes. Why did he take the ten Kiwais with him?

A thorough plan had been devised on the island during the night to slaughter anyone who came ashore. Twelve men came ashore and were all killed in a concerted attack, though Navagi was sufficiently alert to grab a club and despatch one attacker before he fell. Meanwhile those Goaribaris in their canoes beside the *Nuie* swarmed aboard and looted her before the rattled captain (from Roratonga) and crew (all Kiwais) were able to get her away.

Chalmers, Tomkins and their late students were cooked and eaten with sago. The Administrator Sir George LeHunte's comment that "Mr Chalmers has won the death he would have wished for of all others" makes it questionable whether just misjudgment was responsible. However, the train of events put into motion by Chalmers's death was just gathering momentum.

LeHunte stormed ashore on 2 May with a heavily armed party, shot at least thirty-four Goaribaris, burned houses and destroyed some large canoes. He returned to Port Moresby with a skull believed to be that of Chalmers. It is significant that for this blow LeHunte had requested assistance from the Queensland government. In the assault party he had included a detachment of soldiers from the Thursday Island garrison, who had arrived on the S.S. *Parua*, in addition to the six armed Europeans and thirty-six armed natives on the *Merrie England* (a vessel belonging to the Papuan administration). Afterwards LeHunte was obliged to send a telegram to the governor of Queensland explaining his regret at what had been done but that the "action was absolutely necessary and best in the end".

On Thursday Island Chalmers's many friends subscribed towards a plaque which was subsequently mounted on a Baptismal Font at the Quetta Memorial Cathedral on Thursday Island, where it may be seen today.

LeHunte's successor C. Robinson, who was chief judicial officer and acting administrator, felt the people of Goaribari could not be forgiven till the murderers were apprehended and Tomkins's skull recovered. In a visit to Goaribari in 1904 at least another eight Goaribaris (some claim a hundred) were shot, the acting administrator's enthusiasm in the massacre provoking disparaging remarks from other Europeans present. These remarks subsequently became the basis for a royal commission into the affair — all of which was too much for Robinson. On the morning of 20 June Acting Administrator Robinson shot himself, "whilst temporarily insane", beside a flagpole outside Government House, Port Moresby. He was later posthumously censured for his conduct at Goaribari.

By 1907 Tomkins's skull and a bundle of human bones claimed to be those of the two missionaries had been produced by the humbled Goaribaris. They were given a Christian burial at Daru.

In 1904, the year of the royal commission and Robinson's suicide, Hubert Murray returned to Papua and within four years was lieutenant governor of Australian Papua (the Papua Act of 1906 having changed the territory's name and the nation responsible for its administration). It is impossible that he was not affected by the sensational train of events.

In 1911 the resident magistrate at Daru reported that the

natives of the Western Division were inclined to be sullen but were easy to bring under control, intelligent and industrious. He went on to claim that a minimum of patrol work was being done due to the unavailability of suitable vessels. Murray however was concerned primarily with the lack of restraint shown by patrol officers out of Daru, so that patrols often took the form of punitive expeditions. Between 1908 and 1910 scores of Papuans had been shot by police or European officers and at least one village burned.

Murray's scheme for the "scientific aspect of pacification" was eventually spelt out in unmistakeable terms. He railed against officers who took the easier and more violent method of using the lives of ignorant bushmen to compensate for their own lack of initiative. He went on: "In practice the natives always have the first shot, for the Government party does not open fire until it is attacked, and not even then . . . even if spears are poised and bows bent, there is still a chance of preserving the peace and making friends. But it is a chance a timid man would not take". Murray had no time for timid men. Perhaps the shootings and repercussions of Goaribari Island did have a beneficial effect, after all. The notorious events surrounding the deaths of Chalmers and Robinson ensured that they would not be forgotten throughout the remaining history of European rule in P.N.G.

In another less obvious manner the Torres Strait Islanders may have helped to shape the future of Papua.

C. Seligman visited the strait with Haddon in 1889. Like Haddon, he was influenced by the biological theory of evolution when enquiring into the origins and development of native societies. After spending some months of intense study in the Torres Strait he went to Port Moresby. At this time Murray as the magistrate was wrestling with the relationship between customary and European law. Together Murray and Seligman visited Hanuabada and other Motu villages. Eventually Murray became convinced that the customs of native societies were worthy of respect. Seligman used his experiences of Melanesian society, primarily from the Torres Strait, in assisting Murray to conceive the even-handed policy which was to dominate his rule during thirty-two years as lieutenant governor (1908-40). In fact Murray found that the carry-over of affairs in the Torres Strait intruded constantly, though not always favourably, into the administration of the Western Division.

In the settled, more stable societies which developed on the islands after 1871, chiefs were recognized by the government and known as "mamooses", though generally there was little or no traditional justification for such recognition. Nevertheless the recognition of leadership as an institution was a considerable advancement on the loosely organized societies of the semi-nomadic Papuans in the Trans-Fly. However as the terror raids along the Papuan coast subsided and permanent villages were established, recognition of a village official or "mamoose" gradually became accepted. The Papuans even borrowed the Island term in places.

Just as the mamoose was becoming established in Papua so the islands were being introduced to a new form of government. Initiated in 1907, the council system was radical for its day. Each island community was to have its own elected council, which was at first guided by Europeans, but with the ultimate objective of creating self-governing communities, and whereas the gap between the concept and its implementation as such was quite formidable, it could be appreciated by all as a progressive step. As early as 1913 the Kiwais had imported independently their own councillor organization from the Torres Strait Islands. But where the Islanders found their councils receiving official encouragement, the Kiwais found their attempts to create a form of local self-government frowned upon by the European authorities in Papua.

The resident magistrate in Daru did not regard the councils as an advancement. Under his jaundiced eye they were simply a cover for indolence. He claimed everyone wanted to be a councillor but instead of seeing this as as healthy sign he chose to take it the other way. So for eight years the administration sought by completely ignoring the councils to kill them. In this they were unsuccessful. By 1921 it was found necessary to officially recognize the councillors and subsequently committees were formed to assist the constables appointed by the administration. By 1929 they had been introduced, for better or for worse, throughout the rest of Papua. The role of the councillors was frequently confused by European officers who utilized the village council as an instrument of administration control. It was noted however that the Kiwai councils were quite effective, as were those of the Motus around Port Moresby.

For Murray his problems with Daru and the Western

Division, though unimportant overall, were a nagging problem. Through lack of finances little government expansion could take place. As late as 1930 Madiri (in the Fly estuary) and Daru were still the only European settlements in the whole enormous area of 90,000 square kilometres.

In 1928 the anthropologist Williams, working in villages on the Morehead, discovered that religious meetings were being conducted by deacons from Boigu. He was astonished for these missionary activities were totally unknown to the administration. In fact they were so removed from European direction that the Papuans were reluctant even to admit their association with Christianity at a time when there was no administrative or church post in Papua west of Daru. It was a grass roots movement motivated by the initiative and courage of these Boigu men who had succeeded in appointing village deacons to conduct services on a regular basis. Although the theological knowledge of these village deacons was less than rudimentary, they performed their duties earnestly. When missions finally moved in they must have found their task immeasurably easier due to the efforts of the early Boigu missionaries.

During the 1920s the northern Western Islands of the Torres Strait continued to suffer from Tugeri excursions though these had declined to almost nuisance value. If a strange foot print was found on the beach, or the shadow of a canoe seen at night, then special care was taken. On Saibai the women and children were sent to the church which was being constructed as a solid lime, block structure and was easily covered by rifle fire. On one occasion the men then dressed as women, concealing rifles and shotguns under their dresses or in gardening bags, before straggling off to the gardens inviting an attack. Unfortunately the Tugeri did not fall for the trick.

In 1932 the people of Mabadawan sent a message to Daru stating that they were being attacked by Tugeri. The government launch was hastily made ready and departed but, on arrival, found no evidence of the elusive Tugeri. Since the Mabadawans were unable to help it was considered that a few large nipa trunks floating round the point from Saibai, could have been interpreted as canoes full of Tugeri, by a stretch of the imagination. However, it is a measure of the awe the Tugeri inspired that such a mistake could have been made in the first place.

In 1931 seventeen people from Werendai about two hundred kilometres from the mouth of the Fly were killed and eaten by men from the Suki lagoons. The success of the attack was, typically, due to the treachery employed. The Sukis, professing their friendship and intention to barter, waited till the sheepish Werendais had brought their women and children out of hiding. In the ensuing massacre some of the Werendai men escaped but many of those butchered were women and children.

Fortunately Murray had one of his best officers on the spot. Jack Hides was a Brisbane boy and had represented Queensland as a swimmer when at school. He was cool and experienced, though his later career was to be clouded by bitter controversy. Quickly Hides tracked the Sukis to their homeland — a series of swampy lagoons connected by a maze of creeks and channels to the Fly.* Hides and his police arrested a number of the guilty men, in spite of impossible conditions, through sheer tenacity and wit. There was no fighting.

Officially this was the last raid on the Lower Fly. However another story may be heard on Daru. It is said that some years later the Sukis tried to ransack Madiri plantation. The only European present, a professional hunter and crack shot, barricaded himself in the house and shot at any Suki he saw until finally the raiders had had enough.

One of the problems with Daru was its European population, which was always small with little opportunity for recreation beyond drinking and tennis. Consequently quarrels, disputes and disagreements frequently occupied the time of the officers on Daru to the detriment of their work. The lieutenant governor commented upon this officially on at least one occasion. So this further hindered progress in a region which already had considerable natural obstructions. The only two factors which assisted Daru were its proximity to the Torres Strait and its proximity to the Fly River — the key to exploration across a great proportion of Papua.

In 1926 Ivan Champion, who had been educated at The Southport School near Brisbane from 1914 to 1922, and Charles Karius launched from Daru their momentous effort to cross New Guinea from coast to coast. After six months they returned, having failed, but in September 1927 they left Daru

---

* The Sukis had been given their name by early traders who took their call "*suki*", which meant iron, as a label for the tribe.

22. Papuan constables on the Fly River in 1935. From Jack Hides, *Papuan Wonderland*, 1936. Reproduced by permission of Angus & Robertson Publishers.

once again. Four months later the two stood at the mouth of the Sepik, having travelled up the Fly and crossed the 2,750 metre high mountains which lie between the two great rivers.

In 1935 Hides and O'Malley departed from Daru on an equally hazardous enterprise. They penetrated the unknown area between the Strickland (a tributary of the Fly) and the Purari — the last major piece of exploratory work to be undertaken in Papua.

But the Fly had not seen the last of Hides. Following his resignation from the administration in 1936 he led a private prospecting expedition from Daru into the Strickland area. The trip was a disaster. Hides's European companion, Lyall, collapsed bleeding from the mouth, and confessed to Hides that he was suffering from a stomach ulcer. Desperate to save Lyall, Hides left his party, paddling down into the Fly estuary in a canoe with the sick man and one Papuan. Here their canoe was upset by the tidal bore which Hides in his haste had forgotten. At certain periods the tide builds up so much that a wall of water more than a metre high sweeps areas of the Fly delta. By

the time Lyall reached Daru it was too late. His coffin was borne
on a carriage by members of the Papuan constabulary through
the streets of Daru and buried in the European cemetery near
the mission. Hides, shocked and weakened by beri-beri, died of
pneumonia in Sydney shortly afterwards. Of the Kiwais he
wrote: "They are very soldierly natives and make fine N.C.O.'s
in the Papuan Constabulary. They are an artistic people, and
dance and sing magnificently". He remembered particularly
Sergeant Major Simoi, "a tall, black Kiwai, with an intelligent
Semitic face" and "the most loveable character in all Papua".

In spite of all the exploratory activity, still no development
took place. The one attempt to encourage indigenous enterprise
in west Papua was the village plantation system. However this
suffered from the usual problem, a lack of any real incentive.
After all, the ultimate objective was to make each Papuan pay
head tax to the administration, so that the Papuans, whose
participation would have been less than enthusiastic in the first
place, saw little return for their labour. In 1929 the administration was obliged to admit defeat. The native plantations were
overgrown and untended. The Papuans could see no point in
working to pay their head tax and Murray was forced to realize
that most of the money circulating in western Papua for head
tax or otherwise actually came from labour in the Torres Strait.

In the early twentieth century thousands of Aborigines,
Islanders and Papuans were engaged in the pearl, trochus and
bêche-de-mer industries in North Queensland. Murray did not
like this but there was little alternative, for he was granted only
£40,000 annually in 1904, rising to £85,000 in 1940, for all administrative costs in the whole of Papua. Labour in Queensland,
even at the low wages then paid, provided in taxes a considerable income for the economically backward region of western
Papua.

Murray enquired into the reasons for the spread of beri-beri
and other diseases believing they were brought by boat crews
from the Torres Strait. He suggested that a protector be
appointed on Thursday Island to look after the interests of
Papuan workers (one was), and asked that the reports of the two
patrol officers in the Western Division be put aside for his
special consideration. Beyond this there was nothing really he
could do, although his lack of action amounted to a condoning
of the situation. By the time of Murray's death in 1940, the
exploitation of cheap Papuan labour had become an established
practice — and a practice which continues today.

5

Thursday Island: the Beginning

Old T.I.*

Why are you looking so sad, my Dear?
Why are you looking so sad?
I'm thinking of someone so far away,
In a beautiful place called T.I.

Old T.I., my beautiful home,
Tis the place where I was born,
When the moon and stars they shine,
Makes me longing for home,
Old T.I., my beautiful home.

Take me across the sea,
Over the deep blue sea,
Darling won't you take me,
Back to my home T.I.

T.I., my beautiful home,
T.I., my home sweet home,
I'll be there forever.
The sun is sinking,
Farewell.

Somerset in the early 1870s was being subjected to an increasing barrage of criticism. The anchorage was not only exposed to blustery southeast winds that blew from April to October, but

* This is a very popular song sometimes described as Thursday Island's "national anthem". Although its popularity is waning among youngsters, the song continues to touch the hearts of T.I. expatriates, as it has done for generations.

also to raging tides which forced steamers to throw out both anchors on a normal day. The conditions were in fact so poor that sailing vessels, in particular, actually avoided the port.

Captain Moresby of the H.M.S. *Basilisk* had made a blunt assessment of Somerset's potential during a report in 1873: "I am of the opinion Somerset has failed and is most unsuitably placed for fulfilling the original objects of its establishment." Nevertheless, in the thirteen years before its abandonment by the government in 1877, the survivors of fourteen shipwrecks had found refuge there. Moresby went on to describe, in unflattering detail, the port's degeneration. Buildings were unpainted and ravaged by white ants. Government equipment and supplies deteriorated rapidly due to climate and neglect, many items being so dilapidated as to be useless. Fencing and stockyards were broken down and rotting. Jardine's cattle were to be encountered as much as a hundred kilometres away, running wild.

To his dismay Moresby found that the residents of the "port of refuge" had been eating tinned meat for months, and the only fashion in which his request for beef could be met was by slaughtering three of the settlement's milking cows. Moresby was shocked by the state of the settlement and actively supported the closure of the port, going so far as to report Jardine for alledged misconduct. This led to a board of inquiry into the matter and Jardine's vindication.

At the urging of the Imperial government, which continued to subsidize the establishment and which fretted on Queensland's lack of control over labour abuses in the area, the colony's government began the search for an alternative site.

Moresby recommended a move to the northern coast of Keriri overlooking the shipping channel not far to the north. This site however was rejected by George Dalrymple in June 1874 in favour of a spot on western Keriri where vessels at anchor would be better protected from the northwest winds (November to March) by Gialug and Palilug, and where a reliable freshwater spring was discovered close by the intended settlement. Dalrymple had been appointed officer in charge at Somerset following long years of exploration throughout other areas of coastal north Queensland, for which he was highly respected. Unfortunately his health, already taxed by previous exploits in the tropics, finally and irretrievably broke after he had been on duty at Somerset for only a month. He subsequently left Australia and returned to his native Scotland where he died eighteen months later.

Dalrymple was succeeded by D'Oyley Aplin who in early 1875 unexpectedly suggested an area at the northwest end of Waiben (near Tamwoy) as a site for the new settlement. He died shortly afterwards and was buried on Albany Island.

However after due consideration of the various reports, the colonial secretary and Imperial government, taking into account facilities for marine industries and shipping, selected none of the places previously recommended. Instead, due mainly to the insistence of the portmaster of Queensland, a site at the south-west end of Waiben was chosen. It was felt that the channel south of the island was the only reasonable anchorage in the vicinity, protected as it is on all sides, yet quite spacious.

The decision to move was not made without reservations. Douglas, who was Queensland's premier at the time, remarked in retrospect: "I have often thought, since I have become better acquainted with the locality that a good deal was lost by us when we left Somerset and the mainland. We abandoned with it the chance of occupying some twenty or thirty thousand acres of fine rich scrub land near Somerset, as good as any in North Queensland, and we abandoned also the chance of a railway which might have been pushed through the Peninsula and made our starting point for the East, for India, China and even the Old Country . . . Good anchorage also could have been found in one of the bays between Somerset and Cape York. But the die was cast."

Accordingly in December 1876 a proclamation was made declaring Waiben, or Thursday Island as the Europeans called it, a government reserve for public purposes. Today the name Waiben is applied to the northeast portion of the island alone. It has frequently been stated that Waiben means "no water" or "dry island" in Island language, but this is not true. The Kauralgal may have considered it a dry island and passed on this impression to Europeans who misunderstood them. But this again is difficult to comprehend since Thursday Island has at least two springs and is probably just as well watered as Gialug or Palilug.

By late 1876 the erection of government buildings had already begun. A pearler's hut, constructed of thatched grass, was ordered to be removed and further applications from pearlers to build at the far eastern end of the island were refused. Underground tanks were constructed and gradually a comfortable mansion arose on the hill above Hospital Point (or Vivien Point as it was then known). Included in the original plan was provision for a signal station on Palilug. Signalling apparatus was to be used by the station to convey details of passing vessels to the residency, although in practice Chester, who was to be the first resident, found that a less formal session of lantern signals in the evenings was more convenient.

Before Christmas 1877 Chester was in residence with five water police, a number of tradesmen still completing work and the crew of the Queensland government vessel *Lizzie Jardine.* Douglas had already visited the island and chosen the site for a school and post office. Soon Chester was joined by his wife and, on frequent occasions, entertained officers from visiting ships on the wide wooden verandahs of his residency, buffetted by the southeast winds and overlooking the turbulent waters of his wild domain.

Because the government discouraged private occupation the town grew slowly. There were a handful of married white women living on the island and the first white child was born to Mrs J. Simpson, the gaoler's wife. Another family lived in the signalman's cottage on Palilug.

In 1882 a visitor at Thursday Island was impressed by the beautiful gardens which surrounded Chester's residence. The gardens were maintained by prisoners from the gaol and it was noticed that the severity of sentences varied according to the season and the condition of the gardens. There were four private houses on the island but pressure was growing on the government to allow private investment on the island. By 1885 there were two popular hotels "behind one of which there was a huge mound of bottles". It was in the same year that Thursday Island was finally opened up for extensive private settlement with forty allotments offered for sale. Five years later there were 142 houses and 526 people living there.

The Queensland government had realized from the outset that the success or failure of this new post would be determined only by its convenience for, and attraction to, passing vessels, and the government was resolved that it would not fail, simply because it was felt that the colony's security rested with Britain

23. The residency at Vivien (later Hospital) Point on Thursday Island in the mid 1880s. Note the signalling apparatus. From the *Picturesque Atlas of Australasia*, vol. 2, 1886.

and whoever controlled the Torres Strait controlled Queensland's lifeline to the motherland.

As early as July 1860 the premier, Sir R.G. Herbert, disappointed with the British Mail Steamer service which terminated in the southern colonies, proposed that the Queensland government subsidize a steamer service via the Torres Strait. Queensland at that stage had a population of only 25,000 Europeans, and the proposal, which seemed unnecessarily extravagant, was to be bandied about for the next twenty years. This was unfortunate since it was certainly a far-sighted plan, particularly in respect to migration. Few of the British immigrants landing in Sydney or Melbourne filtered through to Queensland which was desperately short of labour in the second half of the nineteenth century.

Initially arrangements were made with the governor-general of the Netherlands East Indies whereby both governments subsidized a steamer for mutual benefits. However this agreement collapsed, due to conflicting interests, and was followed by two further unsatisfactory collaborations with Asian-based

British firms, till finally in 1880 a contract was negotiated with the British India Navigation Company. Sir Thomas McIllwraith, the premier, had difficulty persuading parliament to approve the agreement and in the end cabled the company on 12 August: "The Legislative Assembly not having disagreed to the mail contract it stands ratified". The company would be subsidized £55,000 per annum for five years, an enormous sum, but it put Thrusday Island on the map once and for all and was to prove of inestimable value in the development of Queensland. On 13 April 1881 the *Merkara* arrived in Moreton Bay with the first direct mail from England (previous contractors had sailed from India or Singapore), and on 20 May 1884 the first overseas ship-ment of frozen meat from Queensland left on the *Dorunda*.

As the colony's first port of call Thursday Island served as a quarantine post. A leper colony and quarantine station were maintained on Gialug from 1887 to 1907 when the lepers were shifted to Moreton Bay and the quarantine station to the north-west corner of Thursday Island. Also the island became a coaling station and several of the rusted, broken-backed wrecks about the Muralug group were once coal hulks.

Thursday Island, as the northernmost of Australia's outposts — facing the Netherlands East Indies and British New Guinea, and visited by German and French ships travelling to colonies in the Pacific — was recognized as one of the areas essential to the continent's defence, since a great proportion of Australian trade and communication passed through the Torres Strait.

In 1887 provision was first made for the island's defence by the formation of a training centre for the Queensland Naval Brigade on the island. The volunteers received gunnery and sea training practice during visits to the area by ships of the Queensland Defence Force, of which there were four. This was only a beginning.

An indication of the other colonies' interest in Thursday Island's defence was the establishment in 1890 of an inter-colonial committee of commandants under an imperial officer, Captain Moore R.N., to discuss the problem. After inspecting Thursday Island and Port Kennedy the committee made its re-commendations. In line with these submissions three six-inch guns and other armaments were offered by the Imperial government and accepted by the colonies. Work began on the fortification in July 1892. A fort was sunk into the crest of Green

Hill with large subterranean galleries serving as magazines and "bombproof" shelters. The six-inch guns were emplaced and, whilst they were in position and capable of firing, no vessel could approach Port Kennedy without the consent of the battery commander. At a lower level in the fortifications two six-pounder guns were sited in cells and fired through steel apertures. Musketry parapets and rifle pits were also included so that, with a strong garrison and its commanding position, Green Hill was a formidable fort. On the southeast coast of Thursday Island a military road was constructed girding Millman Hill with fortifications for a nine-pounder and two mobile heavy machine guns capable of sweeping the eastern approaches to Port Kennedy.

The total cost of this substantial military development was actually in excess of the £17,000 anticipated, but all colonies, except Tasmania, contributed according to their population. The population of Queensland stood at 410,346 and she gave £3,039 towards an eventual total of £23,053.

24. Busy Port Kennedy, seen from a beach on Thursday Island. It was a coaling station and a port of entry for international steamships. From the *Picturesque Atlas of Australasia*, vol. 2, 1886.

The soldiers of the garrison comprised two officers and forty-eight men of the Queensland Defence Force's A Battery, a regular unit which, although based in Brisbane, had another small detachment at Townsville. The men of the garrison were granted twice the normal rate of pay as an inducement to serve in the area. Expenses incurred in maintaining the garrison were again to be met by all the colonies, paying in proportion to their population. The cost was estimated at a total of £4,943 annually. In time of war Queensland was to provide a further two hundred and fifty men minimum, supplemented by local rifle clubs.

Generous precautions had thus been completed for the protection of Australia's vital lines of communication through the Torres Strait. Significantly this was the only permanent post defended by regular Imperial troops for sixteen hundred kilometres. However, the only action the artillerymen saw consisted of some wild nights in Thursday Island's Japanese district and LeHunte's ruthless raid on Goaribari in 1901. The only occasions on which the guns were heard to fire were for the one o'clock time signal each day. The garrison became a Commonwealth unit after Federation and was finally disbanded in the late 1920s.

In 1890 the J.J. Arundel Company, which had some years' experience mining guano on islands in the Pacific, began operations on Raine Island. Barracks, a jetty and tramlines were constructed and a hundred Chinese under the supervision of ten European overseers laboured in the bleak, treeless landscape for two years removing the accumulated droppings from millions of seabirds. Although this enterprise was welcomed it probably had little direct effect on the area's development.

A further limited contribution to local development took place when gold was discovered on Nurapai. In 1894 it was declared a goldfield and mining and crushing began in earnest. Prospectors exploring other islands in the group located and mined gold on Keriri and Tuined though these were never significant. After the initial rush the field on Nurapai stabilized and was to provide an alternative source of income and employment well into the twentieth century.

The new and much praised steamer service lead to a tragedy which rocked the white community of the Torres Strait to a greater extent than any other event up to the Second World War.

25. The R.M.S. *Quetta* at sea. From the *Queenslander*, 15 February 1890.

The regular mail steamer traffic between Brisbane and London (via India) used the Adolphus Channel, generally calling at Port Kennedy on the way into the Arafura Sea. Residents of Thursday Island found the service more reliable and comfortable than that of smaller vessels engaged in the coastal trade. Consequently when the British India Navigation company Steamer *Quetta* of 3500 tonnes approached Albany Island on the night of 28 February 1890 many European residents of the Torres Strait, having spent the muggy, overcast wet season in the south, were on board.

The sea was calm and passengers sat on the deck talking, enjoying a smoke, anticipating the arrival of the ship at Thursday Island early the next morning. It was a bright moonlit night and across a magical sea to starboard the outline of Muri (Adolphus Island) could be seen against a star-studded sky. To port the ragged hills of Cape York loomed dimly, with Somerset lost somewhere in their shadows.

At 9.14 p.m, at a position approximately three kilometres south of Muri, an uncharted rock (later named Quetta Rock) tore the bottom out of the steamer as she churned north. The ship sank in three minutes allowing little time for sleeping passengers to be roused, crew to come to stations or boats to be lowered. In a twinkling it seemed, startled men, women and children were thrown from the security of a comfortable cabin into a dark sea, notorious for its treacherous tides and sharks.

At daylight Frank Jardine at Somerset saw the results of what had happened and sent a message to the telegraph office at Peak Hill twenty-four kilometres to the west. However it was not until 2 p.m. on 1 March that the Queensland government survey ship *Albatross* received the message. With extra stores, a doctor, the harbour master, the Rev. McLaren and ten volunteers, it left Port Kennedy a half hour later.

The S.S. *Victoria* had already picked up four survivors including Captain Saunders, the *Quetta*'s master. The *Albatross*'s company were temporarily elated by the discovery of 160 castaways on Muri, but these were Lascar seamen and with a sinking heart the searchers realized that almost all the Europeans had perished. As dark fell Frank Jardine pulled nineteen-year-old Alice Nicklin from the water and, about the same time, other searchers sighted a Singhalese seamen floating on his back, holding a tiny European child to his chest. During the hot, agonizing day, with the infant almost expiring from exposure, all he could do was push his tongue into her mouth for her to suck. But this was enough and the girl survived. Though her identity was unknown, she was adopted by a Captain Brown at Thursday Island who gave her the name Quetta Brown.

Incredibly another teenage girl, Emily Lacey, was rescued from the sea on the morning of 2 March after a day and a half in the water. She was the last survivor. Among the dead was her eighteen-year-old sister Kathy.

All told 133 people were lost. A few of the bodies that could be found were collected for burial at Thursday Island but Rev. McLaren decided that a permanent memorial to the disaster was appropriate. By appealing publicly throughout Queensland £2,000 was raised to construct a Quetta Memorial Church, which was consecrated in 1893. Then McLaren departed leaving the building to become the object of controversy, for it had never been made clear to which religion the church belonged, if in fact it belonged to any. Since it had been erected as a result of wide public subscription many felt that it should be a union church. On the other hand members of the Anglican Church claimed it since both McLaren and Bishop Barlow of Queensland, who had consecrated the building, were of that church. In time the Anglicans made good their claim and the building is now the Cathedral for the Diocese of Carpentaria. Each year a Quetta Memorial Service is held, although the vast majority of the congregation are Islanders and not a single Islander died in the disaster. Yet the anniversary of the 1899 cyclone in which scores of Islanders perished passes without comment.

At the beginning of the twentieth century Thursday Island found itself to be Queensland's if not Australia's front door step and the centre of a flourishing fishing industry. With a hospital, artillery battery, post office and well-attended school with seventy students and two teachers, the area's white population could look confidently to the future.

6

Government Control

The later part of the nineteenth century saw a drift towards a protectionist attitude by concerned Europeans in regard to the indigenous people of Queensland. Many clergy, such as the Rev. J. Gribble who established Yarrabah in 1892, stated unabashedly that they desired a total disengagement of blacks from whites. Various acts were passed through the Queensland parliament conferring excessive authority upon white "Protectors". The Aborigines Protection and Restriction of the Sale of Opium Act of 1897 was the first significant move in this direction. Opium had been introduced by the Chinese who had earlier inundated North Queensland, though they affected the Torres Strait only marginally.

For some years North Queensland had been under pressure to do away with coloured labour. But for a region which had allowed the Chinese to exploit the goldfields of Cape York Peninsula, and which relied on Kanaka labour in the burgeoning sugar industry, and on South Sea, Malay and Filipino labour in the North Queensland fisheries, this was a very contentious issue.

Though new and fairly rigid laws governed the employment of coloured labourers from the Pacific Islands — who were termed variously South Sea Islanders, Kanakas or Polynesians — the lack of a common language between recruiter and recruit (except for the vagaries of "pidgin"), the recruit's lack of experience in such a situation, and often the avarice and

26. Islanders at Badu about the turn of the century. From John Douglas, *Past and Present of Thursday Island and Torres Straits*, 1900.

brutality on the part of European recruiters, made problems inevitable.

In 1884 Rev. MacFarlane at Mer was surprised by the arrival of five men from a plantation at Mourilyan a thousand kilometres to the south. They had stolen a small boat and were attempting to sail home to the Lydia Islands off New Guinea. Totally disillusioned with plantation existence, they had risked their lives in their desperate flight, but were inclined to believe that in so doing they had at least escaped death by disease or ill-treatment at Mourilyan. Meanwhile another twelve labourers from the Basilisk Islands had turned up on Thursday Island in a vessel stolen from a Chinaman. They were from the same plantation and voiced similar complaints. Chester was of the opinion that the runaways had been deceived as to the nature of their three-year contract and the conditions involved. When the schooner *Elsea* called at Thursday Island in November he prevailed upon the government agent aboard to return the men to their home islands. It is interesting to compare Chester's considerate treatment of these absconders with his harsh punishment of D'Albertis's Fijians some years before.

The agent on the *Elsea* complied with Chester's request,

taking the precaution of entering Port Moresby to see
Commodore Erskine. An investigation was made, the labourers
were transferred to a naval vessel and, with Rev. Chalmers as an
interpreter, they departed Port Moresby for their islands.

A subsequent Royal Commission on Recruiting Polynesian
Labourers in New Guinea and Adjacent Islands, produced an
inconclusive assessment of the Mourilyan case, but the very controversy which it created aided the White Australia forces in the
colony.

The Pacific Islanders Act of 1885 prohibited the further entry
of Kanakas but was repealed seven years later by the same
government that had proposed it in the first place (that of
Premier Sir Samuel Griffith). However with federation on 1
January 1901 Queensland became a State of the Commonwealth
of Australia and immediately came under strong criticism from
southerners who regarded Queensland as the weak link in a
"White Australia". One cartoon by Norman Lindsay, which
appeared in the *Bulletin* in 1902, reveals to what extent un-
ashamed racism was a factor contributing to the debate. North
Queensland had toyed with the idea of secession, originally from
southern Queensland, for more than twenty years as a means of
protecting the use of coloured labour, but on 31 March 1904
Commonwealth legislation effectively put an end to the
vacillations and acrimony by prohibiting further entry of Pacific
Island labour. Also it was decided to exclude those Islanders who
were already in the state. All Pacific Islanders were to be sent
home except for those who had married in Queensland, had
been resident for twenty years or who possessed land or
property. The ones who satisfied these conditions represented a
tiny minority of the state's population but a place had to be
found for them in Queensland's increasingly segregated society.
One move to meet this problem was the establishment of a
reserve for South Sea (or Pacific) Islanders in 1904 on Moa. This
later became St Pauls Anglican Mission.

While all this had been taking place the remaining inhabited
Torres Strait Islands had been languishing under a lethargic administration by the L.M.S. which had made no secret, right from
the beginning, of its main ambition of entering the missionary
field in New Guinea. By 1914 the L.M.S. regarded the Torres
Strait as a backwater, syphoning off badly needed resources from
the massive problems which confronted it in New Guinea. It

THE QUEENSLAND SECESSION PARTY.

27. A Norman Lindsay cartoon from the *Bulletin*, 4 October 1902. Such prejudice and fear led to legislation curtailing coloured immigration.

was with little regret that they handed the islands over to Bishop White of the Anglican Church in that year. White accepted this new challenge enthusiastically.

It is interesting that at this time the population of all the Torres Strait Islands, with the exclusion of St Pauls and Thursday Island, was a mere 2,000, and it must be remembered that many of those on Erub, Mer, Badu, Masig and Mabuiag were actually South Sea Islanders or their descendants. In 1850 the population of only three of these islands, Saibai, Erub and Mer, would have exceeded this total. Thus it can be seen by what a slim thread Torres Strait Islanders escaped total extinction. The fact that they did survive may be attributed in part to the firmer role church and administration had played in protecting them from exploitation. Yet, if physically they had survived, their culture had all but vanished and what pieces remained continued to be trampled down by mindless ethnocentrism.

Administration of the islands, whilst paternalistic, was enlightened for its day. The earlier Mamoose, or chief, system was replaced in 1907 by the election of representatives to form a council on each island. The enthusiasm this innovation aroused may be appreciated by the manner in which it spread to coastal villages in Papua, and Mapoon and Cowal Creek on Cape York Peninsula, within two decades of its introduction.

Each council supposedly wielded considerable power on its island, allowing the feelings of the people to be voiced and taken into account. But in practice church representatives and officials of the administration, usually resident European teachers, continued to dominate proceedings.

Bishop White in 1914 complained that old customs and heathenism persisted on Mer. All through the period of "the light" Waiet, in his cave up on the side of Waier, was visited clandestinely by devotees. As elsewhere in the Torres Strait Christianity rarely replaced the old religions — they just went underground, working on the principle that what the whiteman could not see would not concern him.

In 1928 the teacher on Mer, A. Davies, had some Islanders take him by dinghy to Waier. While they fished he clambered to the cave and looked upon Waiet — the first European known to have done so. The image was composed of turtle shell, human bones, vegetable fibre, shells and had a decoration of coconuts. Certainly it must have been an impressive sight, and Davies promptly threw the lot in a bag he had taken with him for the purpose. Back on Mer there was consternation when word of the desecration spread. Island leaders approached Davies's house and requested that Waiet be returned to his place. Davies refused. In desperation *pouri pouri* was tried and Davies threatened with death, but he remained firm and the magic had no effect. Davies, unperturbed, left the island in due course and took Waiet with him. Later it came to rest in the Queensland Museum where it is located today.

What prompted Davies to such an act of piracy? Was he a Christian zealot bent on obliterating heathenism in the islands? Was he a keen but thoughtless amateur anthropologist? Despite these puzzling questions, the episode reveals the total lack of practical authority of the island council and its members. Davies, the only European on the island, was able to safely defy the entire Meriam community — numbering several hundred.

In line with protectionist policies a system evolved whereby unauthorized whites were gradually excluded from the islands and Torres Strait Islanders excluded from Thursday Island. Boats working the Eastern Islands unloaded at Thursday Island but their Island crews were not permitted on the island during the hours of darkness. This was becoming common in Queensland with Cooktown, Charters Towers and Bowen being among other towns which hunted indigenous Australians from their streets at sundown. However, in fairness to the authorities, there may have been some justification for these strict measures in the case of Thursday Island at least. George Morrison returned home to Australia in 1915 after fifteen years away. His port of entry was Thursday Island but the *Aki Maru*, on which he travelled, had the misfortune to berth on St Andrew's Day. Most of the population was "more than usually drunk", including pilots, officers and policemen. The Japanese master was furious, and Morrison humiliated, as a dishevelled, drunken policeman attempted to take the thumbprints of the crew. Thursday Island appeared to deserve the derogatory title "Thirsty Island" which Morrison used to describe it.

Boats from the Western Islands were encouraged to call at Badu where Rev. F. Walker, a far-sighted L.M.S. man, had resigned from the mission and in 1904 established the Papuan Industries Ltd. Through a large store on Badu this company bought marine produce from the Islanders and sold any goods which they might desire to purchase with their hard-earned cash. Slips were constructed and Badu became the focus of activity throughout the busy western straits. The island's population increased due to natural causes as a result of greater affluence, but also due to the migration to Badu of men entering the cash economy and bringing their families. There was a thriving primary school with a European head teacher and a large troop of enthusiastic scouts. A scout detachment went to Thursday Island in 1927 to take part in a pageant commemorating the fiftieth anniversary of the founding of the town. A spectator observed: "In an intermediate position marched the native boy scouts and rovers from Badu Island in regular order, looking remarkably well and smart in their clean,

28. A procession up Douglas Street led by the town band celebrating the fiftieth anniversary of white settlement at Thursday Island in 1927.

29. Island dancers on the oval near Hospital Point during the anniversary celebrations in 1927. Fifty years later the grandsons of these men play rugby league on the same oval.

neat costumes, while near by came a particularly fine squad of native school boys and young men from mission stations and island settlements, looking clean, healthy, disciplined and active — an altogether exceptionally fine turnout".

A primary objective of Walker's company was to assist groups of Islanders to buy their own luggers through a pay-as-you-work plan extending over a number of years. From the Islanders' point of view the scheme was a great success and many Island communities soon possessed their own boats which operated on a communal basis. Captains were selected from amongst the experienced men, but the young men still went to work on

European-owned boats since most "company boats" were manned by older married men who went out for shorter periods when convenient. As a result of this cottage industry outlook the "company boats" rarely took the quantities of shell that European-owned luggers did but this was not important, for through these boats Island communities were given a measure of economic independence and the opportunity to manage their own enterprises. Unfortunately the long-term effect on Papuan Industries Ltd was ruinous. Although devised as a philanthropic scheme it was unable to pay even the modest 5 per cent interest on capital which had originally been envisaged and the company was in trouble. Copra and rubber plantations at Madiri and Daru in Papua helped to float it along but were subject to extreme price fluctuations which often exaggerated rather than stabilized the situation.

However, if it had been an unprofitable venture from the investors' viewpoint, Papuan Industries largely fulfilled the aims first conceived by Walker. In 1930 the Queensland government bought the bulk of the company's assets at Badu and the plantations in Papua were sold. The government tried to extend the effectiveness of operations by starting stores on other islands, however government administration also produced tension. Further protectionist legislation had given protectors the responsibility for controlling the personal income of each Aborigine or Islander under his authority. When applied to "company boats" it meant that the Island crews saw little direct result from their efforts and, adding insult to injury, was the fact that Aboriginal crews were receiving a higher wage at this time than Islanders. Resentment grew as well from interference by the administration in the running of the boats. On New Year's Day 1936 the crews of "company boats" went on strike, causing a ripple of concern in the white bureaucracy, although a compromise was reached. Island councils would henceforth supervise the running of the boats and selection of the captains and crews, but the protector would continue to control finances.

Despite the problems, Papuan Industries Ltd.'s operations at Badu from 1904 to the 1930s gave the island a boost which carried it through to the 1970s at which time Badu was still the centre of Island-owned fishing enterprises. These are now primarily aimed at live pearl shell for culture farms and crayfish.

The Torres Strait Islanders Act of 1939 in theory gave virtual

30. A sailing canoe at Thursday Island in 1945. Photograph by courtesy of the Australian War Memorial, Canberra.

home rule to Island communities, but in practice the white schoolmaster or schoolmistress, who also enjoyed the title of government administrator, controlled each island with a chairman and two councillors for assistance and to act as magistrates in village courts. A visitor in 1940 described these councillors: "They have an official uniform consisting of grey trousers, red jerseys with the word 'Councillor' embroidered in large letters across the chest, and broad-brimmed straw hats. They are only too ready at the slightest excuse to exchange the simple lava lava of daily wear for this more resplendent attire. There are native police sergeants and constables. All inhabitants have to be in their homes by 9 p.m., and this rule is rigidly enforced by the Councillors and police, who alone are priviliged to walk abroad after this hour. They also inspect the houses and see that the laws governing their cleanliness are observed". To the Islanders it must have seemed a bizarre, discouragingly regimented existence.

Community leaders, dressed in outlandish costumes, were apparently unable to prevent anomalies like the nine o'clock curfew, and keen policemen enforced such ridiculous rules. During inspection on village days a strange whiteman, half the age of village elders, was entitled to tell them what to do with their homes on the land where their ancestors had lived for centuries. It should have been obvious that the government had over-reacted to the turmoil of the late nineteenth century and that the islands were now being over-governed. Yet this did provide stability in a time of change, and the Islanders' natural resilience and good humour helped to cushion the impact of the more oppressive regulations.

Some elderly people still lived much as their parents had lived, but the communities generally were better off than they had been fifty years before, and they hoped to be even better off in the future. Lugger crews had demonstrated their independence by going on strike in 1936 but the results were largely inconclusive and war with Japan was on the horizon. With the war much would change.

7

World War II

*The Song of the Torres Strait
Light Infantry Battalion*

Ngittha ngalmun kalakawananu ina*
Torres Strait Light Infantry Batallion.
Jacky Jacky Main Road Sig. Sig. J. J.
Pioneer Company A B C D Company
Artillery Water Transport.

In September 1939 Australia went to war. The war in Europe must have seemed far away for Charles Turner, government teacher on Saibai, until a German arrived by canoe from along the Papuan coast. Turner promptly arrested him with the aid of Island policemen. The German, without a radio, had not known about the war and was naturally surprised. Subsequently he was interned.

Back on Thursday Island many of the local white and mixed race men joined up and, in the following years, served in the Middle East, Europe and the Pacific. Bill Turnball, who had been born and educated on Thursday Island, joined the R.A.A.F. Later in the war he participated in the Dambuster raids on Germany and was awarded the D.F.C. H. Carse, a Torres Strait pearler, became Lieutenant Carse R.A.N.V.R. In 1943 he captained the commando raider *Krait* in an attack on Singapore

* This line is in Badu dialect: "You have left us behind here". The song is popular among children.

in which seven Japanese ships (totalling 65,000 tonnes) were sunk, and received a Mention in Dispatches for his services.

However, during the first years of war, things changed little in the Torres Strait. Some goods were now difficult to obtain and the shipment of shell was disrupted by wartime priorities and circumstances. Underlying the outward calm however was the strong apprehension that Japan would enter the war. Though the consequences of Japanese entry could not have been anticipated, most concern centred on the hundreds of Japanese who lived on Thursday Island and worked on the boats. Japanese had been working in the area for generations and many who had an intimate knowledge of the strait were now in Japan where they would be available to Japanese intelligence. At this time luggers searching for trochus sailed down the Great Barrier Reef as far south as Mackay. Since large areas of the reef were unmapped such local information provided by expatriate Japanese would be of considerable value.

In December 1941 Japan attacked Pearl Harbour and simultaneously invaded British Malaya, thereby involving Australia in the Pacific War. Few luggers had radios so in the days and weeks that followed, as the luggers came in to anchor, they were met by members of the Queensland Police Force and the Japanese members of their crews were interned. European managers of the companies which owned the luggers working out of Thursday Island were also there to meet them as they arrived and to supervise the sad job of arresting men who, through their sweat, had made Thursday Island the prosperous town it was. This was virtually the end of pearling till after the war. Other Japanese residents of Thursday Island had already been rounded up and placed under guard in a stockade at the site of what is now the Wongai basketball court. Later they were sent to camps in southern Australia — from which few returned to Thursday Island.

On 23 January 1942 Rabaul fell and 2,000 Australians went into captivity. Then on 3 February Port Moresby was bombed. Six hundred European noncombatants had already been evacuated and now most natives decided to evacuate voluntarily, by going bush. The ill-prepared Australians found themselves with a serious labour shortage.

On 15 February Singapore fell and 17,000 Australian troops were captured. The allies, desperately fighting to contain the

31. Spitfires of no. 79 squadron and other R.A.A.F. planes at Nurapai. Photograph by courtesy of the Australian War Memorial, Canberra.

Japanese advance in the Dutch East Indies, staged American planes and allied shipping through Darwin. Hundreds of Dutch civilian refugees came south to Perth or through the Torres Strait to the east coast. Those on Thursday Island who saw the weeping women and haggard men, crowded together without possesions on their evacuation ships, could have had few doubts as to the fate which would shortly overtake themselves. Evacuation of European and mixed race noncombatants had already begun.

Darwin was subjected to a savage bombing attack on 19 February in which 240 people died. Eight ships were sunk in Darwin harbour, but this was obviously a back-up raid for the fighting in the Netherlands East Indies. With the fall of the Indies Darwin would be in the front line but its strategic importance would diminish since the Japanese army had aleady decided against invasion. The most crucial area strategically for Australia was New Guinea where the Japanese were advancing south, and obviously far north Queensland would play an integral part in the coming battle.

Airstrips at Iron Range, Jacky Jacky (an airstrip near Cape York named after Kennedy's companion) and Nurapai were already operational as ferrying stages for the short-range fighters and bombers of the U.S.A.A.F. However here the general lack of allied preparedness was to have immediate consequences.

In late April 1942 thirty-five Airocobras left Townsville to fly to the airfield on Nurapai, and from there to Port Moresby. At this stage of the war many American pilots were hastily trained and few were experienced in navigation which was difficult enough anyway in the cramped cockpit of a single-seater fighter. So it was arranged that the Airocobras were to follow a B17 bomber. Very soon though the inexperience of the pilots led to difficulties in maintaining formation and this confusion increased when the aircraft hit heavy cloud. Radio transmissions were disrupted by atmospheric conditions near the tip of Cape York and many planes in the broken formation became lost. The planes had left Cairns about 1 p.m. By 4.30 those which had not landed at Nurapai were running out of fuel and beginning to come down all over the top of Cape York Peninsula. Eleven crashed that day and another flight of six Airocobras all crashed the following day in the same area. One pilot was killed and others spent up to four days in the bush before being rescued by a launch from Nurapai. Most planes that reached Port Moresby were quickly outclassed and destroyed by superior planes of the Japanese air force. (Ten inexperienced American pilots had been shot down over Darwin during the raid of 19 February.)

Later some American bombers crashed off the end of Nurapai runway and were stripped by unofficial Australian divers before they could be salvaged. There is also a record of accidents at Iron Range with casualties among U.S.A.A.F. personnel.

Meanwhile in 1941 the first Torres Strait unit of company strength was formed of men from all islands. It was officered by Queenslanders of the Australian army and designated the Torres Strait Infantry Company. The Torres Strait Employment Company and the Torres Strait Labour Company also came into existence. However in 1943 it was decided to amalgamate and expand the force. It became known as the Torres Strait Light Infantry Battalion as part of Torres Strait Force. There were four companies A, B, C, and D. The men of A company were from Erub and Mer, B from Badu, Kubin and Mabuiag, C from Poruma, Masig and Iama and D from Saibai, Boigu and Dauan. They were mainly engaged in training, guard duties and work parties around Thursday Island.

On 14 March 1942 Nurapai, already on the alert after the attacks on Moresby, Broome and Darwin, was bombed for the first time. A Hudson and two other aircraft were damaged on the ground. Another attack was made on 29 April and again on the 30th when a B26 and two Wirraways were damaged and a soldier killed. Although there were few casualties in the first raids, the effect on the people was similar in some respects to the impact of bombing on Darwin's inhabitants.

The first raid on Nurapai was a great shock to those civilians who remained — mainly white men and mixed race. Arthur Filewood, who had worked on the Thursday Island wharves for over twenty years, ran from his modest bungalow in Hargreave Street to shelter under a nearby concrete culvert. Another European resident ran from his shop in Douglas Street to a slit trench dug in his back yard to find it already occupied by an Aborigine. The fellow had streaked across from where he was working two hundred metres away, in less time than it had taken the European to move twenty metres. The *Nancy*, a small Island cargo vessel, was moored at the Engineer's Jetty on Thursday Island. The raid caught its four Island crewmen near the Federal Hotel and they found shelter in a drain. However no bombs fell on Thursday Island in these or any other raids.

The Japanese bombers which made the attacks were all land-based planes requiring additional tanks to conserve sufficient fuel for the return trip. After the raids discarded silver belly tanks littered the channel between Thursday Island and Nurapai.

The night of the first raid and the days following saw the un-official evacuation of many of those civilians who were still about. They simply threw stores aboard boats and left. One group crept out of harbour after dark on a nine-metre sailing ketch. Without authority for the move, they were afraid of being spotted and challenged in the dark. It says little for the alertness of the garrison at this time that they passed out of Port Kennedy without being detected. They eventually reached Cairns. Filewood escaped to Cairns on a lugger with some South Sea and mixed race people shortly afterwards.

A curious feature of the raids was the way the Japanese pilots, in their determination to bomb the airfield, totally ignored the numerous ships and small craft scattered about the anchorage. Many, tied up to wharves unloading at Thursday Island and Nurapai, were sitting targets. These shallow-draught wooden vessels could have easily been destroyed by machine gunning or near misses by bombs (as shown at Darwin). The loss of these boats, essential for free movement in this area, could have created difficulties for the allied forces, spread as they were across six islands and the two mainlands to north and south.

Subsequent air attacks on Nurapai were as follows:

12 June 1942	One Wirraway destroyed
7 July 1942	Slight damage, fires started
30 July 1942	Heavy damage to two Hudsons, three others slightly damaged
1 August 1942	Bombs fell three kilometres south of Nurapai
25 August 1942	Bombs fell between Muralug and Nurapai
18 June 1943	Bombs fell between Muralug and Nurapai

The inaccuracy shown by the Japanese in the last three raids was not a reflection on the declining abilities of Japanese aviators alone, but rather evidence of strengthened Allied defences.

A radar unit had been established at Long Beach on the north-western corner of Muralug, thus allowing ample time for fighter aircraft on Nurapai to scramble, employing tactics which were to be used repeatedly throughout the Pacific against the highly manoeuvrable Zeroes. By climbing above the attacking aircraft, slower allied fighters then used their diving speed to advantage against the Japanese planes which were still encumbered by auxiliary fuel tanks and full bomb loads. One Japanese plane crashed on the northern side of Keriri and at least one other is said to have fallen into the sea near Gialug.

The T.S.L.I. witnessed the various air attacks in their capacities as labourers, or in transport, or as guards. In the slit trenches on Nurapai, Island soldiers experienced their first bombing just as thousands of other Australian soldiers did in many other places during the war. During one raid Private Calorus Isua took great interest in the activities but his companion Private Isau Ibuai slept through the whole event, thus acquiring a notorious and continuing reputation as a heavy sleeper.

Unhindered by these abortive raids a steady allied build-up was taking place in the Torres Strait. Blockhouses had been constructed on Thursday Island and surrounding islands. Around the back of Thursday Island (near Tamwoy) mudflats, which are exposed at low tide, were festooned with pickets and barbed wire. Machine guns were set up. The T.S.L.I. trained hard in the scrub on Muralug. Six hundred negro troops of the American army camped at Cowal Creek, immediately establishing a close friendship with the Island soldiers.

32. An inspection of C company of the Torres Strait Light Infantry battalion. Photograph by courtesy of the Australian War Memorial, Canberra.

33. Two drivers servicing a truck during the war. Photograph by courtesy of the Australian War Memorial, Canberra.

The object of all this activity was to safeguard the supply lines to Papua and so the small transports passed constantly across the strait. Many luggers and their former crewmen were pressed into service in the waters they knew so well. Frank Narua, now resident in Daru P.N.G., worked as a crewman on sailing luggers between Thursday Island and Daru, an area which is mapped inaccurately in parts, or not at all. The journey generally took about three days. However the main shipping route from Port Moresby to Thursday Island lies across the Gulf of Papua past Bramble Cay. It was here that a tragedy, little known today, occurred.

By August 1942 Port Moresby had been severely and repeatedly bombed. General Morris ordered the evacuation of all remaining European and mixed race noncombatants. The *Mamutu* slipped from the wharf with some eighty distressed men, women and children aboard — only a handful of them Europeans. In spite of rough weather and reports of submarines, the voyage went ahead. In the harbour the apprehensive travellers saw the burnt-out hulk of the *Macdui* sunk by Japanese bombing in June.

The course to Daru caused the *Mamutu* to steer north of Bramble Cay, where on 6 August it was found by a Japanese submarine. Four shells were more than sufficient to sink such a small vessel, and survivors are supposed to have been machine gunned in the water. Only one man, a European engineer, escaped by shamming dead. Among those killed was Henry Matthews, an Australian Anglican priest from Port Moresby. He could have left earlier but had preferred to stay till the evacuation of the last noncombatants. With him was Leslie Gariadi, his Papuan assistant. The names of both these men appear in the Book of Modern Martyrs kept in St Paul's Cathedral, London.

The question arises as to what a submarine was doing so far north of the regular shipping lanes, in shallow water that would put it at a distinct disadvantage if attacked.

During the war crews of ships coming up from Cairns sometimes came to an isolated island to find the remains of a camp and other evidence of occupation which they supposed was made by Japanese. And it has to be remembered that the Japanese had access to detailed information regarding the waters of north Queensland. It is perhaps surprising that they did not make more use of it than they did.

The assault through eastern New Guinea having stalled, the Japanese began reconnoitring the southwestern approaches. The allies responded by sending a mixed Australian/American force to Merauke where an airstip was quickly completed accommodating some fighter aircraft and Australian Dauntless dive bombers. Contact with the Japanese was sporadic with some minor sea battles between Japanese and Australian barges along that flat, swampy coast. The overextended Japanese were unable to maintain the effort and so this threat faded. But even as it did, servicemen were reminded of another danger when an Australian soldier was clubbed to death by savage tribesmen in the swamps. In July and August 1945 parties of the T.S.L.I. were sent to serve in this isolated outpost.

The strength of the T.S.L.I. was between 450 and 500, representing a considerable proportion of the total population of the islands and, as the weight of recruiting had not fallen equally on all islands, some islands were denuded of their young males. A visitor to Nahgi during the later part of the war found thirty-seven women and children and one old man. Every other male adult had volunteered or been conscripted into war service. Across the islands this was to have serious repercussions.

Over the years many Islanders had become used to new foods — rice, tinned meat, flour — and European-style clothing. Hurricane lanterns were in widespread use. As the war developed European staff were withdrawn and island trade boats pressed into war service. The people of the islands were left largely to their own devices. One observer, commenting on conditions at the time, said that many people on the islands left their houses and went to live in the bush for shelter. At night no lights were allowed and all cooking had to be done in the day time.

Most islanders were thrown almost entirely upon their own traditional food resources. The old sago trade with the coastal Papuans was revitalized but when it came time to hack new gardens out of the bush, catch dugong and turtle or shoot ducks, the young men were not there. For some families the war years were years of considerable hardship. At the end of the war twelve of their men did not return. Their names are shown in the Roll of Honour in the Australian War Memorial Canberra, with illness and accidents being recorded as the causes of death.

On Thursday Island, as in all towns under army occupation,

widespread looting had occurred which discouraged the return of some evacuated civilians. Others had made a new life in the south. Many had married. Few of the Malays or Japanese returned. Before the war no Islanders had been permitted to reside there but afterwards, perhaps in recognition of their contribution to the war effort, the Department of Native Affairs* built a "model" settlement at Tamwoy for Islanders, beginning the exodus from the Outer Islands and ultimately changing the destiny of a race. Thursday Island became the gateway to the south and by 1975 half of all Torres Strait Islanders would be living in the south.

The Torres Strait was never the same after World War II. An Islander serving in the T.S.L.I. was quoted as saying: "The Army has been good for us coloured boys. In the Army we meet good white men. They talk with us. We are friends. Some white men are good. The Education Officer on T.I. helped us coloured boys a lot. We get any book we want in the Army. We treated like white men in the Army."

Today when a couple of old T.S.L.I. men get together you may hear stories of bombs, or their friends the negroes, or Merauke, or how they first learned to drive a truck. And on Anzac Day the T.S.L.I. turn out in their numbers to march proudly from the Thursday Island post office to the small memorial park opposite the Torres Strait Hotel.

---

* The D.N.A. in 1965 became the Department of Aboriginal and Island Affairs and then in 1975 the Department of Aboriginal and Islanders Advancement (both D.A.I.A.).

The Border Problem

The extension of the Queensland border to the coast of Papua had originally been motivated by a desire to protect Queensland fishing enterprises in the northern Torres Strait. Associated with this was a recognition of Queensland's responsibility to regulate interaction between outsiders and the indigenous inhabitants of the region. A further consideration was the absolute necessity to secure the shipping channel through the Torres Strait which was crucial for Queensland's livelihood and not unimportant to the other states of eastern Australia.

The act of 24 June 1879, urged by Premier J. Douglas but finally confirmed by Premier T. MacIllwraith, can be readily understood in these terms. The absence of any administration in Papua allowed Queensland to fix a line close to the Papuan coast without regard to international convention. But the motives which had induced this arrangement also clearly demanded that Papua should not become a German possession and so Queensland was compelled to encourage annexation by the Imperial government — a request to which Britain finally acceded in 1884.

With the creation of British New Guinea, Queensland achieved the security she had been seeking in the far north for twenty years, ever since the establishment of Somerset in 1864.

The mainlands on both sides of the Torres Strait were under British administration and, since the Colonial Conference in 1887 arranged for the Queensand governor to guide the ad-

ministration of B.N.G., both mainlands were therefore
responsible to the governor of Queensland. As the problem had
been resolved in this way it seemed apparent to most observers
that an adjustment of the border was necessary and would not be
difficult to achieve under the circumstances. Appropriately it
was Douglas who first voiced concern on the matter.

In 1884 Douglas had been appointed resident magistrate to
Thursday Island and was for a short time special commissioner
for British New Guinea, based in Port Moresby. These dual
appointments (there was an acting resident magistrate at
Thursday Island) enabled him to view the border question in a
more balanced fashion — certainly it brought home to him the
inequitable nature of the problem when viewed from the
Papuan side. He now found himself in the difficult position of
trying to move south the border which he himself, only six years
before, had been largely responsible for moving north. To
Douglas however the question was not so much whether to
move the border south again but rather how far. He actually
recommended at one time that all the islands of the Torres
Strait, including Thursday Island and the Muralug group,
should be transferred to British New Guinea. Nationalist
sentiment in Australia made this suggestion hypothetical
though its justification was simple. The Islanders were
Melanesian village dwellers similar to the Papuans and dis-
similar to the nomadic hunters of mainland Australia. Douglas
found Queensland laws framed for Aborigines clumsy and ir-
relevant, particularly in the northern islands where Papuan
influence was stronger: "It is difficult, nay impossible to apply
our Queensland laws to such islands as Saibai, Dauan and Boigu.
To the magistrate at Daru, with his native ordinances, and his
proximity to these islands, it is another matter altogether." He
despaired of effective administration of the islands — "unless we
can induce the Queensland Parliament to transfer some of them
to New Guinea".

Eventually Douglas advocated the tenth degree south latitude
as the border line. This seems the most rational departure from
the 1879 border and was based on possession of equal parts of the
strait and its resources by each administration. On a cultural
basis also it was fairly satisfactory since the northern Western
Islands, northern Central Islands and Eastern Islands, which
comprised the more sophisticated societies Douglas probably

had most trouble applying Queensland laws to, would all be part of British New Guinea with its special provisions for indigenous customs and land tenure. Possibly the only significant cultural anomaly was that the border fell between Mabuiag and Badu which were the homes of two very closely related peoples. However in the late 1880s it was a solution which, if accepted, would have caused a minimum of disturbance at the time and prevented the dispute which arose during the 1970s.

That the proposal was never accepted is sometimes attributed to a lack of general interest in the subject or to its political unpopularity. Many of the best trochus, bêche-de-mer and pearl shell grounds lay north of the 10° latitude (Darnley Deeps, Orman Reefs, Warrior Reefs) and a convincing argument would be necessary to prise them from Queensland. Such arguments mainly rested with Douglas's sociological reasoning.

In 1893 Sir Samuel Griffith, who was then premier of Queensland, toured the islands with Douglas and was impressed by Islanders on the northern islands "such as those at Saibai who differ in few if any respects from their neighbours on the mainland of New Guinea". Griffith consequently sought to eliminate the most obvious discrepancy by advocating that the border be moved south of Saibai, Dauan and Boigu, thus uniting the inhabitants of these islands with the Papuans under a British administration.

Sir William MacGregor, administrator of British New Guinea, approved Griffith's proposal with qualifications. During the term of his administration he frequently visited these northern islands in the couse of exploration and pacification. These visits permitted him to collect a number of Torres Strait artifacts, some of which he donated to the Queensland Museum whilst governor of Queensland. Yet his concern was not limited to the border's sociological implications, for he also insisted that in any readjustment of the border the crucial Warrior Reefs should be included in British New Guinea. In this he was clearly thinking into the future. Griffith's proposal, even if adopted in 1893 would not have prevented the 1970s dispute for although it corrected the most obvious blunder of the 1879 act (Saibai, Boigu, Dauan), it did not allow a fairer distribution of resources. MacGregor's shrewd proposal, if accepted, would have given the prolific fishing area of the Warrior Reefs to Papua. It is unlikely that Papua then could reasonably have asked for more — although it is just as unlikely that Queensland would willingly have parted with them in the first place.

Queensland's obduracy meant that any further initiative would have to come from the British government. However a special Colonial Boundaries Act passed by the Imperial government in 1895 provided that the consent of a self-governing colony was required for any alteration of its border. This confirmed the 1879 border and in effect gave the Queensland government final authority to decide on the border question.

In June 1896 the British government recommended that the border be moved south of Saibai, Boigu and Dauan. However MacGregor protested strongly that this did not amount to any redistribution of resources, particularly in respect to the northern Warrior Reefs which were a traditional Papuan fishing ground. A compromise agreement, with Queensland holding all the cards, led to a proposal that the border be altered so that Saibai, Boigu, Dauan, Buru, Gebar, Bramble Cay and the northern Warrior Reefs be included in British New Guinea. The British government issued an order in council in May 1898 along these lines fully recognizing that the approval of the parliament of Queensland was necessary. Such approval was not forth-coming and in 1901 Queensland became a state of the Commonwealth of Australia. Under the Commonwealth Con-stitution the alteration of a state border requires not only the approval of the commonwealth parliament and the state parliament but also a referendum in which the majority of the electors of that state approve the change. This added qualification effectively ended any hopes of an adjustment in the first half of the twentieth century.

The nearness of the Queensland border, the fishing industries and their attendant problems concerned the Australian adminis-tration of Papua at various times though little could realistically be done about it. So the dispute lay dormant through the years till the nation of P.N.G. began to prepare itself for independence in the early 1970s. Nationalist politicians, both in the Western Province and nationwide, understandably resented the proximity of the Queensland border and regarded it as an obsolete colonial border denying Papuans access to their share of the strait's resources.

34, 35. These dancers' elaborate costumes show the time spent in preparation. Many dances emphasize the traditional hostility between Papuans and Torres Strait Islanders. Ironically, the man's drum, bird-of-paradise and black cassowary feathers were obtained from Papua. The tinsel, wristwatch and bright paint are from Australia. Photographs by courtesy of P. Berends.

Much dubious publicity has been made of traditional borders. There is a bank to the northwest of Saibai called Saibailgau Maza where a traditional leader named Alis was fatally wounded by Papuans and which is claimed as a traditional border. This may be correct but twenty-four kilometres to the east Papuans hunt dugong, crabs and fish well south of this on the island of Saibai itself and have done so for generations. Yet *this* traditional border is hardly acceptable to the people of Saibai. Similarly the reefs north of Moon Pass are a traditional Papuan fishing ground. Islanders in small aluminium dinghies with outboard motors can no longer travel as widely as their large sailing canoes allowed in the past. Today few Islanders are even seen in the northern Warrior Reefs area except as crew on European or Asian owned fishing vessels, whereas Kiwais regularly sail canoes about these reefs often staying out for days at a time. Much of the 25,000 kilogram catch of crayfish processed through Daru in 1971-72 actually came from reefs which are inside Queensland waters. These northern reefs are just fifty kilometres south of Daru but a hundred and sixty kilometres northeast of Thursday Island. No solution to the border problem would therefore be possible without an allowance for legal access by Papuans to the fishing resources of the Warrior Reefs.

Apart from fishing resources it is possible that exploration could reveal deposits of petroleum or natural gas offshore. Geological data suggest that conditions may be favourable although a single drill operated by Tenneco Australia Inc. in 1969 at Anchor Cay was unproductive. All the Torres Strait is covered by various mining leases, excepting the area about the lower Western Islands. These lower Western Islands are granitic and are not covered by a lease since the chances of discovering petroleum there are negligible.

No further drilling has taken place following the Tenneco attempt because of an embargo by the Queensland government on oil drilling on the Great Barrier Reef. This in turn has led to a lack of geological information. In late 1978 there was a brief controversy over alleged mining interests in the Torres Strait by the Queensland premier, Joh Bjelke-Petersen, and this was followed by the suggestion that the state cabinet was re-considering oil drilling on the Great Barrier Reef.

It is difficult to decide to what extent the possibility of oil being discovered has actually affected the course of negotiations on the Torres Strait border issue, however it does illustrate the important distinction between seabed resources and fishing resources.

The sociological issues that troubled Douglas and Griffith have now been resolved to some extent. Today the Island way of life is different from that of Papua though the Islanders themselves in some cases have changed little. They are still predominantly Melanesian by race and culture, and linked to Melanesians in Papua, often by direct relationship or descent. However their lifestyle has been distorted by their participation in the fishing industry on the labour-for-cash principle (although often there was much labour for little cash). This coupled with large-scale integration with the white Australian community, and the all-pervasive influence of the Australian Department of Social Security and the Queensland D.A.I.A., has created a different type of Melanesian from that found on the Papuan side of the border. The Islander is sedate, confident, perhaps possessed of a quiet dignity, yet somehow he seems to lack the humble diligence of the Papuan and the individual initiative and energy that Papuans may display in pursuit of opportunity. But then there are a few opportunities in Papua and probably the Islander is entitled to feel more confident than his Papuan neighbour.

It is significant that most Europeans cannot distinguish between Papuan migrants and Torres Strait Islanders. Indeed after one decade in the Torres Strait the Papuan migrant may have learned to speak an Island language, to perform Island dances, to use Island mannerisms and to look at life in the same quietly confident manner as the Islander.

It is the security of life as part of Australia that has transformed Island society and it is surprising how quickly Papuans are also transformed when placed in the same environment.

When negotiations over the border first began there were few Islanders even prepared to discuss alterations to the border. "Border Not Change" was the slogan of a remarkable political movement which united Torres Strait Islanders to an extent never before experienced. Although marked by a naivete, which weakened its impact, it was a genuine movement which enjoyed the support of a vast majority of Islanders. It was the Islanders' own intransigence on the question which permitted the Queensland government to adopt the firm position it did over more than five years of negotiations. Without their overwhelming support the state government would have been unable to maintain such a stand.

In P.N.G. there was a surprising divergence of opinion. Those Papuan villages with traditional and continuing contact with the Torres Strait Islanders generally approved of the 1879 border since it allowed them to use facilities on the islands which their own government could not provide. One group from Buzi (near Boigu) in 1976 were even reported to have asked that the border be moved north to include their village on the New Guinea mainland.

Complicating the matter was the existence in P.N.G. of a minority who were committed to moving the border south, as far as possible and as soon as possible. I was amazed at the strength of feeling expressed by some young Papuans (Western Province, Southern Highlands and Port Moresby) in this respect. While traditional communities appeared unconcerned, the newly educated elite, disciples of rising national sentiment, pressed strongly for a change. Perhaps the most vocal was Ebia Olewali, a Kiwai from Tureture, who has been a cabinet minister in the Somare government for a number of years.

This group dominates education, administration and politics and clearly it would be a mistake to under-estimate their influence. Continued attempts by Queensland to delay an alteration to the border could only lead to belligerence. The victory of the Somare government in the P.N.G. elections of July 1977 meant a continuation of moderate influence, but the time would come when pressure for change became irresistible.

The legal issues involved are extremely complex. There are no specific international conventions which satisfy the peculiar problems of the Torres Strait dispute. As early as 1974 a possible solution was being suggested involving a median line drawn between the two mainlands for allocation of seabed resources, with island enclaves under Queensland administration and a negotiated agreement on the utilization of fishing resources perhaps along traditional lines. Such an arrangement would depend upon appropriate and continuous supervision. In the March 1974 *World Review* R. Lumbe proposed the establishment of a Torres Strait Maritime Commission consisting of representatives of Australia, Queensland and P.N.G.

The Whitlam federal government, before its demise in late 1975, had made noises which Torres Strait Islanders interpreted as indicating a sell-out. The situation developed into a political battle between Prime Minister Whitlam on one side and Premier Bjelke-Petersen, claiming to represent the Islanders' interests, on the other side. However the premier's visits to the Outer Islands, often in conditions of some discomfort, greatly impressed the inhabitants. Whitlam's failure to conduct similar visits was widely resented. How could he make such crucial decisions regarding the islands' future when he had never taken the trouble to visit them or talk to their inhabitants? A visit by Bryant, then federal minister for Aboriginal Affairs, was a disaster. At least one council ignored him, others received him with cold courtesy. A public meeting at the town hall on Thursday Island degenerated into a farce in which Bryant belittled Tanu Nona O.B.E., a prominent Island leader, obviously in the belief that he was not present, only to learn to his embarrassment that Nona was standing within several metres of him. At that time a more damaging action can scarcely be imagined.

Bryant was later replaced by Cavanagh who generated somewhat less hostility among Islanders. Nevertheless the Whitlam years represented a low point in relations between the Islanders as a group and the federal government. After 1975 the situation steadily improved though Islanders remained wary of a Canberra which still appeared determined to alter the border — a concept which the Islanders claimed to oppose totally and unconditionally.

Getano Lui, chairman of the Islander Advisory Council and a leading Island spokesman, rejected the proposals for both a seabed boundary and for island enclaves in Papuan waters — "if you take our water and the seabed then you take our lives." He went on to explain the traditionalist philosophy of resources use: "We are happy to share what we have in the Torres Strait, but we will not give — not a teaspoon of water, not a grain of sand." It is remarkable how much the coastal Papuans and Islanders appreciate each other's positions and how cordial discussions between the groups have been. Left to the traditional inhabitants there would be no dispute, however time has caught up with the Torres Strait and its peoples. Politicians in Canberra and Port Moresby, whilst sympathetic to traditional practices, were committed to a treaty based on international, rather than intertribal, custom.

In fact among the first foreign affairs matters to which the new Fraser government devoted itself were negotiations on the Torres Strait border issue with P.N.G. In March 1976 Somare and Fraser met in Port Moresby and agreed that it was important to reach an equitable and permanent settlement. Following this, in May, the foreign ministers of each country conferred and announced in June that they had reached general agreement on some basic points. Prominent among these was acceptance of a proposal for a seabed resources line running through the Torres Strait. There were even details of its location. This was despite the fact that Islanders on every occasion had made it known that they would refuse to accept such a line. When Fraser visited Thursday Island and then the Outer Islands to discuss the matter with Island chairmen and representatives he received the unanimous refusal he must have expected.

In P.N.G. Prime Minister Somare seemed prepared to wait for Australia to cajole the Torres Strait Islanders into accepting a change. Despite passage through the P.N.G. parliament of the national seas legislation, by which P.N.G. could theoretically take action, Somare's government and the Australian government came to an understanding that no such action would occur pending further constructive negotiations.

In late 1978 Andrew Peacock, Australian minister for foreign affairs, visited the islands to discuss the business with Island leaders once again. His proposal was little different from the one Fraser had put forward two years before. It involved establishing the far northern islands as Australian enclaves, with separate borders for fisheries and seabed resources further south, and provisions for traditional movement. However, Peacock had one crucial advantage which Fraser had lacked. The Queensland premier, Bjelke-Petersen, who accompanied Peacock, had changed his whole stance over the border question and was now prepared to recommend that Island leaders agree to the proposed settlement. In fact, the Australian government had adroitly side-stepped constitutional issues by emphasizing that there was to be no alteration to Queensland's land border, whilst simultaneously asserting the commonwealth's authority over the territorial sea and its resources. Papua New Guinea had meanwhile been persuaded to accept the enclave idea.

At the meeting with Peacock the previously unshakeable Island representatives followed Bjelke-Petersen's lead and accepted the proposed agreement.

On 18 December 1978 Fraser, Peacock, Bjelke-Petersen, Somare and Olewali, now P.N.G.'s minister for foreign affairs, met at Papua New Guinea House in Sydney for the official signing of the treaty and, it was hoped, a conclusion to the problem that had troubled politicians in Queensland, and elsewhere, for a century.

There are however some indications that the agreement is not universally popular. Many Islanders, and not a few white Australians, were dismayed at the sudden collapse of the Border

Not Change movement. Actually it only demonstrated once more the Queensland government's continuing influence over Islanders and their representatives. This time though voices have been raised in opposition.

When Bjelke-Petersen arrived at Papua New Guinea House for the signing of the treaty, Carl Wacando, a native of Erub now resident on the Australian mainland, presented the premier with a high court writ challenging the treaty's validity on a legal technicality. On Thursday Island, Eti Pau of Erub sought to rally opposition to the treaty amongst ex-servicemen by advocating the reformation of the Torres Strait Light Infantry. Certainly the border settlement is unpalatable from the Islander's point of view, even if it may be considered inevitable, for they have lost waters and resources which they had been encouraged to regard as their own.

It was no coincidence that at the time the treaty was signed P.N.G. had just contracted a north Queensland company to expand fish processing and storage facilities on Daru. Papuan fishermen now have access to substantial new fishing grounds in the northern Torres Strait and the P.N.G. government is committed to exploiting them.

Similarly, it was no coincidence that within a week of the signing the Queensland minister for mines announced that drilling for oil on the Great Barrier Reef would again be considered.

If a small number of Islanders alone voiced opposition to the treaty there would be few complications but there is also some dissatisfaction evident in P.N.G. The treaty is, without question, a personal triumph for Olewali, but the very fact that Bjelke-Petersen described the treaty as "a just and honourable settlement" must raise doubts in the new nation.

In an article in the *Australian* on 30 December 1978 the newspaper's Port Moresby correspondent stated: "The Torres Strait border agreement with Australia, presented as the year's crowning triumph of government diplomacy, seems to most people in Port Moresby a ludicrous 'cop out' leaving black 'Australian' citizens on 'Australian' islands within a few miles of the P.N.G. coast, just as they were before." It would be unreasonable to expect that nationalist politicians in P.N.G., after their success this time, will not seek to renegotiate the border terms on a future occasion — whether it be in ten years or fifty.

As if to irritate P.N.G. nationalists still further the common-wealth undertook to return illegal Papuan migrants in the Torres Strait to their homeland about the time the treaty was signed. Initial reports suggested that more than a hundred people had been repatriated, eliminating some of the more blatant instances of cheap labour exploitation on fishing boats and on Thursday Island. The government in P.N.G. probably hopes that many of the returnees will find employment in the expanded fishing industries. It is clear, however, that all Papuans in the Torres Strait have not been repatriated.

The most intriguing point concerns the timing of the repatriation drive. Why was the move not made years ago? If the drive was linked to the treaty what was the reason? Surely it must have been anticipated that the impact in P.N.G. would be negative in the extreme, unless the move was an attempt to maintain credibility in the eyes of the Islanders. The *Australian*'s correspondent believed that the repatriation of P.N.G.'s nationals from the Torres Strait Islands emphasized "the old white master's sneering continuity of sovereignty over the whole sea".

In these circumstances it is difficult to state with any confidence that a satisfactory and permanent solution to the dispute has been reached. A change of government in P.N.G. could easily result in a new, less moderate administration pressing for renegotiation of the treaty. As it was in late 1978 the Somare government avoided, by a very narrow margin, being displaced. The complexity of the agreement, which is considered unique because of the lack of a natural or traditional border, requires the active goodwill of both sides if it is to succeed.

THE PEOPLE ~ THEIR LIFE

9

The Sea

Taba Naba*

Taba naba naba norem,
Tugei pe neiser mi, dinghy ge nabatre,
Mi ko kei mi serer em nebewem,
Taba naba norem.

For a resident of the Torres Strait the sea is a road to other places
— to islands, reefs and mainlands. The indigenous people have a
special relationship with the sea and its creatures and many to
this day are required to fish in order to provide protein for their
families. Outsiders are surprised that Islanders generally eat
smaller fish which they say taste "sweeter" than larger fish. This
preference also could be motivated by convenience since this is
subsistence fishing and small fish are caught more easily.
Another consequence of the subsistence philosophy is found in

---

* The translation is:
  Come let us go to the reef,
  While morning low tide, let us go in the dinghy,
  Let us wade to the edge of the reef,
  Come let us go to the reef.

This is the Wed-Meriam Mer (that is, Eastern Island Language from Mer)
version of a popular and spirited Island song. A sit-down dance is normally
performed to this tune with the participants seated *barbuk* (cross-legged) in
a circle facing each other. The dance consists of rhythmic clapping and
gesturing with the body swaying back and forth.

36. A morning's catch of bream, catfish, mullet and barramundi taken in a
small-gauge gill net along with the shark.

the variety of fish eaten. In fact there are few fish in the sea
which cannot be eaten.

This is not to say that large fish are not sought but since most
Outer Islanders have no refrigerator to preserve large catches
they are distributed throughout the family in the traditional
manner and consumed while fresh.

Fishing has been so fundamentally important to Islanders that
a host of customs and traditions has developed. On some islands
when a boy catches his first fish there is a great feast and
celebration. This signifies the first occasion on which he has con-

tributed food for the family meal — a significant step on the road to manhood.

When large numbers of fish are caught there is extreme reluctance to throw any edible fish back. Partly this is because almost no fish is too small to eat and any surplus will be given to relatives. Also however there is a mystical justification — a notion that these are gifts from the sea and throwing any back shows a frivolous ingratitude which must invite bad luck.

In estuaries there are sluggish, brown eels, growing to three metres in length. If Islanders fishing from a dinghy sight this repulsive animal they all instantly spit into the water. This prevents the eel interfering with their fishing. Here also catfish are caught. Today pliers are frequently used to break off the poisonous spines on the catfish's back and flanks but I have also seen girls tear the dangerous spines from wriggling catfish with their teeth.

Naturally the other creatures of the sea are known intimately by the Islanders and are accorded the esteem or fear they deserve. The dugong is one of the most important. Dugong are mammals which are found in suitable areas of the Red Sea, Indian ocean and around north Australia. There are few places where they remain as plentiful as in the Torres Strait, however it must be realized that even here their numbers are dwindling.

In the nineteenth century it was widely believed that dugong fishing in southern Queensland would become a viable long-term industry. No part of the dugong could not be used — skin, bones, meat and the oil, which sold for as much as £3 a gallon. One herd of dugong in Wide Bay was described as being five kilometres long and a kilometre wide.

Dugong fishing however never became the "source of industry and wealth" as was hoped and in fact dugong all but disappeared because of commercial fishing, often by Aboriginal spearmen working for whites.

Throughout the Torres Strait these guileless and inoffensive animals are hunted relentlessly. Much of the hunting is commercially based: openly on the P.N.G. side; discreetly and illegally on the Queensland side.

The dugong of the Eastern and Western Torres Strait are different in some ways. Those of the west are lighter in colour and, it is claimed, must surface every quarter hour or so whereas those in the east may stay down for periods considerably longer.

Whether this is true or not, most dugong are speared in the Western Torres Strait.

In certain places it is known that the dugong will occur in large numbers at certain times. Each herd has a leader. In Saibai language dugong is "dthungal", and the herd leader is recognized and known as the "whistle dugong". As the tide rises and the dugong are coming onto their feeding ground, which is generally in marginal areas where access depends on a high tide, the lead dugong will swim ahead. Alone he will investigate the grounds while the herd wait patiently in deep water. When satisfied he whistles clearly so that the herd, and any men nearby, will hear. The herd then follow their leader onto the feeding ground. The same procedure is followed when they are leaving the ground and dropping off into deep water.

In the past wooden platforms were built in places where dugong could be expected, and they were speared from these stands. Today all dugong are speared from boats and many hunters prefer to stalk them at night. On a quiet evening the exhalation of the dugong can be heard for hundreds of metres, and the phosphorescent splashes are easy to locate. Some skilled hunters can smell the air which the dugong has exhaled, hanging in the still atmosphere over the feeding grounds.

During the day dugong can be detected even when not visible. As they feed in the shallows they root about the slimy bottom with their thick, bristled lips, and send billowing clouds of sediment to the surface.

Spearing a dugong is not a job for beginners and can be dangerous. Although large and seemingly sluggish, the dugong is a powerful animal. The spear shaft is a straight length of mangrove, up to two and a half metres long and hand carved, with a bamboo extension sometimes giving it added length. At one end it widens to a hand's width in diameter. In the centre is a hole in which is fitted a metal head. This is a three-cornered file on which the edges have been worn into serrated barbs. A rope is tied to the file.

The dugong must be approached very carefully — drifting on the tide, by oar or sail. The slightest sound and the animal will disappear. When close enough the attacker leaps from the bow of the dinghy, lending his own weight to the power of the thrust. The file bites deeply, the wooden shaft falls away but is tied by a loose loop to the rope so that it is easily retrieved. The rope tautens immediately and streaks away. If the boat is small it may be pulled some distance but if the file and rope hold, the dugong must tire and, as it does so, it can be pulled in hand over hand. A rope is tied about the powerful tail and the animal may be held upside down over the side till it drowns.

A chubby dugong is butchered carefully by slicing with razor-sharp knives down the whole length of its body. Strips are then cut from the body so that each has a layer of meat and an outer layer of rich fat up to ten centimetres thick. The meat may be roasted or boiled, and is tasty and quite tender — often being compared favourably with veal. Islanders find the fat delicious, sometimes preferring to chew the cooked blubber rather than the fine meat which accompanies it.

The old people in the Torres Strait, after eating dugong, smeared the fat and oil over their bodies and in their hair, believing that it enhanced health and strength. For the men, constantly in and out of the water and forced to work in the wind and the rain, this was also a practical measure insulating them against cold. In fairly recent times this tradition has been carried through with Island children being dosed with dugong oil by the spoonful in the same way that European children were fed castor oil.

There is no doubt that in the past dugong were an extremely important food item. They frequently appear in Island legends and accurately carved models of dugong were even discovered in the Eastern Islands where they were comparatively less important. The hill of Gelam on Mer traditionally represents a dugong. Gelam is claimed to have journeyed from Moa to Mer in the guise of a dugong.

The market on Daru Island is right on the muddy foreshore. It is a small cement slab and corrugated-iron structure. Sago and bananas are almost the only crops sold there, but rarely a day passes, weather permitting, without hundreds of kilograms of dugong meat being offered for sale. As a town worker, an un-skilled Papuan in 1975 could expect little more than twenty kina a week. From one dugong however he might expect a hundred kina. With this incentive it is not surprising that dugong hunting in the Western Province of P.N.G. has developed into a highly competitive local industry. The only thing that seems likely to halt this is the decreasing number of dugong.

Frequently Queensland dugong end up as Papuan dinners. At present this is not resented by the Islanders who regard it as a sort of traditional fishing arrangement. The eastern end of Saibai is a favourite hunting ground for the Papuans at Mabadawan, who later may take their catch to Daru for sale.

On Thursday Island word spreads that dugong is for sale at Tamwoy or Boigu Camp or even on the main beach at the front of the island. It may cost anything up to a dollar for a string with something less than half a kilogram. It is illegal, and extremely profitable, but no action has ever been taken to stop it.

Whilst dugong is popular, it is doubtful if it is more popular among the Islanders than the green turtle.

During the months before and after Christmas the female green turtle, immediately distinguishable from the male because of her shorter tail, comes up to lay her hundred or so eggs in the sand. She is quite selective. The position must be above high tide mark and is generally among the loose scrub and grasses at the top of the beach.

As her tracks are readily observed from a distance, she usually wanders around making several trial holes. These holes inevitably mislead anyone searching for eggs but not for long. Thrusting a stick or spear down through the sand, the searcher discovers a wet mash indicating the buried eggs. Those eggs which humans do not get the goannas probably will. The young turtles which do succeed in hatching must then run the gauntlet down the bare beach to the water. Gulls and larger fish take a massive toll of them.

In some areas turtle are often captured by Islanders at night as the animals blunder about seeking to lay eggs. Generally however turtle cannot be obtained frequently and reliably enough in this fashion and if Islanders wish turtle they must hunt them amid the reefs and sandbars. A century and a half ago Islanders used a sucker fish (gapu) for this purpose.

This fish is sleek, muscular and black with white stripes running the length of its body. On top of its head is a large oval-shaped suction plate, which the fish uses to attach itself to a large host. It will eat the scraps of its host's meal.

When Islanders caught a sucker fish it was secured with a coconut fibre rope about the tail and allowed to attach itself to their canoe. They devised some method by which the fish would fix itself to the shell of a moving turtle, then hold fast as they dragged on the line slowly pulling the turtle to the canoe. This old practice has now fallen into disuse but it is known. Today turtle are speared with a dugong spear though a barbed file is not thought necessary and a tightly bound trio of long nails is sometimes used.

On some Islands it is the custom to kill or stun a turtle before butchering by giving it a number of heavy blows on the bridge of the nose. This is by no means universal practice and struggling turtle are often cut up while living. Those who do kill the animal beforehand sometimes deliver scathing commentary on the barbarism of their neighbours who do not. Always the bottom shell plate is cut away first revealing a mass of quivering innards. Most meat is situated about the chest and shoulders of the fore flippers, but everything is eaten. The intestines are emptied of sea grass for cooking, unlaid eggs are collected, the layers of rich fat are especially prized. Usually the turtle will be cooked in its shell after butchering. The cooking is done with hot stones, and the lot covered with coconut or banana leaves. There may be variations, a hole may be dug, or sheets of galvanized iron used, but they are all known as "Kap Mari".

Apart from the laying season, most turtles are taken about July and August during the mating season. "Turtle fast", or a pair of mating turtle, are found almost anywhere between Papua and Cape York, but some places seem to be popular as traditional breeding grounds. The sea from the southern end of Muralug to Cowal Creek on Cape York Peninsula appears to be one of these spots, and it is possible to travel the whole distance without being out of sight of a pair of mating turtle.

Turtle farming, initially under the direction of Dr Bustard, a marine biologist, has begun on Erub, Mer and other islands. The requirements for a successful turtle farm are turtle eggs and suitable food. The young, growing turtle feeds on small fish such as sardines and chopped clam meat, whereas the adult turtle becomes vegetarian. Though these two islands appear to meet the prerequisites, it is extremely doubtful whether the farms are economically viable.

Before the war, and before the turtle was protected, several unsuccessful attempts were made to exploit the green turtle by the erection of soup canning factories on islands of the Capricorn Group, which is the other great stronghold of the green turtle. Green turtle shell was never valuable and today most demand for such material is satisfied by plastics. Furthermore the prospects for large-scale production of turtles for meat do not appear favourable. The islands' isolated position, the effort required to find feed for the turtles and the typical "cottage industry" approach may well doom the venture to economic failure.

In spite of the commercial nonprofitability of the present scheme, it may be a useful conservation measure if the turtle's high natural mortality rate during growth can be reduced. It could thus be used to conserve turtle numbers whilst perhaps catering to the Islanders' preference for turtle meat.

The shark also deserves a mention. Island legends tell of pack assaults by voracious sharks which even intimidate small, isolated islands causing them to flee to the safety of larger island groups. On Mer the Beizam le (shark god people) are reputed to have been the security arm of the Zogo le (priesthood). Appropriately it was the shark sect which supervised ceremonies and ruthlessly traced and punished those who transgressed.

Since 1900 there have been six recorded cases of fatal attacks by sharks in the Torres Strait. Three occurred on the Warrior Reefs, one at Boydang and two in the vicinity of Thursday Island. For each recorded fatality there were several attacks which were not fatal and an unknown number where a shark may be presumed to have been involved in someone's disappearance. The arrival of almost any large shark will cause divers to leave the water but the tiger shark and hammerhead, in particular, have evil reputations. Another possible danger is the sluggish groper. Lurking in dark caves the groper, which may grow to 360 kilograms weight, will cruise serenely forward to confront divers. Much more justified is a fear of sea snakes. Divers have mentioned a black snake with red eyes which occasionally menaces them. This may be the moray eel. Almost any variety of Australian sea snake is extremely venomous and, though normally quiet, can be very aggressive at times such as the mating season.

Crocodiles in Australia were, at one time, found as far south as the Northern Rivers of New South Wales. Very few still survive in these southern areas. However in the dense swamps on the black deltas of the tropical north the crocodile has thrived. River estuaries, tidal creeks, fresh water billabongs and sand beaches from North Queensland to Western Australia teemed with several distinct types of crocodile.

The estuarine, or saltwater, crocodile is a squat, powerful brute which may grow to six metres or more. It will grow thirty centimetres a year for the first seven years, then its growth rate slows to only a few centimetres annually. A big crocodile could be a hundred years old, its longevity being attributed to its extreme economy of movement. It will lie absolutely motionless — to all appearances inanimate — half covered with mud, amidst rotting wood and mangrove roots, or with just its ugly, gnarled grey head protruding from brown water at the water's edge. It is in no hurry, for a large crocodile requires only a few kilograms of putrid meat a week to keep going.

Although a crocodile may remain perfectly still, it can move like lightning to seize its prey. If a medium-sized crocodile takes a large boar by the snout, the pig may push his feet in, not allowing himself to be pulled into the water. The crocodile simply throws the whole weight of its body into a roll, felling the pig.

The freshwater, or "marsh" crocodile is a distinct species found in New Guinea. It is similar in appearance to the estuarine but smaller and inoffensive. Its average length is about two metres though it may grow to more than three. Its skin is lighter in colour but the chief physical distinction is that from the base of the skull down the centre of the back it has a series of enlarged, horny plates. Another important distinction for the hunter is that the freshwater belly scales are much larger than those of the estuarine, resulting in a much lower price. The freshwater preys exclusively on fish and smaller animals and represents no threat to man. Another harmless type is the slender Johnstone River crocodile of northern Australia.

It should be noted that a crocodile found in freshwater is not necessarily a freshwater croc. Estuarine crocodiles are hatched far up rivers and may subsequently spend all their lives there without ever seeing saltwater.

The large saltwater crocodile, able to travel long distances at sea, has always been present about the Torres Strait Islands. The large, flat, deltaic islands of the northern Strait provided the most suitable environment for crocodiles though they could have been found on all islands at times. The Islanders held them in great respect paying them the compliment of adopting them as gods.

On Saibai there was a crocodile clan (Kadalaugudalgal), a snake clan (Tthabuaugudalgal) and others. The members of each clan worshipped the animal, coming to know its habits and thus perhaps fearing it less. On Mabuiag the Kadalaugudalgal used a crocodile headpiece, claimed to be made of turtle shell, for their worship. The headpiece was originally a gift from another clan who mistakenly killed a crocodile during a dugong hunt and sought to atone for the offence in this manner. A headpiece from the Western Torres Strait in the British Museum, which has gaping jaws but a fish tail, was probably used for ceremonial purposes. Elaborate headpieces are still used on occasions. Worship of the saltwater crocodile was not confined to the Islanders. The Koko-Jao group of Aborigines north of Princess Charlotte Bay in eastern Cape York had the Iwai (crocodile) cult which is supposed to have been introduced from the Torres Strait.

Commercial shooting has driven the crocodile in Australia to the edge of extinction. Shooting had been going on for years, but it was not till the collapse of the Congo, which had supplied 80 per cent of the world's skins, that the industry in Australia boomed. During 1963 the price of skins soared from six shillings a belly inch for estuarine to twenty-three shillings. Much of the demand was from Chinese buyers for distribution through Singapore and Asia. Overnight croc shooting had become a goldmine. Many who sought to cash in on the boom were inexperienced and many were new Australians.

In a couple of seasons the easy shooting was over. Some shooters moved to Papua where the slaughter continued for a few more years. Gill in 1872 noted that the Oriomo "was swarming with crocodiles" and D'Albertis in 1876 had lost his hunting dog to one. But a great drought about 1972-73 all but finished the crocodile in the lower Fly area. Thousands of crocs were isolated in rapidly dwindling swamps. Whereas a crocodile can in an emergency lift his entire body and tail clear of the ground and run at great speed, it can do so only for a short distance. During these seasons thousands of skins were processed through Daru, but it was the last flurry of a dying industry.

In the swamps of Cape York Peninsula, Papua and the Torres Strait the survivors learnt to dive at the sound of an outboard motor, or at the sight of a human being or spotlight. By extreme caution they managed to live often in close proximity to man without being detected. They remain today a very real feature affecting life in the Torres Strait region.

Frequently vessels travelling the straits are accompanied by schools of sleek dolphins. Arranged in identical formation to port and starboard of the bow they easily pace the boat at maximum speed, sometimes streaking ahead diagonally across the bow or underneath to appear suddenly on the other side.

All the creatures of the sea, whether foods, hazards or company, comprise part of a unique environment. Getano Lui, chairman of the Islander Advisory Council, put it this way: "We came from the sea; our history and culture is tied up with it. Even winds, tides, currents, the air, the cays and reefs are part of our culture." The sea dictated the conditions under which the distinctive, sea-orientated societies of the Torres Strait Islands evolved and, acting as a kind of moat, it also ensured that Melanesian culture (with, for example, its pigs and cultivation) would not easily spread to mainland Australia.

Today the emphasis has shifted from subsistence harvesting to surplus production. Pearl, trochus and bêche-de-mer fishing over the last century did not affect basic subsistence resources though they may have led to upheavals in Island society. The exploitation of Torres Strait resources in the last two decades however has begun to eat into those fundamental resources which are important to Island communities, including crayfish, mackerel, and barramundi. It is naturally unfair for the Islanders not to share in this exploitation and recently the state government started a scheme whereby freezer facilities would be made available to Island communities with a view to producing a surplus for sale.

If this enterprise is to succeed a solution must be found to the special problems of Island communities. When an individual profits financially the rewards are traditionally distributed throughout the family, thereby affecting incentive and efficiency. The scheme will never operate in the way aggressive, independent non-Island fishermen might operate it. Also, despite the enthusiasm of some younger Islanders, more traditionally inclined elders are less interested and even openly opposed to the concept.

As a consequence it is primarily white Australians who have battled for fishing resources in the area against increasing foreign competition. In the past Papuan, Malay, Japanese and European boats have taken advantage of the strait's resources but in the last decade the ships of two nations in particular have irritated local seamen.

The intrusion of the Russian super trawler *Van Gogh* into international prawning grounds in the Gulf of Carpentaria during the 1968 season caused consternation among Australian skippers with their smaller boats and more modest catches. Protests were made that the *Van Gogh* plunged through the local trawlers without regard to working convention and, because of its heavier equipment, was taking a huge quantity of prawns. After what the Australians claimed were repeated provocations an Australian fisherman on a boat in international waters fired several shots to warn off the Russian vessel. There were immediate international repercussions and talk of "piracy" and a "Prawn War".

The man who claims to have fired those shots is not Australian-born, like many other prawners, but comes from an East European country which has been occupied by Russian troops within the last quarter century. He said he spoke by radio to officers on the *Van Gogh* in Russian, which he learned at school, warning them that there was danger of an emergency arising if they continued on their course which would take them across the bow of an Australian vessel. When his warnings were ignored he fired three shots from a .303, using bullets with cut-off noses to maximize effect (being unstable they shriek as they tumble through the air). Two shots were aimed in the air but the third had as its aiming mark the *Van Gogh*'s radar scanner. The *Van Gogh* sheared away from the threat and at the end of the season left, never to return. Though sensational, these events are insignificant beside the massive and continuing depredations of Taiwanese boats.

In the late 1960s and 1970s many of these fishing vessels were captured by the R.A.N. and taken into Thursday Island. They were motorized wooden hulls exhibiting classical junk lines — high bow and stern, with the deck dropping away almost to the waterline amidship. Up to eighteen crew slept on the deck or in tiny wooden shelves in the foc'sle. At that time most of the crew were dark, stocky Taiwanese. These were the men who risked their lives gathering clam meat from the Great Barrier Reef. The skipper and radio operator were generally slim, lighter-skinned Chinese — more sophisticated and sleeping in relative comfort on mattresses on the floor of the radio shack.

Working among reefs continuously, not particularly seaworthy, often lacking maintenance and thousands of kilometres from home, many of these wooden vessels have simply disappeared. Sometimes survivors stumble ashore or are discovered, completely by accident, marooned on a reef or sand cay off the Queensland coast. Each year as many as seventy of these vessels operate solely on the Great Barrier Reef. In the two years 1969 and 1970 only three were apprehended for the illegal poaching of clams which supposedly enjoy complete protection in Australian waters. Increased surveillance by the R.A.N., R.A.A.F. and private vessels has led to an increase in the number of those apprehended. One Taiwanese boat was detained at gunpoint by Australian fishermen at Lizard Island near Cooktown. Others have sought to intrude into the rich waters of the Torres Strait and people in the Eastern and Central Islands are constantly on the alert for them. In 1976 one vessel was arrested near Erub and another near Poruma after being detected by Islanders. Recently it is the steel-hulled and more efficient stern trawlers which are the menace. Stretching a huge net between pairs of vessels, whole fleets of these boats operate within sight of the Australian coastline. In the two years 1975 and 1976 a total of fourteen clam boats were taken — most being subject to heavy fines or, in some cases, forfeiture of the boat and repatriation of the crew.

In late 1976 there were five Taiwanese vessels anchored under guard in Port Kennedy and because it frequently takes months to repatriate the seamen detained, there were anything up to one hundred Taiwanese roaming the streets of Thursday Island. Naturally they were patronised by the local Chinese community. Some obtained jobs with businessmen moving goods, labouring and painting, and by working for forty dollars a week they undercut local unskilled labour (mainly Islanders). Several Islanders, in fact, lost employment because of this cheap competition.

The fishermen from the steel-hulled vessels tend to be more sophisticated than the clam gatherers. They drink at the hotels, frequently acquire Island girlfriends and are accepted by the community with its usual hospitality. Some even moved into houses on the Tamwoy Reserve as the guests of sympathetic Islanders. Surprisingly there seems little resentment about the lost jobs, for as one Islander put it: "They come from a very poor land and we are sorry for them." Unemployed Europeans on Thursday Island felt differently and in 1976 protested strongly to the federal government though without apparent success.

The sea affects the whole lifestyle of people in the Torres Strait. However in a wider sense it has not just dominated but has determined the course of history in the region. Cook, Bligh, Chester and the other Europeans who left their mark on the region came only because the strait offered a vital passage from the Indian to Pacific Oceans, or to help fish the wealth from its depths. Without doubt the sea will continue to direct the course of social and political development in the region.

10

Magic and Death

*Apoo**

Gaogao apoo senobee.
Koolai, koolai,
Kai ngin gutsumpa!

On Mer the legend of Gelam is the basis of traditional beliefs. Seen from the north the hill behind the village is said to resemble a dugong. Rising from the east this hill culminates in a craggy cliff at the western end, dropping away to the rocks and the sea hundreds of metres below. On the face of this cliff are two holes which are said to be the dugong's nostrils. They are in fact the entrances to caves, difficult of access and so sacred that even today we may only guess at what lies within.

A giant snake with a red light blazing from its skull issues forth to protect the cave from intruders, for this is the cave of

* The translation is:
Mangrove devil woman is coming
Watch out, watch out,
She will catch you.

When small children are restless or misbehave this verse may be sung. It is not a traditional song or even widely used but is simply one of hundreds of short, functional verses used daily on the islands of the Torres Strait. Imagine a woman sitting cross-legged on a coconut mat, by the fitful glare of a hurricane lamp, with a whimpering child on her lap. The verse is intoned slowly with relish gradually building towards the climax — "gutsum*PA*!" The child cringes, whimpers cease.

Gelam. In living history one man, a Rotuman sorcerer (or *pouri pouri* man), has entered this cave. He emerged to talk of piles of jewels and cascades of crystal water, but no one has verified his claims.

During the dry season the thickly grassed sides of Gelam Hill were set alight. Sometimes, if care was not taken, the fires burned too far to the west and, deep down in the rock caverns, Gelam awoke. The whole of Mer shook with earth tremors and frightened people fled to the lower slopes to escape Gelam's wrath.* At night the village streets were empty for surely Gelam would come out. Some people have seen Gelam, a young man in a red *lava lava*, picking his way down from the caves, to the western villages. At a spot on the empty track marked by a tree, he changed into a large black dog and stalked between the silent houses. Doors were locked, windows closed, but occasionally a listener heard the heavy padding of his paws and the whisper of his breath as he passed.

Seven or eight years ago a village policeman walking near the cemetery at night, saw the dog disappearing along a track in the forest towards Deaudepat (a valley). Armed with his torch he rashly decided to follow. Somewhere in the thick scrub a black cat leaped at him from the dark and raked his arm. He required treatment at the aid post for the injury and his accident also served to revitalize the Meriams' faith in their traditional spirits.

Haddon recorded the rituals followed by the Zogo le on Mer prior to 1871. These men guided their society, enforcing its customs by the judicious use of *pouri pouri*. Part of their power they derived from the dead through ritual cannibalism. Male corpses were placed on platforms and, after they had ripened for several months, portions such as the fingers were eaten.

With the arrival of Christianity some members of the Zogo le entered the Christian church and, in time, even entered the priesthood. So the elements of mystery and magic were passed on.

Today the practicioners of *pouri pouri* may be divided into two groups. There are those who exercise the dark art for non Christian and evil purposes. These people will kill, maim and entrance others. The second group, which may include

* Curiously the first Christian church built on Mer by the L.M.S. was reportedly destroyed by earthquake — an extremely rare event in this area.

dedicated, practising Christians, uses knowledge of magic to cure the evil inflicted by the first group. For this they are highly respected by their people. It is not unusual for an Anglican priest or church warden to engage in mysticism when combating *pouri pouri*. Symbolic of this marriage of the old and new is the Meriam word for the Christian church building, which is "Zogo meta" ("meta" means house). Many Islanders quite frankly see it as a contest between Christianity and *pouri pouri*, an idea the church may have unconsciously reinforced.

Good sorcerers provide certain other services such as warding off unwanted rain or predicting, with some success, the arrival of a boat or an impending death.

The evil groups follow rituals of magic descended from the Zogo le including, it is rumoured, cannibalism. Some Eastern Islanders today claim that bodies in the cemetery on Thursday Island have been exhumed and the hearts eaten by sorcerers. Initiates to the cult are carefully chosen. The experienced sorcerer supervises the trainee as he kills fowl and other small animals. Meetings occur secretly at night and power may be transmitted by sexual intercourse without regard to age or family relationship (and Island incest laws are, in many cases, stricter than European custom). This immorality underlines the cults' essentially anti-Christian nature.

Finally the evil sorcerers may move against a human. Magic chants (in an ancient, almost forgotten language) and force are used to overpower the victim (for this purpose the *pouri pouri* cultists prefer to work in groups). Then the victim is magically maimed. Intestines may be torn, a brain bruised or a leg broken. When the operation is complete the wound is temporarily repaired and the victim's memory of the incident erased.

At a predetermined time, perhaps a week later, the victim's intestines will suddenly burst or he will suffer a stroke or his leg will collapse. A European doctor may be called or the casualty taken to Thursday Island Hospital, but a good sorcerer may also be consulted. If recovery takes place the white doctor often gains little more prestige than his black counterpart.

The majority of deaths about the islands are attributed to *pouri pouri*, though the circumstances vary from community to community.

Certain people are sometimes suspected of using *pouri pouri*. The suspect's conduct may be strange or inconsistent and they may find themselves trapped in compromising positions — such as lingering in the dark outside the home of an ailing old woman. Often they are linked to a recent illness with jealousy or envy as the motive (for example, a respected Councillor may be struck down by arthritis and forced to retire). Gradually resentment and fear build up, friends fall away or are suspected themselves. Because the power can be passed through sex, girlfriends, wives and children are also suspected. However a sorcerer's power need not prevent physical assault. Out of concern for the safety of the children and the elderly, young men may attack him.

Precautions can be taken to guard against the evil magic. The inhabitants of some islands take extreme care with the disposal of fingernail clippings and cut hair, either burning them or casting them on the sea. If a sorcerer were to obtain these he could work powerful magic against the owner. Curiously the inhabitants of other islands discard the same items without the least precaution or fear. However even amongst Islanders who are not particular about the disposal of cut hair there persists a notion connecting strength with hair length. A baby for example does not have a haircut for four years or more. To cut the hair earlier might cause the child to weaken or become sick. Similarly a mother who has "big hair" at the birth of her child might not cut her hair for some time for fear of producing similar results.

Customs and features of witchcraft differ from one island to the next and even within the one community. On the northern Western Islands sorcerers fly about at night and have been seen sometimes capering naked in the dark with flames flickering from their anuses. On occasion the sorcerer's reputation is so strong that he terrifies the entire community. On Thursday Island in 1970 complaints were received from Mabuiag of an old *pouri pouri* man from whose head a light was seen glowing in the night. In the end the situation may necessitate the removal of the *pouri pouri* expert and throughout north Queensland dozens of suspected witches and sorcerers are found exiled from their islands, simply because they are not wanted. It is said to be impossible for a sorcerer to retire, for once a man or woman is committed to *pouri pouri* then the evil power within them will multiply and, if it does not find release on a victim, it will slowly poison the body of the host himself.

Pouri pouri permeates Island society and can explain illness, death, success and failure. Life to the Islander thus has an extra dimension which is generally hidden from the outsider to avoid misunderstanding or derision.

A man from the Outer Islands visiting Thursday Island briefly was given a large trumpet shell by another Islander. This unusual and unsolicited gift was immediately suspect as the giver had a dormant reputation as a *pouri pouri* man. The shell was wrapped in newspaper inside a cardboard box but no one dared unwrap it. It was decided, after some discussion, to take the shell to a *pouri pouri* expert from Boigu who was known to be drinking in the Federal Hotel at that time. This man apparently knew of the matter even before it was broached. He immediately agreed to examine the shell in private. Six adults sat cross-legged in a circle on the kitchen floor, watching anxiously in silence as the shell was gingerly unwrapped by the Boigu man. Words were said, ritual observed — yes, the shell was a trap. The receiver had narrowly escaped sickness and perhaps death.

News spread rapidly and soon the whole community knew, thus strengthening the giver's evil reputation. The shell was now treated like a defused bomb, disquieting though no longer dangerous. In the end the Boigu man took it.

Such minor incidents concerning *pouri pouri* occur daily throughout the Torres Strait. It is little wonder that Islanders think differently from Europeans.

Sorcerers may carry poison beneath their fingernails which they can easily drop into drinks at a hotel or food at a feast. An elderly Aborigine advised that if approached for a cigarette one should give a single cigarette but not the box of matches since whilst selecting one a sorcerer could poison the others. This would be a particularly dangerous form of *pouri pouri* as the cigarette smoke is drawn deep into the lungs. Sometimes agents, including dogs, cats and large spiders, or an item such as a trumpet shell, may be used to deliver a curse.

When a person dies a wake is held with the female relatives wailing lamentations for hour on end and frequently for more than a day. Burial takes place quickly but the deceased is not forgotten, for throughout the Torres Strait and the rest of Australia relatives are being called upon to contribute to his tombstone which might be unveiled a year or two after his

death. Wealthier families conduct big ceremonies with hundreds
of guests for the unveiling of an elaborate cement monument
over the grave. Many pigs, turtle, dugong, fowl and deer may be
consumed in an afternoon with three sittings necessary to allow
all the guests to eat. Newcomers are often surprised to discover
that little, if any, fish is served. Islanders eat fish and rice almost
every day. A feast demands meat. Families often try to out-do
each other, amassing thousands of dollars over several years for
this one extravagant day. But increasingly more modest
ceremonies are held with a cemented headstone, plastic flowers,
ceramic tiles, perhaps a photo or painting of the deceased on the
stone, and later a quiet family gathering. The Anglican Church
recognizes this ceremony and invests the memorial services with
the dignity they deserve.

Early travellers in the Torres Strait had noted what appeared
to be fastidious funerary customs among the Islanders. Captain
Edwards saw a grave on Muralug decorated with dugong and
turtle bones, two human skulls and a paddle. Later visitors
recorded that the Kauralgal lopped fingers off to mark the death
of a child in the family. On Mawai another grave was observed

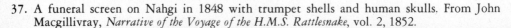

37. A funeral screen on Nahgi in 1848 with trumpet shells and human skulls. From John
Macgillivray, *Narrative of the Voyage of the H.M.S. Rattlesnake*, vol. 2, 1852.

surmounted by dugong bones and human skulls, and again on Tutu with just dugong bones. Because these sites are festooned with dugong and turtle bones and as many of them occur on high points, it has been suggested that they were the graves of successful hunters and that, if used as lookouts for turtle or dugong, they might increase other hunters' chances of success.

Among the Islanders of Erub, Mer and Ugar, hand and foot preservation was practised, as well as the more exacting art of mummification. There are rumours of mummies on Mer but perhaps they were destroyed or wisely hidden away by the inhabitants. Two mummies, a male and a female, were taken from Ugar late in the nineteenth century and placed on exhibition in the Queensland Museum. The mummies are still held by the museum.

Nothing appalls an Islander more than to visit an Aboriginal community such as Yarrabah (near Cairns) where the bare, neglected earth mounds stretch for two hundred metres along the beach and back into eighty years of history. The gravesite of an ancestor, suitably marked by a tombstone and well tended, is a link with the past and, as a symbol of continuity, has become a cornerstone of Island society, more treasured even than the new material wealth.

11

Pearling

Running through the history of the Torres Strait like a thread is the fishing industry. From modest beginnings in the 1860s with a few bêche-de-mer boats, it expanded dramatically in the 1870s, boosted by exploitation of the pearl beds.

By 1880 there were 102 boats operating in the strait, 68 of which were apparatus boats and 16 of which were swimming. As well there were 18 swimming boats that preyed exclusively on bêche-de-mer. The fleets were serviced by about 800 men including 215 Malays, 340 South Sea Islanders, 9 Chinese, 30 Europeans and 215 indigenous Australians, with no distinction being made between Islanders and Aborigines.

A station run by Lamb and Co. was established at Wai-Weer, not far from Thursday Island, with a slipway, jetty, barracks and flourishing graveyard full of South Sea Islanders and Japanese, most of whom died violent deaths in their early twenties. Twenty-five boats with 164 men operated out of this tiny island.

Other stations were found at Albany Island (twenty-one boats), Mabuiag (ten boats), Somerset (eight boats), Palilug (Goode Island — ten boats), Endeavour Strait (ten boats), Gialug (Friday Island — six boats), Tuined (Possession Island — four boats), Muralug (Prince of Wales Island — four boats) and Thursday Island (one boat).

When pearling first began shells were easily collected by diving in shallow waters, and many local Islanders were employed as divers. Some white masters preferred to employ

38. Islanders sorting and drying bêche-de-mer at a station on Tutu about 1895. This was the first marine industry in the Torres Strait, beginning some time in the 1840s and continuing well into the twentieth century. Photograph by courtesy of the John Oxley Library, Brisbane.

young Island women, thinking they made better divers than men. Ten to fifteen swimmers were used on each boat, diving in water up to seven metres deep. Two swimmers a year were usually taken by sharks, whilst being paid only £1 a month for an eight month season (the southeast). It was obviously not a career with much of a future, since if an Islander pursued it for five seasons he had to continually face the dangers of sharks, sea snakes, crocodiles, stingrays, stone fish, and could gross at the very most only £40 over the five years. Still this provided some purchasing power where previously there had been none, and accustomed the Islanders to European food. Salted beef, tinned meat, pickles, flour, sugar and tea were standard rations on a lugger at that time.

However the majority of shell lay below the reach of these "swimmers", and the helmeted apparatus diver had already made his appearance in 1871 when the Rev. MacFarlane conducted a service over the body of a white diver at Gebar. The man had drowned when his air pipe burst.

An apparatus boat about 1880 required an outlay of £400 and a further £40 to transport it by mailsteamer from Sydney, where they were built, to the Torres Strait.

Each boat had a diver/skipper and a mate/tender with about

four crew. By 1880 no white divers were employed because South Sea Islanders, Maoris and a few Norfolk Islanders (including Fletcher Christian's grandson) were found to work harder and longer. These coloured divers were in total command of their boats, answerable only to their employers. Usually they signed on for the season's work in either Thursday Island or Sydney. This, incidentally, led to endless difficulties since contracts made in Sydney under New South Wales law were often repudiated by Queensland officials acting under

39. Part of the pearling fleet during the mid 1880s. From the *Picturesque Atlas of Australasia*, vol. 2, 1886.

Queensland law. The Colonial Office believed that the contracts made in New South Wales should be respected in Queensland, but the problem persisted for a decade till the industry finally became locally based.

The diver's pay usually depended on the weight of shell he

collected, which again depended on weather, crew, and his own initiative and luck. Few divers at this time earned less than £200 annually and some earned as much as £340. Originally any pearls found theoretically belonged to the European manager, but this led to such subterfuge and deception that in the end most managers allowed the diver captains to keep them. Among the lugger crews however pearls caused endless trouble with rumours of "accidents", theft and death.

The Torres Strait Island and Aboriginal crewmen received a maximum of £1 a month but, unlike those on the swimming boats, were able to work a twelve month year.

That all was not well with the industry was emphasized by the debate which preceded the passing through Queensland parliament of the Native Labourers' Protection Act in 1884. The main concern of this bill was to regulate the employment of indigenous Australians and Papuans on vessels in Queensland waters. Recruitment was often less orthodox than pearling masters would have people believe, a particularly odious practice being the abduction of Aboriginal and Island girls. But this was rampant throughout the colony and an act of parliament could not stop it overnight.

It became apparent that the limited fields about the Torres Strait were being over-fished, and in 1885 part of the fleet shifted to Western Australia, exploring the shell beds off Broome. There the highly professional Queensland fleet gave impetus to the local industry, yet the fields off Western Australia did not fulfil their promise and by 1890 many boats had shifted back to the Torres Strait.

Another response to over-fishing was the development of the "mothership" idea. Due to the scarcity of shell, luggers spent more and more time at sea searching for workable patches of shell, and sailing further afield in order to exploit them. Also poor facilities at several of the stations restricted the number of craft which could harbour and unload at any one time (for example Wai-Weer). Consequently some companies began employing schooner "motherships" to service fleets of up to a dozen boats. Increasingly the fleets were obliged to sail further and further down the east coast of Australia, and operational luggers rarely saw Thursday Island during the season at all, relying almost entirely on schooners for unloading shell and victualling. Such an innovation, which revitalized the industry,

40. The pearling station on Goode Island. All the boats in the picture were lost in the 1899 cyclone which devastated Princess Charlotte Bay. From *The Pearling Disaster*, 1899.

also contributed to its greatest disaster, for it allowed eighty-two boats to anchor in Princess Charlotte Bay on the night of 4 March 1899.

As was the custom, luggers captained by Japanese divers collected together, those captained by Malays and Filipinos (or Manilamen as they were known) gathering in similar groups. The fleet was enveloped in an uneasy calm, made all the more uncanny because of the weeks of blustery southeast winds which had preceded it. Dinghies plied back and forth as men took advantage of the opportunity to visit friends on other boats. The voices of men and women drifted across the lazy swell of the sea with conversations in a dozen languages discussing shell, people, and recent events. Not a few would have mentioned the weather, for along the eastern horizon lightning danced continuously beneath heavy, black clouds.

On board the nine motherships and tenders the few white men with the fleet looked with concern to their barometers. As well they might, for in a few hours this area of the Queensland coast was hit by the most devastating cyclone ever recorded along the coast of Australia.

The cyclone came from the Coral Sea. About midnight the wind about the slumbering luggers suddenly rose and within the hour all crews were fighting for their lives. Luggers were smashed to pieces by huge waves, others broke their chains, collided and sank. Some were pounded to matchwood on reefs. Most crews took the only course open to them, going below deck and closing up the ship.

About 4.30 a.m. the eye passed over the surviving vessels. The barometers had dropped alarmingly but worse was to come. When the wind resumed it blew from the opposite direction with unequalled ferocity behind an incoming tide. The result was a spectacular tidal surge which swept inland for some distance. Most luggers that had hung on so far were torn from their anchors and crushed against the shore.

Sammy and Muara Lifu, newlyweds from Erub, were on the schooner *Silvery Wave*. Sammy was washed overboard to his death, and shortly afterwards the schooner went down. Muara began swimming for shore three kilometres away. On the way she encountered two struggling whitemen and, despite her own exhaustion, she helped them to reach land. For saving their lives she was subsequently awarded the Royal Humane Society's Gold Medal.

By midday Sunday it was finished. The grey sea was littered with the pathetic flotsam of sixty-six wrecked luggers and seven tenders. Over three hundred people had died at sea, including twelve Europeans. Many bodies were never recovered as the swirling tide drew them out to sea, leaving beaches strewn with all manner of dead animals — wallabies, snakes, sharks, porpoises and birds. During the lull at the eye of the storm Aborigines camped along the shore had come down to pull feeble survivors from the sea, only to be overwhelmed by the great tidal surge which followed. About one hundred were carried out to sea and drowned.

Few Europeans or Asians escaped death in the cyclone except by remaining on a floating vessel. The strong Island swimmers by comparison often survived the foundering of boats in which whites perished.

Two Mer men, one of whom was Douglas Pitt's son, and their wives swam for twelve hours with each woman supporting a young child. After persevering for more than twenty kilometres they finally came ashore, but both the infants were dead.

When rescue vessels arrived from Thursday Island and Cooktown they were surprised to find groups of Islanders swimming from reef to reef far from the scene of the disaster, living on the raw marine life they picked up from among the coral as they went. Five Mer men swam twenty kilometres before being rescued. Five days after the cyclone a man and woman from Erub were found on a reef thirty kilometres from where their lugger had gone down.

The catastrophe was a hard blow to white investors, and a tragedy for the coloured community on Thursday Island and the Islanders of the Eastern Torres Strait, who made up most of the crews at this time, but it could not stop pearling. At the turn of the century there were 260 boats and 1,600 men employed in the fishing fleet out of Thursday Island, despite the recent losses at Princess Charlotte Bay.

Smaller "chicken shell" — young shell — was still found by swimming boats in some quantities along the Ormond Reefs stretching fifty kilometres from Mabuiag north to Buru.

Older, larger shell was fished from grounds to the west of Mabuiag and through the central straits. Though heavier and theoretically of more value, these shells were sometimes riddled with worms.

Staying at sea for weeks at a time, the crews could read the waters like a book. I recall once when travelling south of Buru by speedboat in foul weather, how an elderly Island companion had directed us to a safe anchorage within a tiny lagoon. No land was in sight and no reef could be detected till the boat was on top of it. Thirty years before he had worked on luggers which had used the lagoon to clean their hulls. At times three or four luggers were crammed together while their crews splashed and dived in the clear water, scraping weed and shells from the wooden hulls. Some sixth sense had given my old companion the location of the lagoon admist the welter of spray and rain.

Such qualities endowed Torres Strait Islanders with a formidable reputation and they were to be found working as crewmen on boats from Mackay to Broome.

Vic Hall, a policeman in the Northern Territory, described the wreck of a lugger in which he was a passenger off the territory's Crocodile Islands in the early 1920s. This lugger was based in Darwin and owned by a half-caste Aborigine named Reuben. It included in its crew "two giant men" from Badu named Yoran and "Carpu" (a nickname meaning "good" in Western Island language). "Yoran, the biggest, was a genial colossus who roared with laughter at every opportunity. Both were like porpoises in the water. There were four more coloured men on board, two of them being members of Reuben's crew and the others being passengers to Milingimbi Mission. Both Yoran and his mate Carpu wore murderous looking Malay knives in their belts, and Reuben also wore a sheath knife." When the boat went down on a reef six kilometres from shore, Hall was thankful for their swimming ability as, menaced by sharks, Yoran towed him the last three kilometres to the beach. No lives were lost.

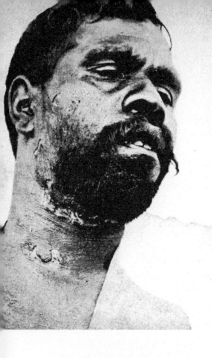

41. "Treacle" who survived a shark attack while swimming for pearl in 1914. From T.C. Roughley, *Wonders of the Great Barrier Reef*, 1951. Reproduced by permission of Angus & Robertson Publishers.

Swimming boats operated right down the Barrier Reef. Old men today often regale the young with stories of diving on the outer reef. In the Torres Strait there is seldom more than a swell or chop, but the competition in earlier days forced boats out onto the edge of the Great Barrier Reef where men swam amidst crashing breakers and foam.

Sharks also remained a worry though it was mainly the swimmers who suffered. Helmet divers sometimes released a cloud of air bubbles from under their sleeve or from their release valve to frighten sharks. For the swimmer, more likely to attract sharks in the first place with his splashing and surfacing, the only course was to swim to a dinghy or to dive deep and hold himself motionless against a wall of coral till the dark shadow had passed.

From 1901 to 1968 there were forty-five recorded shark attacks on divers on the Great Barrier Reef, of which twelve were fatal. This represents something of an improvement on the two fatalities per year in the late 1870s. Most, if not all, of the victims were coloured and are known to have included Aborigines, Papuans, at least two Japanese and a number of Torres Strait Islanders.

An Aboriginal named Treacle or Teapot, earned fame locally on Thursday Island after an accident in 1914 while swimming for shell. A shark had taken Treacle's head completely within its mouth then released him, leaving ugly lacerations encircling his head and shoulders. After a month in the Thursday Island Hospital he recovered, but the scars were clearly visible.

T.C. Roughley recorded a series of attacks in the 1930s which illustrate what pearl and trochus diving meant to the men in the water. In 1933 a Torres Strait Islander was seriously injured by a shark but lived. In 1934 a Papuan diver was killed and the following year another diver killed and three injured by sharks.

In 1937 Iona Asai from Saibai had a similar experience whilst swimming for pearl shell near Mabuiag. He dived twice returning to the lugger each time with a shell but on the third dive he came face to face with a shark which immediately bit and held him by the head. With remarkable presence of mind Asai thrust his thumbs into the shark's eyes causing the shark to release him and allowing him to escape to the surface where friends pulled him into the boat. Two hundred stitches were required to mend massive wounds about Asai's neck and shoulders. Later the broken tooth of a tiger shark was removed from an abscess at the back of his neck. Curiously this is supposed to be the second occasion on which he was attacked by a shark. Nineteen years before he had suffered some injuries when attacked at a reef near Cairns.

But it was the sea itself which was the real danger and year after year it exacted a steady toll of lives. The annual cyclone season from November to April along the open coasts of eastern Australia continued to cause casualties. In 1934 several luggers were wrecked with the loss of seventy-five lives, in an intense cyclone that crossed the coast near Port Douglas on the morning of 12 March. Among these were two luggers whose entire crews were lost, including three Japanese, five Papuans, and five Aborigines. Several luggers had narrow escapes as they raced to port barely ahead of the storm. Some elderly Island men today recall weathering the storm on their boats near the Port Douglas Jetty where a two metre tidal surge occurred.

Even on dry land caution was necessary, for the mainlands to north and south were untouched wildernesses. As late as 1931 the fourteen-man crew of a Japanese lugger were massacred by Aborigines and their boat looted in the Gulf of Carpentaria. The following year five more Japanese were killed in the same area and a white policeman investigating the killings was also speared to death.

As if all these dangers were not enough, the incessant competition for shell eventually led to the fishing of the Darnley Deeps (southeast of Erub), which involved divers in almost suicidal plunges into the depths. In 1915 Hockings presented a trophy commemorating what he considered to be the first successful dive to forty fathoms. It is said by some old men today that the Japanese sometimes went down to fifty or sixty fathoms. Many divers suffered from the "bends" or "diving sickness", resulting from too rapid a descent or ascent. The bends are brought about by the nitrogen, which the diver has absorbed under pressure, being released in the bloodstream as bubbles during decompression. As a result a diver may be crippled or killed. Initially an ignorance of the problems involved caused appalling casualties, and the Darnley Deeps came to be known as the "Diver's Graveyard". In fact the losses were so severe that in 1897 the Darnley Deeps were closed to diving.

By the early twentieth century the principles of staging — that is, gradual descent/ascent — were generally known and losses considerably reduced. To work for half an hour at maximum depth, an hour might be required on the descent, and three hours coming up. And even then accidents were not impossible. What if a line fouled as the lugger drifted down tide? What if an air pump or compressor failed or the diver were attacked by a sea snake?

If a diver surfaced quickly another was immediately suited up and sent down with him to help him stage, for even with the bends upon him there was still a chance to properly decompress. There followed hours suspended in the silent green, the assistant clutching his perhaps mortally injured companion. In the end the victim might die, but if he recovered his legs might be weak and bent outwards at the knees (hence the "bends"). He might never walk again.

One Malay diver was brought back to Thursday Island before the war, crippled and bed-ridden. The white doctors at the hospital expressed hopelessness at the case but friends gave him "bush medicine" and encouragement, which he probably needed even more, and with the aid of a walking stick he struggled down to the beach resolved to dive again. Months of hard diving later he arrived back on the island, threw away the walking stick and never used one again. But nothing could cure completely the "bends" in his legs which mark him to this day. Vic Hall stated: "I had seen a Japanese diver undressed and the sight had shocked me. From the waist down the man's body had been practically a skeleton, as a result of the immense pressure in

42. A pearling lugger with two divers down and the mothership in the background. The centre scene shows the cleaning of the enormous pearl shells for which northern Australia is famous. The sea creatures portrayed are fanciful. From the *Picturesque Atlas of Australasia*, vol. 2, 1886.

deep water". Early in the twentieth century the Darnley Deeps were reopened and shell collecting began once again, using hardy Japanese divers. Dozens died and were buried, some on Erub, so crushed and twisted by the bends that they were buried in their diving suits. In 1935 alone four divers died while working the Darnley Deeps.

The work of a diver was tough and fraught with risk. Little wonder that divers enjoyed themselves with furious abandon when on Thursday Island. The Japanese quarter, or "Yokohama" as whites sometimes called it, was situated along the flat northeast of the present post office. The Japanese Club was directly opposite the post office and still stands today between Seehops Bakery and Seekees General Store. The hard drinking, free spending atmosphere bred trouble and men were sometimes found dead in the dark alleys or along the beach. However the white administration rarely interfered.

An additional hazard was venereal disease. An official report in 1879 had described it as the "chief sickness among shellers" but had gone on to say that "At all stations a plentiful supply of medicines is kept, and the venereal and other diseases are generally successfully treated". Twenty years later the situation had deteriorated to an alarming degree. The incidence of venereal disease was especially high among divers, particularly the better divers who received better pay. Consequently periods of rough weather when boats were layed up in port were often followed by periods when, although the weather had improved, many luggers were unable to work due to the incapacitation of divers. The financial losses were so serious that in 1902 the government resident at Thursday Island called for the state government to proclaim the Contagious Diseases Act 1868 in the area. This act involving compulsory medical checks on prostitutes and the imprisonment in lock hospitals of those infected with V.D. was in force in Brisbane, Rockhampton, Maryborough and Cooktown. It was the subject of such controversy and had proved so expensive that the government was reluctant to accede to the resident's request despite the loss of revenue. Eventually the resident had to be content with medical examinations to which the local prostitutes agreed to submit voluntarily.

The Japanese had begun to enter Queensland in large numbers after 1892, in response to opportunities provided by the Anglo-Japanese Alliance. Although this immigration was restricted after 1898 by passport controls, the tenacious Japanese diver by then was already dominating the pearling industry. A visitor in 1900 felt that Thursday Island was "more a Japanese settlement than a British colony", noting that 3,100 Japanese were at that time working on or out of the island in the fishing industries. White employers were in favour of the Japanese since strict ordinances governing the employment of coloured (that is, South Sea Island or indigenous Australian) labour had become increasingly irksome. Yet moves were also taken to prevent any but British Subjects obtaining a license to fish. This effectively prevented the Japanese from obtaining any measure of control in the industry. However moves were also afoot to prevent them from even obtaining employment. White nationalists, having already denied the pearling industry the use of South Sea Island labour, sought to forbid the employment of all nonindigenous coloured labour. More specifically they objected to indentured workers from Japan and the Dutch East Indies who comprised the backbone of the pearling fleets. Commonwealth government legislation advised that after 31 December 1913 no coloured labour would be permitted to enter Australia for employment in the pearling industry. For a number of years white divers were engaged but proved unsuccessful and, following World War I, the government realized that the Japanese and Malays were essential and allowed the employment of indentured coloured labour once again.

So the Japanese stayed as divers but found it difficult to settle, since they were unable to invest in the fishing industry and the dry, rocky islands about Thursday Island did not encourage them to agriculture, even if they were interested. Nonetheless some managed to establish themselves. Kametaro Taguchi early this century was operating a shipyard on Thursday Island producing medium-sized wooden vessels for local use and as late as 1940 observers commented on the monopoly on boat building held by the Japanese at Thursday Island.

The main problem for the Japanese however was the dearth of female companionship. Few Japanese women entered Queensland and most on Thursday Island were prostitutes imported as such through Australian immigration. Some men, in the absence of women of their own race, lived with Malay or mixed race women and slowly amidst the hard living, transient community a stable core developed. The Anglican Church employed a Christian Japanese missionary to work among them, but curiously most of those who remained became Roman Catholic or, joining the Malay community, became Moslems.

Above Yokohama, at the base of Millman Hill, was Malaytown with its strong, enterprising community relying almost entirely on the men's ability as tenders and crewmen on luggers.

In 1877 Chester had tried to exclude business activity from Thursday Island supposedly reserving this for the administration. This decision was later completely reversed and the government sought to centre the fishing industry on Thursday Island and Badu, so that reserve islands would only be visited for recruitment, or shelter if necessary.

This scheme was by no means popular. It was inconvenient in some respects for fishing operations, and it severely limited the area available for development and the nature of that development. A visitor in the 1920s recognized this problem and complained of the lack of secondary industries: "It is nothing short of a great blot on the national character and a reflection on the enterprise of the people to have to admit that we are not in a position to utilise locally the pearl shell, trochus shell, and other associated products now exported to other markets in London, America, Japan and China."

Why did such development not occur? The visitor attributed it directly to the protectionist policies of the state government: ". . . the position cannot be otherwise, as employment of white labour would prohibit the establishment of any such industries in the islands of Torres Strait."

The first part of the twentieth century saw the founding of the great pearling dynasties — Duffield, Hockings and others. At one time there were dozens of luggers lining the beach in front of Waitoa and the Federal Hotel. The streets bustled with a motley crowd; wide-eyed Aborigines and Papuans seeing civilization for the first time, trim Japanese skippers in neat white shirts and trousers, Chinese gardeners with baskets of vegetables and tropical fruits, sleek Singalese shopkeepers — the craftsmen who shaved and polished the pearls — and resplendent in white suits and pith helmets the European bankers, shippers, managers and administrators, striding through to lunch at the Grand Hotel with its panoramic views across Muralug, Nurapai and down to Cape York.

During the late 1920s the industry experienced a boom. In 1927 pearl shell was worth £190 per ton in London, trochus £75 per ton locally and bêche-de-mer £320 per ton. The value of pearl shell alone exported from Australia the following year was £167,916, with the Torres Strait and Western Australia producing more than half the world's total.

These were hearty, heady days which could not last forever.

In 1928 new shell grounds west of Muralug were discovered though they were not extensively harvested till the following year which saw 1,400 tons of shell fished from this ground alone. The industry in the Torres Strait was never to produce more in a single season than in 1929. However this glut of shell, falling as it did in 1930, had disastrous results. Those companies in Britain and the U.S.A. which bought the shell thus had large quantities of surplus shell available at the start of the depression. In 1931 the market collapsed and production of shell was restricted to 350 tons. Many luggers ceased work and hundreds of men were unemployed. The industry never really recovered, although it struggled back briefly in the late thirties with almost a hundred boats working in the Torres Strait area. The beginning of the war with Japan in 1941 ended the old pearling days forever. At the war's end the Malay community never returned to its previous strength and few Japanese came back. Many pearling companies had lost heavily. Angus Brooks, stationed on Nurapai during the latter part of the war, remembers numbers of luggers rotting on the reef near the jetty which could have been bought for ten pounds a piece.

Following the war, a world starved of resources competed strongly for the pearl shell available. In 1948 790 tons were produced at Thursday Island bringing £435 per ton. In the channel between Muralug, Nurapai and Thursday Island on occasions the lugger crews enjoyed fiercely-fought sailing races. With government assistance Torres Strait Islanders bought and operated forty luggers of their own, but for the first time the pearling companies came to rely on Island divers. Islanders disliked the full diving suit and took to wearing the helmet and boots with just heavy woollen shirt and trousers protecting the body. This was more convenient but it encouraged divers to "throw their helmets" when they got into difficulties. Of course this practice led to casualties and at great depth was suicidal. Island divers to this day reject the full dress though it is still worn by pearl divers in Western Australia.

Even in the late 1940s over one third of luggers on the north Australian coast employed swimmers, another third employed divers with just a helmet and the remainder employed suited divers. However the apparent revival was to be short lived. Within a decade of the war's end the pearling industry went into an irreversible decline.

Some managers, harking back to the halycon days before 1941, urged the government to allow the reintroduction of Japanese divers and in 1958 a number of Ryukuyan divers, known locally as Okinawans, were brought into the industry. They began diving the fringes of the dreaded Darnley Deeps, where Islanders were reluctant to work; however many were inexperienced and they were only partially successful. Within a few years most were repatriated, though a handful remained and were absorbed into the polyglot community on Thursday Island.

In 1966 buyers were still paying £600 a ton for mother of pearl and £450 a ton for trochus, yet the industry was on its last legs. By 1970 the value of shell produced through Thursday Island had fallen from $537,000 in 1956 to a mere $107,000, and trochus from $297,000 in 1956 to zero. There were twenty-one luggers remaining in 1970 but many were in need of repair and others did little work. Those that did work were simply uneconomical, due partly to the Islanders' refusal to work at the low wages prevailing.

The main cause of this decline was the popularity of cheaper, oil-based plastics which, for a fraction of the cost, replaced the famous pearl-shell button. But, once again, the Japanese entered the industry, shifting the traditional emphasis of pearling from the shell to the pearl.

For centuries men in Asia had experimented with the pearl oyster to see if pearls could be artificially induced. The technique was finally perfected by Mikkimodo in Japan. There had been earlier attempts in the Torres Strait to cultivate pearls artificially (such as at Albany Island in the 1920s) but it was not till 1960 that the Japanese brought their superior knowledge to the area, establishing a number of stations at carefully selected spots.

There are two major considerations in the cultivation. There must be a sufficient supply of healthy plankton on which the oyster feeds. As the shell baskets are suspended from rafts of a wooden framework supported by oil drums, fairly stable conditions are required. Consequently most stations are situated between islands where the strong currents clear the water and supply plankton, and the rafts are protected from the open sea where they would break up.

To produce the pearl a particle of foreign matter is introduced to provoke the oyster into retaliation. Smooth, rounded portions of a muscle shell found in the Mississippi River are commonly used. The oyster secretes a fluid which coats the foreign particle and solidifies into a clean, gleaming surface — the pearl. The larger the seed, the longer it takes to produce a large pearl. So different shells are seeded with different-sized seeds, and so have different "incubation" periods. The Japanese use northern Australia to take advantage of the area's unique shells which are the largest in the world.

In 1970-71 the export of cultured pearls from Thursday Island was worth $834,000. However it seemed that oil was determined to complete its destruction of the pearling industry, or what was left of it, for the same year the oil tanker *Oceanic Grandeur* struck an uncharted rock in the main east-west shipping channel near Mawai. Interested spectators on Millman Hill at Thursday Island watched through binoculars as one side of the *Oceanic Grandeur's* deck went awash and thousands of litres of oil seeped through the tears in her side. A second tanker arrived and took off part of the oil and finally the *Oceanic Grandeur* survived. However, the oil lost, and the detergent used to combat its spread, caused serious results.

Some pearl culture stations were directly affected but also a mysterious disease, attributed by some to the oil spill, spread through the seeded shell stock killing the oysters. Years later the industry was still recovering.

If you go to Thursday Island today you will probably see luggers riding at anchor in Port Kennedy. Some are cargo boats or work boats (such as the Q.G.V. *Stephen Davies*), and others have been fitted out with freezers for crayfishing — an extremely lucrative industry at times. A few continue to go out to the pearling grounds and send men down in helmets for shell to be processed through the I.I.B. Shell Store on the waterfront, or else they may collect live shell for the shell dump at Poid for distribution to pearl culture stations. And it can still be dangerous. In 1974 a young diver from Boigu was flown south for treatment in a decompression chamber. In 1976 a Papuan diver was attacked by a sea snake, threw his helmet and also had to be evacuated south by the R.A.A.F. for treatment. Fifty years ago both these men would have died or remained badly crippled.

Most of the old white pearling families are gone. Hockings left a ramshackle ghetto at Hocking Point — sub-standard, dilapidated accommodation now rented to Islanders. Farcquer's Store is no longer known by that name. For many the only memorial to their passing is in the old European part of the cemetery where they lie beneath ageing tombstones.

Operational luggers are now dominated by the Nona family from Badu, though European and Chinese owned boats continue to struggle along in an industry which is dead but will not lie down.

12

Portrait of Three Islands: Muralug, Saibai and Nahgi

Muralug

The Kauralgal (otherwise known as Kawalgal or Kowreragas) were a loosely knit, semi-nomadic tribe which had the misfortune to inhabit those same islands desired most by the Europeans.

The islands of Tuined, Palilug, Nurapai, Gialug, Keriri, Waiben, Mawai, Zuna and Muralug were their regular stamping ground. They were relatively unsophisticated and, though racially Melanesian, were very closely related culturally to the Aborigines of the Australian mainland only thirty kilometres to the south.

The Kauralgal travelled regularly between their island group and the mainland. Their motive for this movement often may have been raiding for heads or women but generally their easy relationship with the Aborigines of the peninsula gave them a vital position in the trading system across the Torres Strait. It was possibly for this reason that they were tolerated by their aggressive neighbours on Badu and Nahgi.

Muralug has perhaps the most potential of all islands in the Torres Strait. It is almost twenty kilometres by thirteen, with crumpled, rocky ridges separated by greener valleys and flats. In several places permanent water may be found. Yet, according to a nineteenth century observer, this largest of the Torres Strait islands had an estimated maximum population of around fifty. The Kauralgal were mainly hunters and gatherers. In their nomadic existence they showed a striking divergence from other Torres Strait Islanders, with whom they had many other things in common including language.

Muralug in Western Island language means "everybody's place". This may suggest that the nomadic Kauralgal were unable to defend their tribal land against other groups. It is known to have been visited by other Islanders from Badu, Moa and Nahgi and by Aborigines from the Australian mainland. In fact, through inter-marriage with Aborigines over a period of time, many Kauralgal came to resemble Aborigines rather than Islanders. Other Islanders considered them to be relatively unsophisticated, referring to them as Wera Kauwagal (Island Aborigines) in recognition of their similarity to the Kauwagal (mainland Aborigines).* Not all contact with the mainland Aborigines however was friendly for within the framework of their relationship based on trade there was still room for hostility. Barbara Thompson told of an occasion when an Island man camping alone was speared by Aborigines who had stolen across from the Australian mainland in their frail canoes (presumably in good weather). A retaliatory raid was launched by the Kauralgal and seven Aboriginal heads taken, including those of two women and a small girl.

A favourite camping spot was at the mouth of North West Creek. Here between craggy, frowning hills a wide permanent stream empties onto a large reef which stretches half a kilometre out to sea and is a haven for crayfish, shellfish, fish and seabirds. The shallow creek at times is brimming with shoals of mullet dark against the sandy bottom, and in the trees above succulent black flying foxes hang from the branches (Papuans about Daru regard flying fox as a delicacy). The seed pods of certain mangroves were crushed and made into a paste, probably used during the leaner periods when other food was scarce.

On a long white beach, under the casuarinas beside the creek, the Kauralgal made their camp. Areas of burnt and broken shell testify to their tenancy. In the valley behind were goannas, turkey, pigs, roots, honey and wild fruits. It would not have

---

* The Western Island Language word "kaurug" means "troublesome" and could be the origin of these terms which are still in use today as far north as the Papuan coast. Alternatively "kerauwag" means "does not know" and this certainly sums up the attitude of present-day Islanders when applying the word "kauwag" to Aborigines.

43. A rare photograph of a dancer from Muralug probably taken before the turn of the century. The man's decorations are a fine example of Torres Strait art work. Photograph by Charles Kerry, by courtesy of the National Library of Australia, Canberra.

been a difficult life for them. An intriguing feature was the absence of coconut trees. None grew on the Muralug group of islands at this time despite the fact that the Kauralgal obtained coconuts in trade from Nahgi.

The arrival of Europeans could at first have caused little trouble, although the Europeans who came were not the kind to compromise and may have provoked attack. Display of the wealth of goods in their possession — knives, steel, clothing, glass — may have been sufficient provocation. In any case sailors moving through the area learnt to keep moving.

In 1843 the cutter *America* was in the Torres Strait attempting to salvage drums of whale oil lost in a shipwreck. A crewman of the wrecked whaler, failing to locate the wreck, was marooned on a sandbank. Two other members of the crew were mysteriously drowned. This left Thompson (the master), his wife Barbara and one other man to handle the ship. Barbara, who had come to Australia with her parents from Scotland, was a girl of sixteen.

A storm caught the under-manned cutter against the south coast of Muralug. Barbara later stated that after the boat struck a reef her husband and the other man died trying to swim ashore. After the storm had abated Kauralgal, out turtle hunting, found her on the wreck. It has also been claimed that the two men were in fact killed by the Islanders but, whatever the case, her situation was perilous for she was a "markai" or ghost. Here her youth was to save her. She was recognized by Pacquey, a tribal leader, as the spirit of his dead daughter Gi'iom. Henceforth Barbara, now Gi'iom, became part of Pacquey's family. Soon she became the wife of a young stalwart named Boroto, learned the language of the tribe and was apparently a great favourite.

Ironically the most serious problem which arose for her over the next five years was posed by a whiteman who, like herself, was living with Islanders. Wini, otherwise known as the "wild whiteman of Badu", was a white renegade who is credited with introducing some innovations to Badu in the areas of gardening and housing, but who ruled Badu absolutely and regarded his fellow whites with implacable hatred. Apparently he dreamed of a white dynasty controlling Badu and invited Barbara to join him. However Barbara, with no intention of sacrificing her new found security to join the mad whiteman, rebuffed all approaches. Wini persisted in his efforts and on one occasion descended on Muralug with two hundred warriors in sixteen canoes. The strength of his entourage was intended to intimidate the less populous and less sophisticated Kauralgal but perhaps Wini underestimated Barbara's Scottish stubbornness for she hid amongst the tangled scrub and ridges till Wini, in exasperation, returned to Badu.

In 1847 the H.M.S. *Rattlesnake* was conducting a survey around this area in an attempt to make it less dangerous to shipping. A ship's boat sent ashore took note of certain native customs, observing among other things the extreme accuracy of the men with their Aboriginal-made spears and woomeras at distances of well over a hundred metres.

One day as the party climbed out of the boat a naked female ran towards them pursued by several male Islanders. She threw herself at their feet but, not wishing to interfere in a local dispute, the naval officers were not prepared to take any action until in strangled, halting English the woman — not without difficulty — explained her position. Barbara Thompson was so burnt, ragged and worn that even then the officers were not easily convinced, until she reputedly cried "I am a Christian. I am ashamed." Taken on board the *Rattlesnake* she told her story.

Over the next few days a procession of Island acquaintances, including her husband, came to the ship begging her to return. She in turn was firm but sympathetic in her refusal. It may be assumed that it was the way of life rather than the people that had been unkind to her during her stay. On board the *Rattlesnake* MacGillivray recorded certain Torres Strait legends related by Mrs Thompson. One hundred and thirty years later these same legends are still being told in the Torres Strait.

Barbara Thompson went to Sydney where she married a merchant (she was only twenty-one) and perhaps lived happily ever after. The Kauralgal unfortunately did not for they were fast acquiring a reputation which would prove ultimately disastrous for their tribe.

In 1857 the *Sapphire*, travelling from Gladstone to Calcutta, was wrecked at Raine Island southeast of Torres Strait. The crew set out for the East Indies by small boat but imprudently stopped at Gialug to take stock of their situation before entering the Arafura Sea. Their arrival did not go unnoticed. In a sudden attack Kauralgal massacred all the men in the captain's boat. The shaken survivors made for Booby Island, where stores were kept for just such an occasion, and they eventually reached safety.

In 1869 the schooner *Speerweer*, skippered by Captain Gascoigne, anchored in the passage between Muralug and Gialug. Gascoigne sent his twelve-year-old son and thirteen of his Asian crewmen ashore on Gialug to look for water. He apparently suspected no danger though past events and the official publication *Sailing Directions for the Torres Strait* advised him otherwise.

Islanders in canoes approached the *Speerweer* under the pretext of trade. Suddenly they turned on Gascoigne and the two Asians who had remained on board, killing them.

At this time captains did not make a practice of arming Asian boat crews, for on occasions they had proved more dangerous than the Island natives. So when the poorly armed shore party straggled back onto the beach they were cut to pieces. The party's few muzzle-loaders were useless against the Islanders. Under a shower of spears and arrows the survivors fled into the bush to be hunted down, clubbed and beheaded later.

The resident magistrate at Somerset, Chester, hearing of the incident through Aborigines of the Gudang tribe on Cape York, embarked his native police aboard the government frigate *Blanche* and investigated. There was no trace of the missing crew on the broken, pillaged hulk of the *Speerweer*. What had happened to them was not doubted, for it was believed that these Islanders were cannibals. Some ship's gear, including Gascoigne's log, was found on Muralug along with a portion of the boy's body pierced with a steel-tipped arrow. However Chester, from the evidence available and information provided by the Gudangs, felt that visiting Islanders from Nahgi (the Kulkalgal) were responsible for the attack. Sailing to Nahgi he was able to gather most of the population together. Incriminating booty was discovered in the huts and the Gudangs pointed out three leaders who were supposed to have been involved in the affair. The three were tied to trees and shot. Some accounts suggest that Chester, a number of Gudangs and seamen from the *Blanche* trapped the Kulkalgal on a beach at Mawai. It is generally agreed that three leaders were executed, though in one version another died trying to escape.

But this was not the end of the business for in 1871 Frank Jardine was reappointed to the position of police magistrate at

Somerset. His father John had occupied the post during 1864 and 1865 and he himself had occupied the position previously during 1868 and early 1869. Frank had a tough reputation in his dealings with Aborigines, and he had shot many. The massacre of seventeen sailors within sixty kilometres of Somerset must, to him, have seemed an intolerable outrage. In retaliation he is supposed to have gathered all the forces at his disposal — including Aboriginal police, South Sea boat crews and what Europeans he could find — and then enthusiastically set about eliminating the Kauralgal menace forever.

Although this version appears undocumented it is known that within a decade of the *Speerweer* massacre pearling stations were being established on islands of the Muralug group without fear of interference from the Kauralgal. Obviously they had been neutralized by someone or something in the meantime. In any case they no longer comprised a threat and by the turn of the century the survivors were living on Keriri. In 1921 those who remained were moved to Moa, which was conveniently uninhabited except for an Anglican mission for Pacific Islanders established at the eastern end in 1904.

It is claimed that the people of Moa were exterminated in the course of a long war with Badu. Through the wreck of the H.M.S. *Antagonist* near Badu in 1863 the Badulgal had gained possession of a number of cutlasses and some quantity of tobacco. The cunning Badulgal saw how both these things could be used to advantage. A meeting was arranged where the people of Moa and Badu could sit down unarmed and discuss an end to their long quarrel. The Badulgal even sent along some tobacco as a gesture of their goodwill.

The Moa people, who were semi-nomadic and had been faring badly in the quarrels, were happy at the prospect of a negotiated peace though they could not have trusted their volatile neighbours. However, when the Badu warriors arrived at the beach they carried nothing but the crates of tobacco from the *Antagonist* and their tightly rolled sitting mats. The tobacco was distributed generously by the grinning warriors to all and sundry. The unfortunate Moalgal did not notice until too late that as each Badu man unrolled his mat he drew forth a gleaming cutlass. Only one woman and her baby boy are supposed to have escaped the massacre in which all the rest of their people died.

One explanation for the movement of Kauralgal Islanders from Keriri to Moa in 1921 was that Keriri was a "barren speck" and Moa "more fertile", though this seems hard to accept.

The Kauralgal were hunters and gatherers dabbling in agriculture only with reluctance. By the turn of the century their traditional lifestyle was no longer possible and Keriri, only a kilometre from Thursday Island, the bustling "sink of the Pacific", was too close for them not to be seduced by its obvious temptations. The segregationist/protectionist policy of sympathetic whites led to the remnants of the "Wera Kauwagal" being located at Poid on Moa opposite Badu village with its Papuan Industries Store, slipways, extensive gardens and famous troop of boy scouts.

Keriri in 1933 was chosen as the site of the only Roman Catholic mission on the Queensland side of the Torres Strait. Described as a "half-caste" mission its residents were mainly people of Filipino descent though mixed race people of all extractions found refuge there.

Eventually the site at Poid was deserted and today is occupied by a Japanese pearl culture station. Most of the Kauralgal descendants shifted to Kubin, some distance to the south, from where on a clear day, across a maze of reefs, their old home islands could be seen.

The two villages on Moa — Kubin in the west and St Pauls in the east — remained separate. The people were not of Moa and if asked said they came from St Pauls, Poid or Kubin, whereas other Islanders would give the name of their island. After the war some "Wera Kauwagal" shifted back to Nurupai where they live today. These descendants of the Kauralgal on Nurupai and at Kubin still maintain relations with the Aborigines around Cowal Creek and Bamaga.

Today Muralug or Prince of Wales, as it is commonly called, once again has people living on it. Scattered around its rough perimeter, tucked away in beautiful isolated coves, are shacks and houses thrown up on leasehold blocks. Most are in the northeast corner facing Nurupai or Thursday Island. Many of these are the permanent homes of Island and mixed race families. On the rugged hills above the beaches land has been cleared for gardens and domesticated pigs wander about the houses.

At the southern end a pearl culture farm has been established.

An Island family lives an idyllic existence on Packe Island watching the rafts which are moored between this small island and Port Lihou on Muralug a couple of hundred metres away. Packe (named after Barbara Thompson's adopted father or vice versa) is a high island. The ramshackle wooden wharf thrusts out from a golden beach which is thick with coconut palms. On the beach is an old sailing junk brought from Hong Kong by a traveller. Originally intending to go to southern Australia the owner found it necessary to push it up the beach at Packe. There it remains today, its graceful lines adding to the natural beauty of the place.

Port Lihou a century and a half ago had been popular with the Kauralgal for it had permanent water, swamps and was close to both Packe and Zuna. At one time Europeans cleared the scrub in a small cove enclosed by craggy ridges, and commenced a coconut plantation. The trees remain as do the graves of two whites. In the 1960s a mixed race family of part Samoan descent lived on the old plantation in two corrugated-iron sheds, attempting to grow vegetables and produce coconut oil, but today the site is deserted.

In the late 1960s an American purchased the cattle lease on Muralug. Immediately he insisted that there be no shooting on the island since technically it is a reserve. To understand the impact of this decision it is necessary to realize that most men (particularly Malay and European) who have been married on Thursday Island have taken deer and pigs from Muralug for their weddings and afterwards to offset the high price of meat, which in many cases has been thawed and frozen so many times as to be almost tasteless. In fact many non-Island families in the Torres Strait today live entirely on fish and wild meat.

Rusa deer it is claimed were brought from the East Indies by Hockings. Deer had already been introduced by the Dutch into West New Guinea where their numbers increased rapidly in the monsoonal savannah country that makes up much of that coast. Hockings had holdings in the Dutch East Indies and some say he imported the deer himself. Others say that a boatload of deer intended for southern Australia was apprehended in 1912 at Thursday Island under quarantine regulations. At that time Hockings had a lease on Gialug and he suggested releasing them on Gialug. From there the deer swam across to Muralug — a swim of half a kilometre through turbulent waters infested with sharks and, in those days, crocodiles. An even more difficult swim was across to Hospital Point on Thursday Island where an exhausted, dripping stag wandered ashore in 1972. After prowling about for a while, startling hospital staff and passersby, he realized that he had made a mistake, plunged back into the water and swam away.

In New Guinea the deer stampeded eastwards over the border, swimming to islands such as Saibai, so that this is another Torres Strait Island which has deer.

The Rusa have adapted admirably to the rugged environment of Muralug. I have seen a rare seven-point antler in the southern Torres Strait but eight points are claimed (and are common in Papua) while on Saibai a massive nine-point antler hangs in a house at Rose Bay Village. The venison is rich but can be tough. Each year perhaps five hundred deer are taken from Muralug, yet herds of a dozen or more are found without difficulty close to the beach. The deer will always thrive as long as they are able to retreat to the rugged sanctuary at the centre of the island to breed up. Shooters can only land on the beaches and move up valleys for a kilometre or so from the beach. The deer feed at night moving back into the hills before dawn. The hills are heaps of loose, fragmented rock held together by a web of barbed vines and low trees. Once inside this the deer are safe. Hunters may stalk them here but few deer are shot.

At times deer are seen on a beach in the brilliant sunlight of noon, but this is rare. The time to see them is just after sunrise, when they are moving up into the hills, and at sunset, when they are moving down again. During the wet season they seem scarcer and, in fact, are dispersed since feed is abundant. During the dry season the tall grass disappears leaving red rocks and dust, and by August the deer must gather where there is still feed. Fresh surface water is available in no more than half a dozen isolated places.

Even more abundant than the deer are the pigs. The tendency is towards the large-shouldered, savage, black razor backs, though frequently white and black spotted specimens occur. They are probably descendants of Papuan pigs brought down through the islands at some stage. This however is a controversial point. Pigs had definitely been present in southern Papua for a thousand years and were running wild on Saibai in 1873. It therefore seems unlikely that some were not included in the trading between Australia and Papua, yet they never appear in an Island myth or legend. Early Europeans found gardens on Mer guarded by stout fences as if to protect them from a foraging animal such as a pig, but found no pigs. Perhaps in comparatively recent times they were introduced, found to be too much trouble and all killed. It has been proposed that the pigs on Cape York Peninsula are descendants of those left by Cook, but it is more likely they arrived somehow from Papua.

The valleys and adjacent hillsides on Muralug are a maze of well-trodden animal trails leading from sanctuaries deep in the hills to a beach, swamp or water hole. They follow a logical pattern crossing saddles at the lowest point, cutting the bends from streams and avoiding rocky outcrops. Around the edge of the swamps the soft ground has been ploughed and furrowed by platoons of pigs for hundreds of metres. At level places in the hills the lying places of deer dot the bush. Some trees have the bark stripped from their trunks up to waist level where the stags have been rubbing the moss from their antlers. Before these trees are bare, dusty squares where the grass has been crushed and trampled by stags' hooves.

Pigs and deer are the most obvious animals but others may be found without difficulty. Big, brown wild horses crash away through the scrub when surprised. There are brown or black turkeys, and goannas and snakes. In the evening masses of coloured parrots flock to the paperbark trees above the swamps.

The Muralug horses are not tough, shaggy brumbies though, being descended from thoroughbreds. George Joyce and then his son Frank had the lease on Muralug, utilizing it for beef production for the local market and also for the breeding of horses. Frank, after his father's death, successfully exported horses to southern Australia and the Netherland East Indies. Frank drowned when his dinghy capsized between Thursday Island and Muralug, but his horses, still looking like thoroughbreds, run wild.

The wet season from November to March sends cascades of water streaming down smooth, water-worn rocks to the sea. The white streaks of waterfalls against the red rock can be seen around the coast but inland there are giant cataracts and enormous waterholes sunk into gorges. The most impressive of these waterholes is Dugong Story. By European tradition this is the place where Jardine and his men shot out the Kauralgal. I do not believe the story for Jardine, even with his Aboriginal troopers, could not have caught up with hunted Islanders in the tangled scrub of their own heartland. However, at sunset, with brooding red cliffs on three sides and the black pool below, it conjures up an image of the Kauralgal at their twilight.

Saibai

The Song of Saibai*

> Saibai, Saibai
> Ina ngui muna luggarai
> Ngui muna luggia usulal malu wur wai-ema
> Guba guban naki ngadal asinu wei karigarei
> Ngui muna luggia ngudthei Dthaudthai mata koolai
> Bege-al ttherepima-ei

Saibai is a large deltaic island, twenty-four kilometres long by eight wide, lying only eight kilometres from the Papuan coast. Yet it is still within the Queensland land border. From Saibai village the northern horizon is a long green line of mangroves on the Papuan mainland. Away to the right a slight hillock is Mabadawan Hill, the only elevation between Saibai and Daru eighty kilometres to the northeast. To the west looms the high blue pinnacle of Dauan, a landmark for many kilometres in this flat terrain. Directly opposite Saibai, on the mainland, houses are visible at Sigabada village (pronounced Sigabadur in Papua).

The first men supposed by oral tradition to have lived at Saibai were Melewau and Budia. Shortly afterwards came Nima and Poipoi, arriving by canoe from Sui along the coast to the east.

The people on Saibai Island settled in two groups — one living in the interior at the eastern end of the Island at a place called Aitth (the Aitthalgal), and the other at Saibai village (the

* The translation is:
  Saibai, Saibai
  This is our place
  When the tide rises at our place there is dirty water
  The different winds blowing about here make it look beautiful
  Our place is just before and just like Papua
  Big cumulus clouds gather

Every inhabited island in the Torres Strait has at least one song which expresses the love which the inhabitants feel for their island. This is one of several from Saibai.

Saibaialgal). But scattered at wells and elevated places throughout the island, and according to season, were smaller sub-groups.
All belonged to one of the five main augud (gods):

Oomaiaugudalgal   — the dog god people
Dtheibauaugudalgal— the leaf god people
Samuaugudalgal   — the cassowary god people
Tthabuaugudalgal   — the snake god people
Kadalaugudalgal   — the crocodile god people

Pigs once ran wild on Saibai. Some were domesticated but the
others were hunted down in order to protect the gardens which
were extensive and unfenced. Elderly men still remember the
last pig being shot by a villager armed with a bow and arrows.
Whether domesticated or wild the pig would have been of considerable importance. It is surprising then that a Bur-
umaugudalgal (pig god people) did not exist as such but was
rather a sub unit of the Tthabuaugudalgal. Similarly the
Dtheibauaugudalgal had a smaller sub-grouping which had as
its totem a long-legged swamp bird.

Those gods associated with the Aitth group were dis-
tinguished by prefixing Aitth to their title — for example the
Aitthaukadalaugudalgal (the Aitth crocodile god people).
Though located in the swampy interior, Aitth had a large
reliable well on high ground and adequate gardening land. It is
accessible from the sea through a number of landings. The
nearest landing to Saibai village, a distance of about ten
kilometres, is Danimud.

A hundred metres west of the landing where boats are
moored is a small sandbar exposed only at low tide. On every
low tide a huge crocodile, more than four metres long, is seen
resting there. There are few large crocodiles left on Saibai since
the Papuans came over years ago and slaughtered them, selling
their skins through Daru. The fact that this one dignified
monster — who is approachable to within sixty metres — has
survived at Danimud, the landing once frequented by the
Aitthaukadalaugudalgal (the crocodile god people), is seen as
providential.

The land surface of Saibai may be divided into elevated land,
marginal swamps and perennial swamps. Vegetation consists of
a mangrove fringe around the sea front with eucalyptus, ti tree,
pandanus and grassland predominating in the marginal and
elevated areas. The perennial swamps occupy an enormous area.

In March, after the wet season, they may be waist deep but by September they have become expanses of dry cracked mud, with lukewarm, ankle-deep water in the lower areas. Sometimes as they dry up large fish are caught flapping and splashing in the shallows where they have been trapped. But even in the dried swamps small fish called "kunu" are dug out of holes where they have sought refuge from the sun. Black, slippery and scaleless, they are gathered by the bucketful. These unusual fish have no bony comb running down their backbone like most fish. When the old people dug the fish out they quickly killed each one by biting its head but this practice is no longer continued.

About mid year large barramundi are often speared for the mud flats and swamps of Saibai are an important breeding ground for them. Their departure from the island east along the mainland coast marks the start of their migration, which takes them up the Fly River to Lake Murray and the Papuan barramundi season.

Reeds choke most swamps making walking difficult. Also the Saibai inland swamps have a peculiarly slippery type of clay which is excellent for pottery but which requires experience before you can walk with confidence. The knack is to push your big toe in deep to grip the mud. The uninitiated are often tempted to grip with all five toes at once and immediately disappear backwards as their feet fly out from under them.

In the centre of the island big tracts of land were once drained and cultivated — ideal conditions for the growth of taro. Considerable labour must have been required and the only tools available were hardwood digging sticks about a metre long. However this would have made Saibai Island highly productive — probably among the foremost gardening islands of the Torres Strait. The other Western Islands were high and rocky with little room for ambitious cultivation. The Central Islands were small and sandy, and the Eastern Islands, though highly productive, were very small.

At Waum, Metth, Mug, Kaninub and a dozen other places gardening villages were found for, though all Saibaialgal lived theoretically on the seafront, the time spent on gardening away from the main village necessitated this distribution. Poling easily across the swamps in their canoes to the main village these inlanders could offer garden produce or ducks to the coastal people in exchange for fish, dugong or crayfish. In these circumstances the swamps became a transport convenience. Some of these inner villages were used till comparatively recently and may still be detected by their remaining coconut trees which tower above the lower scrub. Closer examination at each of these sites reveals cultivated fruit trees kilometres from the nearest house today. Obviously Saibai at one time supported a much larger population than the present hundred and fifty.

Captain Moresby visiting in 1876 noted that the population of Saibai village was six hundred. The island's total population then could probably be reckoned at between eight hundred and a thousand. There were large two-storey houses, not found on any island south of Saibai, and pigs were plentiful. The men appeared to have long hair arranged in ringlets down to their shoulders but Moresby discovered, to his surprise, that they were wearing skilfully made wigs and that the men's hair was actually kept close cropped. He was impressed by the gardens which he said "produced an abundance of yams, and other roots, cocoa nuts and fruits". D'Albertis about the same time commented on the large number of ducks seen at Saibai.

The people of Saibai were not Kiwais but were related rather to the Kerakis (roughly west of the Pahoturi River) with regular, open features as opposed to the distinctive, semitic features of the Kiwais and Meriams. The people of Saibai Island and Dauan found themselves united in a war against the Dthaudthalgal (Papuans). From the east came the Kupamal (Kiwais) and from the west came the Tugeri or Sugeri.

A raid has already been mentioned in which warriors from Saibai discomforted the Kupamal who were retiring from a raid on Dauan. However, oral tradition relates the tale of another raid by the Kupamal on Attih, which was to have far-reaching effects of the whole of Saibai.

The Kupamal, having arrived at night, hid their canoes and stealthily approached Aitth across the swamp. All the men of Aitth had gone dugong hunting so the women had taken their children to a refuge, Taiwalnga, which was thought safe. The cunning Kupamal traced them even to this spot. At dawn they attacked massacring with clubs all but one woman and her child, who escaped towards Aitth. The men of Aitth belatedly caught and killed a few raiders among the mangroves. One Saibai man, coming upon the scene accidentally, watched in horror as the exuberent Kupamal, laden with strings of heads, pushed their canoes out.

At one stroke the Aitthalgal had been all but wiped out. The Aitth men realized that the Kupamal had very strong magic to have launched such a successful raid. They resolved to find this magic and, if possible, steal it.

The Kupamal's magic originated from the *adthibuia* (great light), a glowing spherical rock-like object resembling the moon. A beautiful Kiwai girl had become pregnant to the moon when her parents had refused to allow her to marry. The *adthibuia* was the result and thus possessed immense power.

44. A dwelling house on Saibai with a coconut tree, the stump of which can still be found near the school. The houses were designed to give protection against raiders. From W. Wyatt Gill, *Life in the Southern Islands*, 1876.

The Aitthalgal located the *adthibuia* on Kiwai Island, stole it and brought it back to Aitth. From that time on the men of Aitth were invincible, protected by the *adthibuia*'s magic.

At a secluded spot (Diwikal) before a fight, the Aitthalgal performed rituals to gain strength from the *adthibuia*. The traditional form has been accurately recorded in *Myths and Legends of Torres Strait* by Margaret Lawrie. The fight leader would reverently smear the stone with red clay (*parma*), annoint it with coconut oil (*wakasu*) and rest it on a garland of vine (*kedi*). The men in fighting gear would approach the *adthibuia* singly or in pairs. Performing certain rites they could ensure their enemies' defeat in the coming battle.

The Saibai Islanders' first sight of the whiteman would have been a startling experience for them, since they associated whiteness with ghosts. Happily they never found it necessary to match the *adthibuia*'s magic against the whitemans' firearms, since their island offered nothing to attract Europeans. It had no high peak to assist in navigation (such as Dauan), and did not lie close to the pearling grounds (Badu, Tutu, Mabuiag). It was not a vulnerable small island (such as Erub, Masig) to fall easily to marauders. Saibai village itself was backed by impenetrable swamps into which the experienced Saibaialgal could retreat. Its proximity to the notorious Papuan coast further discouraged all but the most adventurous. In this case they were missionaries.

On 6 July 1871 the L.M.S. vessel *Surprise* carrying the Rev. Samuel McFarlane, Rev. A. Murray and a number of South Sea Island teachers arrived at Dauan from Erub, where some teachers had already been installed. On board was John Joseph who worked as overseer for Banner at Tutu. Joseph could speak the Saibai dialect fluently and introduced McFarlane to Nadai, the leader of the Dauanalgal.

Nadai had twelve wives and his brother Saiai, a leader on Saibai, had ten, but McFarlane and Murray were impressed by the general manner and appearance of the Saibai/Dauan group — in contrast to the people of Erub. Such a comparison was unfair for Erub had been the subject of repeated assaults by marauding outsiders. South Sea Islanders and whites had been living there for at least seven years and the indigenous population had been reduced by three quarters. At Saibai on the other hand the missionaries had found a self-contained, confident and traditionally functioning society.

After negotiations, two South Sea teachers and their wives were left at Dauan and two on the neighbouring coast. Almost immediately the teachers on Dauan, inadvertently, became involved in a dispute. As was their custom the Dauanalgal were across on Saibai this day when a schooner called and the crews, finding Dauan island deserted but for Josaia and Sivene (the teachers), helped themselves to the gardens and departed the scene. On their return the Dauanalgal, enraged at the theft of precious food, turned threateningly on the hapless teachers who, hampered by not yet being able to respond in their accusers' language, fled to Tutu. This would have been an interesting voyage in a canoe at the roughest time of the year.

The situation however was resolved when the schooner's master, belatedly realizing what had happened, turned about and at Dauan paid compensation for the stolen produce. Josaia and Sivene were received back into the Dauan community with enthusiasm and apologies, their position more secure than ever.

The L.M.S. missionaries had a tough, practical attitude to the work to which they had dedicated themselves. Through the South Sea teachers, who were rapidly learning the language of the Saibaialgal and gaining their confidence, the Aitthalgal were encouraged to come out of their remote swamp and live at Saibai village. Apparently they left Aitth reluctantly and they stubbornly maintained their identity in the larger village at Saibai (and do so today though there is no hint of discord). Oral tradition contends that McFarlane saw a yellow glow at night in the depths of the swamps. This was, of course, the *adthibuia*. McFarlane battled his way to Diwikal and took the *adthibuia*. Where it went is not known but it never returned to Saibai Island. Without its power to support them the Aitthalgal knew they could not return to Aitth.

The rapid changes which occurred after 1871 were not brought about painlessly. The population of more than six hundred which Moresby had seen in 1876 quickly dwindled as the reins of Island society slipped gradually from the hands of the indigenous leaders. New diseases killed dozens at a time, so that by 1898 the whole of Saibai had a population of only two hundred — an incredible decrease in just twenty-two years. Yet few if any died of bullet wounds, the Saibaialgal still possessed their land and their language, and the L.M.S. was, in all good faith, exerting itself in the Islanders' interests. A school was built on the grassy flat beyond the southern end of the present airstrip and, despite the obvious ill-effects, the changes gave the Saibaialgal an opportunity which their neighbours in Papua were never to have. Access to goods and ability to purchase them (through participation in fishing industries), and increasing sophistication through participation in mission and local government activities came at a time when large areas of the adjacent mainland were uncontrolled. (As late as 1930 the only posts in the Western Division of Papua with Europeans were Daru and Madiri.) Aware of their new-found superiority, the Islanders moved along the Papuan coast and often a good way inland.

Nadai, perhaps the leader who greeted McFarlane, had a son named Alis. He adopted his father's name and became Alis Nadai but he is still commonly known as Alis today. Apparently he was something of a fire-eater and travelled far up the Pahoturi River armed with a rifle. According to present-day Saibaialgal, he "conquered that land".

Alis had experienced the arrival on Saibai of the L.M.S. and lived through the first difficult years of its ministry. But age-old habits and instincts could not be abandoned overnight and Alis had a nostalgia for the old days. When in 1874 a couple of Papuan sailing canoes were seen travelling between Saibai and the Papuan mainland he exhorted the other men to follow him in "one more war". Against the teachings of the L.M.S. and the advice of cooler heads, some men decided to follow him and sailed out to intercept the Papuans.

Their guns should have given the men of Saibai an easy victory. But a hail of well-directed arrows brought Alis down with a bamboo shaft protruding from his lower groin. Papuan arrows were made in two pieces, the bamboo or cane shaft being cemented and bound to the head. A war arrow may have been tipped with an animal or fish bone, sometimes dipped in a decomposing corpse so that one scratch could be lethal. Alis, humiliated by this turn of events, broke the shaft off, successfully concealing the wound from the other villagers, and subsequently died of septicemia. His death simply reinforced the teachings of the L.M.S. and effectively wrote an end to Alis and his wars. (Another version of his death pictures Alis as war chief sacrificing himself, heroically defending Saibai with traditional weapons against invading Papuans.)

Alis's well-tended cement gravestone is found in the middle of Saibai Village today, and served as a focus of emotions during the recent border dispute. The Saibai community claims that the reef, called Saibailgau Maza, where Alis was wounded comprises the natural and traditional border between themselves and the Papuans.

The absence of administrative control in Western Papua meant that life for the inhabitants of the far northern islands

45. The unveiling in 1977 by the then Queensland minister for Aboriginal and Islanders Advancement, C. Wharton, of the tombstone of Alis Nadai who was killed in 1874. Beside him is Saibai chairman, Wagea Waia. The unveiling was part of a shrewd campaign by the Islanders to prevent a change being made in the Queensland-P.N.G. border.

remained hazardous until fairly recently. The story is told of a raid by the Dthaudthalgal (Papuans) in the 1920s which surprised people in one part of Saibai village. They took to the bush in their haste, forgetting a small boy wrapped in a blanket on the floor of a hut. The child came to no harm and today is a middle-aged man living in the same village.

Many were the sleepless nights spent sitting silently in the dark huts with weapons — *gabba gabbal* (clubs) and shotguns — at the ready, listening for the hoarse whistles of a Dthaudthai raiding party in the bush behind the village, for this was where the attacks came from. People on Saibai claim that the Dhaudthalgal signalled to each other by whistling through their noses.

Not all contact though was violent. Trips of exploration in Papua by Islanders penetrated far inland and must have had a considerable influence on local Papuan development. In more practical ways the Islanders assisted the Papuans. The people at Ngau, inside the Pahoturi, did not know how to construct a schooner-rigged sailing canoe until a carpenter from Saibai built them one, presenting it to the village as a gift. Relationships were established which exist to the present day. Through inter-marriage, tradition or the persistent Torres Strait custom of exchanging names with a close friend, some surnames came to be found on both the islands and the mainland.

Many elderly people along the coast of Papua still speak Western Island language fluently today, indicating that in its day it was something of a "lingua franca" along a stretch of this isolated coastline. But today these old relationships are steadily being eroded as young people of Papua look to the east and those of the islands to the south. Billai Laba, a student at the University of Papua New Guinea, from Waidoro village, out-lined the effect of this breakdown of traditional contacts: "The very close and friendly links which Waidoro people have with Saibai Island are threatened by the repercussions of Inde-pendence. This is unfortunate since apart from these links, Waidoro has almost no others. The land is very thinly populated and road transport is non-existent at present, so that links with other mainland peoples are impossible in all but a very limited way."

Saibai was among the first of the islands to be visited by the L.M.S. A post was erected about that time commemorating the occasion and marking the site of the proposed church. The devotion of the Saibaialgal in the construction of their church was inspiring. For years, when time could be spared between the busy rounds of hunting and gardening, men would sail out to the reefs and load ugly chunks of green coral into their canoes. On their return to Saibai this coral was broken up and burned to yield lime extract. Mixed with water and sand it was moulded to shape walls, nave, portico, arched windows. In this way, with their bare hands, the people of Saibai painstakingly built an impressive monument to their own effort. The interior was graced by hand-carved lectern and an eagle, prepared by one of the village craftsmen. The church, with its gleaming white-washed walls, was consecrated in 1938 and is still the most striking building in the village.

There is no bell at this church but the blast of the *boo* (trumpet shell), a traditional Island instrument, echoes around the bay calling the faithful to services which are always well attended.

In the late 1960s a group of Saibai/Dauan men and women were recruited by the Anglican Church to serve at a mission in Popondetta P.N.G. It was tough, uncompromising work. The Islanders participated in gruelling foot patrols through mountainous terrain, visiting villages and people very different from their own. In one village they were offered cooked rat to eat and, conscious of the need to avoid offence, they forced it down. The two "brothers" returned to Saibai some years ago. A Dauan "sister", to her people's astonishment, married a New Guinean and lives in his village. Sister Petta, from Saibai, continues her dedicated work alone today, far from her people but respected by all.

Over the last century of turmoil and confusion, the church has stood as a symbol of unity and strength within the Saibai community, though it has not always done so with ease.

The beginning of World War I provoked a surprising reaction amongst a number of Saibai leaders. Confused by the prospect of one type of markai (white) fighting another and responding to patriotic British appeals for support, they decided to throw their weight behind the Germans (an action which speaks volumes for their opinion of Queensland administration). Thus was born the "German Wislin Movement" with Anu, Wageba and Sagaukus as generals. Just as British churches invoked divine assistance through their prayers and ceremonies, so the German

Wislin group attempted to do the same. Prayers were made to the markai (plural) and wild ginger was chewed by devotees and rubbed on their bodies.

It was claimed that a steamer full of markai from German Town would arrive at Thursday Island and drive out all the British markai (a not impossible event). Having dispensed with this problem the steamer would then go to Saibai, anchoring off Western Point, whereupon the markai on board would be revealed as diseased friends and relatives. A logical development was that non-believers would be punished at this time (which was to coincide with the second coming of Christ), and that believers would be rewarded for their devotion. In anticipation of their rewards German Wislin disciples stopped working. Asa, the deacon on Saibai, was powerless and this cargo cult persisted for two years till finally the people became tired of waiting and things got back to normal.

The generals, though embarrassed at the end by the failure of the cult, had profited while it lasted by charging "fees" for advice given to anxious adherents. If, in their innocence, they had misunderstood the issues and principles involved in the war, then they were no worse off than millions of more sophisticated people throughout the world who could not work out what was going on, or why, either.

The village at Saibai today stretches around a kilometre of foreshore. At low tide there are hundreds of metres of mudflats in front of the village. The twenty or so houses are built on a strip of land between the swamps behind and the sea in front. At places the strip is a mere twenty metres wide. Steady erosion is taking place so that the width of the strip is being reduced. At king tides the sea actually inundates areas of the coastal strip, flowing into the interior swamps. To walk from some of the western settlements to the main village during a king tide involves wading through knee deep sea water in several places.

After the Second World War Saibai was flooded by extraordinarily high tides. Some houses were almost washed away, others were isolated and the occupants rescued by rowing boats. It must have been a frightening experience for shortly afterwards Bamaga Ginau, the Saibai leader, requested the D.N.A. to arrange a transfer to another site of those of his people who wished to leave. In 1948 an area near the top of Cape York

Peninsula was declared a reserve, and it was here that Bamaga and hundreds of other Saibaialgal settled.

The debilitating effect which this move produced on Saibai was irreversible. The demoralized remnants were faced with the problem of maintaining their community when over half the original inhabitants, including many leaders, had gone. The fragmentation of their community resulted in a loss of cohesion which marks the island to this day.

There is an aimlessness about the place. The only employment available is through the D.A.I.A. in jobs designed to merely keep the place going. There is no development, let alone "advancement". Wages are low and unemployment runs at 90 per cent or more of the adult population. Yet this would not be so tragic if a subsistence economy still functioned, but little is produced on the island today. Meals revolve about rice, flour and tinned meat, which are bought at the local I.I.B. Store. The arrival of the cash economy (mutated though it may be) decreased the reliance on subsistence gardening to the point where today garden produce is the exception rather than rule.

Island policemen wear khaki uniforms and slouch hats, and obey the instructions of the chairman which may be according to law, D.A.I.A. directives or personal whim. It is not so long ago that pregnant girls were imprisoned in the school house prior to a "court" to discover the male responsible. However, it is usually impossible to find a policeman when trouble occurs so that fights are commonplace and a rough "rule of the strongest" prevails. Those who are beaten can only grin and bear it and afterwards, with cousins and brothers, plot their revenge. In fact fights and disagreements — and yarning about them — seem to occupy a disproportionate amount of time.

In 1935 Haddon wrote of Mer: "Crimes against the person would be punished by the injured party if he were strong enough, if he were not he would enlist the help of his friends or of a sorcerer. There is no doubt that their general vain-glorious temperament led to frequent squabbles, but as a matter of fact most of the energy was expended in words." This is a remarkably accurate description of the situation on Saibai forty years later.

Island customary law has never been codified and, in the absence of a recognized consensus or effective council system it rests very much on an ill assortment of European law, mission law and Island tradition as interpreted and administered by the chairman through the authority vested in him by the D.A.I.A. Recently wide-ranging incest laws (which include relations with in-laws) were invoked, with strong support from a scandalized community, resulting in the exile of alleged offenders. Later the fibro home of one was badly damaged by outraged youths without any disciplinary action being taken.

It seems that minor skirmishing between youths of different family groups and deliberate destruction of property in certain cases are accepted as part of the natural ebb and flow of a self-contained, self-regulating society. However, with its emphasis on group interaction, customary law may prove difficult to integrate with strictly coded British law and its preoccupation with the individual. This problem is exasperated by the need to work through the chairman/council structure imposed by European administration. The "council" on Saibai consists of only two elected men from the eighty or more adults who live there.

From day to day very little happens. A Papuan canoe may waft into the landing under the coconut trees near the radio shack. The Papuans are industrious capitalists and will sell anything that is saleable. At times they sail to the eastern end of Saibai, catch crabs, bring them to Saibai village and sell them for fifty cents each. A magpie goose sells for a dollar and a basket of mullet for a few more dollars. Also the Papuans are an ever-present source of cheap labour. They might do a couple of days gardening for an Islander at the back of the village for ten dollars and think themselves lucky. Most sought-after are Queensland government jobs, which pay well by comparison with P.N.G., and are sometimes open to Papuans.

None of the Saigaialgal are wealthy, but then they seldom work hard and their needs are few. Once Saibai produced great sailors but today there are no sailing canoes left on the island. Still, using small bondwood dinghies with outboard motors, the few adventurers may visit villages on the Papuan coast and perhaps even do some shooting in the Papuan swamps which swarm with ducks. They may travel to the western end of Saibai and hunt turtle, or go to the eastern end for dugong. But instead of these activities comprising the core of community life they have receded to the fringes and are mere adornments to a slower, more pointless existence that can have only one end — total de-population.

There have been few legitimate births and only one marriage on the island within the last decade. In fact, marriage is discouraged by older men clinging to their traditional authority in approving or disapproving of a wedding match. Customarily a consensus of approval should be sought from the family which is represented, more or less, by the uncles or *barbs*. The eldest of these, *kui barb* ("big uncle"), has enormous prestige and, in the absence of a grandfather, is the family leader. With the migration of young people, partners are not easy to find and the elders are generally reluctant to grant approval in cases which do not measure up to their own rigid ideals. Their truculence is partly responsible for the ruinous marital situation, where even adults in their mid-thirties are prevented from marrying. Some young couples have fled south to marry and presented disapproving elders with a *fait accompli*. Some youngsters drift to Thursday Island to become involved with Europeans or partners from other islands outside the reach of their family. Inevitably this is reflected in the low legitimate birth rate as compared to the alarming number of illegitimate births, of which a steadily increasing proportion have white fathers. There is little or no stigma attached to being an unmarried mother and there is even some envy, for the supporting parent's benefit is substantial.

In view of the serious disabilities Saibai has faced over the last few decades a considerable cultural heritage remains. Each family is aware of the *augud* from which they are descended and their interest in this respect is not seen to conflict with their Christian faith. Characteristics of the Kadalaugudalgal and Tthabuaugudalgal have been mentioned earlier. The snake has a peculiarly strong image, probably because of the abundance of snakes on the island. Brown snakes and yellow-bellied black snakes are regularly killed in and around houses. In days gone by people tapped a length of split bamboo on the ground before them when walking on bush tracks to frighten snakes in their path. It is the Saibai custom to burn a snake immediately it has been killed. To leave the bloody corpse about the house or garden would bring other reptiles, attracted by the smell.

This practice of burning an offensive animal to permanently eradicate it crops up in other Saibai stories. On one occasion a groper attacked and ate a man but was later caught, pulled onto a mudbank, cut up and burned. Another old story tells of an elderly couple who enticed children to their house, then killed and ate them. Finally, when they were found out, they too were cut to pieces and burned.

Members of the Tthabuaugudalgal are sympathetic towards the snake and the death of a snake may cause them to murmur "*Iagar ngau Augud*" (a woman would say "*Iagar ouzzu Augud*"), in English "Sorry for my god", though this would not stop them killing a snake if they had to.

However there are certain places where a snake may never be attacked by anyone. Metth, Mug, Bhuttu (all wells) and Waum are guarded by snakes which are the spirits of those places, called Muroi-ig. The Muroi-ig are the spirits of ancient men which, resident at that well, may assume the guise of any snake, of any size, in the precincts of their well. At the well people should not indulge in horseplay, make too much noise or waste the water, for fear of provoking the guardian.

Metth is the largest and traditionally most important well on the island. The site of an old village, though several kilometres inland, it is still surrounded by coconut palms and native fruit trees. A kilometre to the south are great stands of bamboo where the Saibaialgal have for centuries cut bamboo for spears.

It was at Metth that one of Saibai's modern legends occurred. One day, some generations ago, a man named Babia walked to Metth where he saw a small brown snake in his path. He struck out at it with his stick, leaving it writhing, seriously injured in the grass. But as he returned to Saibai village he himself was attacked by a terrible pain and weakness. He managed to struggle back to his house where he collapsed. To his friends he explained feebly what had happened. The news was received in dumb silence. The elders, most of whom remembered the days before the light, told him bluntly the course he must follow. Having injured the Metthaumuroi-ig he had been similarly afflicted. In order to be cured he had to ask the Muroi-ig for forgiveness, and then receive it directly from the spirit or the snake's mouth.

That night Babia lay apprehensively in the darkened house. The Muroi-ig had been called, with the old men interceding on Babia's behalf. After several sweltering, anxious hours a stealthy slithering and hissing indicated the Muroi-ig's arrival. While

Babia lay rigid with horror, the reptile's forked tongue licked the soles of his feet, slowly moving to his ankles, calves, knees and so on to his head. Then as silently as it had come the Muroi-ig departed. The reconciliation had succeeded and a chastened Babia recovered, giving everyone a lesson in the folly of disregarding the customary spirits of the island. The story is quoted today and the strictures obeyed, for this is as much a part of life on Saibai as Christiantiy.

Mention has already been made of the deer first introduced into Irian Jaya by Dutch missionaries and which then spread east into western Papua. These deer are able swimmers and at some stage during the last sixty years swam to Saibai — a somewhat unlikely and dangerous nine kilometre swim. On one occasion some Saibai men out fishing came across a stag swimming strongly well away from land. They threw a line over its head and pulled it to shore — a very unusual catch for a fishing party.

Until recently deer were rarely shot on Saibai. There are few rifles and anyway the deer, being cautious, live deep in the swamps where during eight months of the year they are impossible to find. With ample water, lush swamp grasses and dense cover they are unapproachable. It is only when the swamps dry in July that they are obliged to congregate about the water holes at Mug, Aitth, Metth, and some even use Bhuttu within two hundred metres of Redlynch village. During the day they disperse, breaking up into small groups. They shelter from the blazing, tropical sun under low trees beside the dried swamps, rarely venturing forth till evening and usually within easy striking distance of the well.

During the very dry Christmas of 1977 Mabadawan ran out of drinking water. Canoes loaded with empty wine flagons arrived at Saibai to be filled from the dams and wells of the Islanders. The people of Mabadawan claim a special relationship with the Saibai people, insisting that Mabadawan villagers first settled Saibai. The Saibaialgal are not as keen to admit to such a relationship but have allowed certain friends and "relatives" to migrate. In January 1978 some 40 of Saibai's 160 residents were Papuans living at a new Papuan camp on the abandoned site of Western Point Village.

The wet canteen (before it closed recently) stood on a small promontory jutting out slightly in front of Redlynch village. It was a small concrete slab and corrugated-iron structure, painted green to blend with its surroundings. The beer — a hundred cartons at at time — arrived periodically by ship from Thursday Island and disappeared in a matter of a week amongst a population of a little over a hundred.

In 1976 the beer was warm because the canteen's fridge had not worked for three months. Most people bought by the carton anyway, picking one up from the mountain of cartons behind the bar and taking it to a table. Outside people sat at tables among grass, driftwood and already empty cans. The mosquitoes droned and clouds of moths fluttered about the lanterns.

At one table there would be some Papuans, immediately distinguishable by their thinner and more ragged appearance and their shorts — Islanders might wear long trousers or a *lava lava* but they would never dream of wearing shorts to the canteen. The Islanders though are sympathetic towards their have-not neighbours and are usually generous, perhaps buying the Papuan group a carton of beer and handing out tailor-made cigarettes — a far cry from the Muruk black tobacco wrapped in newspapers which is the Papuans' normal fare. Communication is in broken English (*not* New Guinea Pidgin) and snatches of Saibai dialect. The Papuans are unabashedly intimidated by the wealth and extravagance of the Saibai men, though such a mean emotion as envy cannot be detected.

Nahgi

Nahgi lies fifty kilometres northeast of Thursday Island. Most days its distinctive triangular shape can be seen looming dark blue on the horizon, but although high the island is not large, being less than two kilometres across.

It consists of a massive heap of boulders and tangled scrub named Mt Ernest (230 metres) joined by a narrow sand flat to a lower but similarly rugged hill to the northeast. The southern side of the island is exposed to blustery winds during the southeast season but on the opposite side Moa to the west, a scattering of small islands (Peenacar, Getullai and Suarji) to the north and extensive reefs provide an attractive and sheltered prospect.

The original inhabitants of Nahgi were the Kulkalgal, a tribe of adventurous seamen who visited Muralug, Moa and Waraber regularly and were well known to the Aborigines on Cape York.

These voyages were no mean feats. During the southeast season the seas to the south, east and west of Nahgi are extremely rough as there are no substantial islands or reefs to windward.

The Kulkalgal were closely linked with the Kauralgal on Muralug by marriage and friendship. In fact they appear to be the only island group with whom the Kauralgal were at ease.

Actually the Kulkalgal seem somewhat more sophisticated than the Kauralgal — a fact which is not easily accounted for. The Kulkalgal cultivated sugar cane, bananas, coconuts and tobacco, all of which they traded with the Kauralgal who, despite close contact between the two groups, grew none of these things. Admittedly there were certain advantages in Nahgi's geographical position: it was more central than Muralug and so possibly was subject to more influences by way of the trading network, but this alone cannot adequately explain the discrepancies.

On occasions the entire Nahgi community ventured out on difficult journeys in their canoes to far islands. Barbara Thompson told of a time when twelve canoes full of men, women and children from Nahgi came to Muralug. This could indicate anything from fifty to a hundred people. The Kulkalgal traded their cultivated crops for fish and wild yams to pay their way during their eight-week stay. Also they brought many items made from bamboo, which once again the Kauralgal lacked, such as tobacco pipes (*soogooba marappi*), water containers (*ngooki marappi*), beheading knives (*upis*) and bows and arrows. Rope (*yegalli*) and plaited waist bands (*wakaus*) made from coconut fibre and coconut shell water containers (*kusu*) were other items traded. In return the Kauralgal appear to have traded only their wild foods as well as spears and ochre which they had obtained from the Aborigines of Cape York.

The Kulkalgal were a highly competent, advanced society with the skills and resources to fulfil their needs and even to produce a surplus for use during excursions. In fact it is probably not surprising that at times they felt a desire to leave their tiny kingdom and wander the island studded sea, there being more than fifty islands within a fifty-five kilometre radius of Nahgi.

While the relatively large population of Nahgi obliged the Kulkalgal to cultivate food their environment was dominated by the sea. Large reefs on both sides of the island abound with crabs, crayfish and fish, and turtle are plentiful. Over the northwest season large sago palm trunks, carried down the Papuan rivers, were driven to leeward, southeast across the Torres Strait. Nahgi and islands to the east received large quantities of sago (*Bisi*) in this manner — a gift from the sea.

However the sea also brought whitemen and other strangers for Nahgi lies on the northern boundary of what has become one of the busiest seaways on the Australian coast. By the early nineteenth century most ships passing through the Torres Strait used the shorter, less dangerous and better charted route passing north or south of Muralug.

In the furore following the loss of the *Charles Eaton* in 1834 Captain Wiseman revealed that when his vessel, the *Augustus Caesar*, visited Nahgi on 31 August 1834, the second mate had come across some wreckage. He searched unsuccessfully for signs of the main wreck but surprised some Islanders on the beach nearby. They fled leaving a fire beside which, according to the mate, were human bones.

In 1844 an unidentified ship grounded on reefs near Mabuiag and was attacked by Islanders. Some crewmen escaped in the ship's boats, but all of those who remained, save one, were massacred. The following high tide took the ship off the reef and it drifted south to ground again west of Nahgi where the Kulkalgal are supposed to have killed the one surviving crewman and looted the ship.

Thus the inhabitants of Nahgi had already gained an unflattering reputation before their involvement in the *Speerweer* massacre in 1869 which led to the execution of three leaders on the beach at Nahgi.

There was a gap of twenty years following this event during which the Kulkalgal dropped from sight. What became of them? Skulls and miscellaneous bones were found heaped in a rock crevice on Nahgi. Some skulls have gaping holes punched in the craniums. Were these injuries made by a club, perhaps before the coming of the Europeans, or by bullets?

Traditional legends imply that the Nahgi community was under some pressure in the nineteenth century from Moan raiders. Some go so far as to claim that the Nahgi community, in spite of strenuous resistance, were all but wiped out in these attacks. This is quite possible since Nahgi, with its relatively small population, was very close to the more heavily populated Moa. Yet the Moalgal themselves were under pressure from

46. A collection of skulls on Nahgi, a beautiful island with a perplexing history. Photograph by courtesy of Thursday Island state high school library.

Badu, culminating in the alleged massacre of 1863. The Kulkalgal were still strong enough six years after this event to kill the seventeen-man crew of the *Speerweer*. Perhaps the Kulkalgal, having already suffered grievous losses in their steady war of attrition with the Moalgal, could not sustain the additional losses delivered upon them by the Europeans. The execution of the clan leaders in particular could have had disastrous effects on such a small group and may help to explain the rapid decline and disappearance of Nahgi's original inhabitants.

In the late nineteenth century a Samoan named James Mills came to the island and, with his arrival, a new era began for Nahgi. The story of the next eighty years was to be that of Mills and his descendants. A Samoan who stowed away as a youth and was stranded in Sydney, Mills knew he had a relative in Queensland and worked his way north to Somerset where he joined his cousin Sania, wife of the resident magistrate at the time, Frank Jardine.

After several years working with the Jardines, Mills came to the Torres Strait where he married his first wife. Through Thursday Island's magistrate John Douglas, a great friend of the family, he acquired a lease on Nahgi Island where he settled with his wife and family. A hard worker with a keen brain, Mills slowly accumulated a fleet of twenty luggers. His first wife died at the peak of his career and he then married Nero Bob, the daughter of one of his lugger captains from Sue Island (also a Samoan married to a Torres Strait Islander). They raised a family of eight children.

At one time there were more than two hundred people living at Nahgi, but during the cyclone at Princess Charlotte Bay Mills lost a number of his luggers and men and never recovered sufficiently to carry on with his fleet. He died in 1916 and is buried at Nahgi along with a hundred others.

WHICH CULTURE?

13

Missions and Reserves of Cape York Peninsula

The Aborigines on Cape York Peninsula suffered to a far greater degree from the impact of European invasion than did their neighbours of the Torres Strait.

Moravian missionaries of the Presbyterian Church commenced missions at Mapoon (1892), Weipa (1898) and Aurukun (1904). Aurukun was founded amongst a nomadic, independent, largely untouched population of about six hundred, but the missions closer to the Torres Strait reflected the worst aspects of European influence and control.

By comparison with Aurukun the open bush about Albatross Bay seemed empty. In its first twenty years the mission at Weipa accumulated only about seventy Aborigines. But it was Mapoon which became the focus of the more repugnant features of Queensland's ill treatment of Aborigines in the far north.

The tribe living on the site where the Mapoon mission became established was the Tjungundji, but even before 1891 the ravages of disease and the depredations of whites and their black mercenaries in the Native Mounted Police had caused the shocked survivors to band together in a way that had never happened before. Many members of the Seven Rivers group (between the Dulhunty and Jardine Rivers), put to rout by the Jardines, had fallen back upon their neighbours to the south.

Port Musgrave, with Mapoon at the southern entrance, became popular with lugger masters as a place where cheap labour and women were available from the demoralized tribes.

Marshall was told by Mapoon people of a time in the 1880s when a crew of Mapoon men were harshly treated by a European master on a bêche-de-mer lugger. They protested to him about his treatment and, when he ignored them, they threw the whiteman overboard to drown, cunningly dumping fishing nets to make it appear that he had died as a result of a fishing mishap. Then, less prudently, they sailed the boat down the coast to their people who happily looted and burned it.

Retribution was inevitable and came in the form of a party of white policemen from Thursday Island who shot some people on the beach and others in the bush behind. When no more live Aborigines could be seen the police withdrew, leaving gifts beside each black corpse as if to say "You've paid for your crime and those of you who are left can be friends again till next time".

It was under these conditions that Rev. J. Ward and Rev. H. Hey started their mission in November 1891. The constant corrupting intrusion of luggers disrupted the mission's activities, though this may have been due in part to Hey's refusal to issue tobacco at the mission, thus obliging Aborigines to seek it from visiting boats. However, whilst Hey was a strict man, he was also something of a realist.

The nomadic life was impossible under circumstances then existing. Any Aborigines living off the settlements were doomed. One woman explained how, after a dispersal about 1893, her uncle joined the mission: "The first child they picked up was my uncle. My Grandmother had to hide him inside a waterhole and cover him with a skin bark, but they heard the little baby crying. I think the baby was two years old. They took the child into the mission and gave him to Mrs Ward."

Hey tried hard to give the local community self-sufficiency (through small, decentralized farming plots) and the ability to enter the cash economy (through the establishment of coconut plantations and cattle grazing). He worked at the mission for twenty-three years.

In 1897 the Queensland Native Mounted Police was demobilized and its white officers refused re-employment, but it had done its job. The Aborigines now needed protection not policing and this was recognized in the same year by the Aboriginal Protection and Restriction of the Sale of Opium Act.

Mere protection soon turned to segregation and surviving Aborigines and halfcastes found themselves forcibly relocated in settlements far from their own country. After 1907 Mapoon was made the concentration area for mixed race children from all over the gulf and peninsula who were thought by their white "protectors" to be living in unsatisfactory conditions. "The government took our fathers and mothers away from our grand-parents," said Jerry Hudson. "Some were six and seven years old. Well, you can guess how our dear grandparents felt about our mothers and fathers who they will never see anymore." By 1914 this dispossessed mixed race group made up most of the population of 110 at Mapoon. Through their common experience they developed as a strong community with a heavy local flavour contributed by surviving locals who taught the orphans some Aboriginal language and customs. Intermarriage took place, tying the mixed race people more securely to a place which they came to regard as their own.

Meanwhile those Aborigines around Cape York, said to be remnants of northern Seven Rivers groups and the Red Island group, are claimed by the chief protector of Aborigines in Queensland in his annual reports to have established "practically unaided and of their own volition" a settlement at Small River (or Cowal Creek).

The village began about 1918 and by 1928 the chief protector reported: "The settlement at Small River, near Cape York, by natives of mainland camps, is interesting as evidence of the growing appreciation by the native of the advantages of the life of industry and order. Until a trained native mission teacher (a Torres Strait Islander) was sent to open school there recently, these people carried on a simple village life, in imitation of what they had seen on the islands of Torres Strait, governing them-selves, working their fishing boats (*Fly* and *Cherrie*) and gardens and doing their trading through the Protector at Thursday Island."

In 1926 the population was 184, increasing to 234 in 1931. "The people are very orderly and manage their own affairs through their councils", the protector reported.

Beneath the alien coconut trees the people lived a life alien to their own. As early as 1928 the *Cherrie* was gone and the *Fly* took less than a tonne of bêche-de-mer valued at only £253, prompting the chief protector to comment: "The mainlander is a good worker under a good captain, but few mainlanders make good masters". Probably the whole rosy picture painted by the chief protector initially was just a public relations job. During the war, the writer Alan Marshall visited the same settlement with a R.A.A.F. doctor from Jack Jacky Strip. At some stage before the war the name had been changed from Small River to Cowal Creek. Marshall wrote:

> Over Cowal Creek broods an immense lassitude. There is no evidence of a directing force — a force to give enthusiasm to the blacks and halfcastes that dwell there. These people are herded here to die, I thought, as I wandered through the village with the doctor. Dirty huts of galvanized iron, miserable hens, children with the pot bellies of malnutrition, old men squatting beneath trees, women in formless garments, girls with sores, a naked idiot boy, babies with running eyes, thin women who coughed gently and quietly while leaning against trees, a well-built church with an altar covered in maroon velvet and a brass crucifix on the wall — this was Cowal Creek Mission, run by the Queensland government.

After the war things changed in a big way. Several hundred Saibai Islanders descended on Cape York, settling several kilometres east and west of Cowal Creek at Red Island Point and Muttee Head. Both sites had excellent fishing, abundant turtle, and soil at least as good as that available on the islands, yet it was decided that, with assistance from the Department of Native Affairs, an area some distance inland could be intensively and successfully farmed with Island labour. In 1948 18,000 hectares, later increased to 39,000, was incorporated into an Aboriginal and Island Reserve.

Some Islanders remained at Red Island Point village and others at Cowal Creek where they mingled with those Aborigines that remained, but most shifted to the new town, ten kilometres from the sea, called Bamaga after the Saibai leader. The camp at Muttee Head was deserted. Supplies of building materials from old army camps and airfields were carried to Bamaga and houses begun. Mosby Creek, named after a descendant of Yankee Ned, was dammed and gardens cultivated. With saw milling, beef production and later poultry farming, there seemed great potential in the project. Soon the development of Bamaga became the focus of Aboriginal policy in the northern peninsula, with the D.N.A. seeking to relocate Aborigines from other reserves in the area.

Mapoon mission was one of the smaller reserves which were difficult and expensive to maintain and, being close to Bamaga, Mapoon was the first to come under pressure. In the 1950s efforts were made to move the people but were successfully resisted by the community. Then in 1958 the axe fell. A mining lease was granted to Comalco and all but 200 hectares ceased to be a reserve. The same lease reduced the Weipa reserve to a mere 125 hectares leaving the population of 170 with no opportunity of self-employment, or even of subsistence activities, except fishing. A town of over a thousand whites rose on the south bank of the Mission River, opposite their village.

At Mapoon the situation after January 1958 is not too clear. Certainly discussions were held between the Presbyterian Church, officials of the D.N.A. and the Mapoon councillors, but the results of these talks are not so certain. Whatever the outcome, many of the people still refused to move and remained at Mapoon through the early 1960s.

Even the Presbyterian missionary was giving the community a hard time. In 1960 two girls who refused to cooperate with him had their hair cropped short, were denied rations and then had their families sacked so that they could not be supported. Another girl was expelled from the mission for the same offence. Some people, seeing the writing on the wall, had already left to settle at Weipa or New Mapoon which was located in the scrub three kilometres from Bamaga and more than six kilometres from the sea. Finally in mid-1963 only a dozen families remained. At this time a D.N.A. official arrived with a detachment of D.N.A. policemen from Saibai Island. Within a month the missionary was gone. According to some Mapoons the store was deliberately allowed to run down, with D.N.A. workers trying to harass the people into leaving.

On 15 November 1963 the *Gelam* anchored off Mapoon with white police from Thursday Island and more D.N.A. police. The aim was to apparently break the back of the resistance. Six families were told to go and they went, though they claim to have been removed under strong protest. After they had been collected (some families were camping down the coast at the time), it is claimed that their houses were burned.

To the Aborigines of the northwest peninsula, perspiration and attendant body odours are a form of personal strength, called *nara* at Mapoon. When a team of men complete a dance, they may take the perspiration from their armpits and smear it over spectators, thus distributing the strength gained directly from the dance amongst everyone, even those who did not or could not participate.* When the houses at Mapoon were burned some old clothes were burned also and as these contained their owners' *nara* then immediately elderly Aborigines began to sicken. Demoralization was complete. Within months all the stragglers had moved and though some went to Weipa and Bamaga, others travelled to Thursday Island, Cairns and Townsville.

There are some among the Mapoon community who suggest that everybody moved to New Mapoon of his or her own free will. On the other hand several attempts have been made to return to old Mapoon. I have spoken to a D.A.I.A. policeman from Saibai who went to Mapoon with white police from Thursday Island to round up Aborigines. On arrival it was found that the people were in the bush behind the beach. Fearing that the approach of European police would startle them and perhaps cause them to flee, the coloured police were sent in to make contact and persuade them to surrender. In this they were successful and the fugitives returned to Bamaga.

In 1924 Anglican workers from Thursday Island had established a mission on the Lockhart River amid Aborigines who had been exposed to exploitation over a longer period than those at Mapoon. At the beginning of World War II, 350 ailing people were gathered there. The death rate exceeded the birth rate by more than 200 per cent. In 1937-38 there had been sixty deaths for seventeen births.

By 1963 the mission was suffering the effects of its isolation. Without sufficient finance from the church and with the collapse of a mission fishing cooperative, it was in bad shape. Approaches to the D.N.A. led to the formation of Umagico on the road from Bamaga to Cowal Creek, where within twelve months seventy Lockhart River people were living. As at Mapoon many preferred to stay at the mission site in their own country, however the point was not pressed and the mission later relinquished control to the D.A.I.A., after which the settlement received substantial independent development.

Bamaga today is a peculiar place. As a result of great capital expenditure there are football fields, basketball courts, a golf course, a new hospital, a powerhouse, a new state primary school, a state high school and a residential college.

---

* On Tutu in the Torres Strait the drinking of the perspiration of a strong or powerful man was believed to endow the consumer with similar qualities.

The primary school is staffed by young Europeans assisted by coloured aides. The high school is in similar position with the college providing boarding accommodation for students from all over the Torres Strait. Unfortunately of the 160 beds at the college only some sixty or so are occupied, and it has become something of a "white elephant". In fact the whole settlement is something of a white elephant.

The hopes for agriculture have all but collapsed. The Island men showed no interest in the project, preferring less rigorous service jobs such as truck driving. What little is grown cannot support Bamaga, let alone be exported to Weipa or Thursday Island.

The poultry project which, given fowl consumption in the Torres Strait and the absence of eggs (chickens are no longer kept on some islands), should be a roaring success is able to supply only a favoured minority at Bamaga. Beef produced at Bamaga must be consumed in Bamaga and frequently risks being totally condemned because of unprofessional slaughtering practices. Certainly the output of the 341 Aborigines, 585 Islanders and 129 Europeans living around Bamaga in 1971 was very small.

The need for efficiency may have led to the centralizing of operations with coloured workers being paid low wages (averaging about $60 a week in 1976) under white overseers. If so, it certainly has not produced efficiency and has discouraged individual incentive. Perhaps a more decentralized system would introduce the private profit motive.

Since most inhabitants are of Melanesian descent perhaps attention should be paid to development projects and co-operative production amongst Melanesian groups in nearby Papua New Guinea. Papuan villages near Saibai and Boigu are today producing tertiary-trained agricultural and fisheries officers to assist in the development of their nation. Where are those from Torres Strait?

Perhaps nothing would work, since the Islanders are seamen and the sea lies ten kilometres away. The new wharf at Red Island Point sees only white-owned fishing boats, some going down into the gulf after barramundi or prawns, others going east seeking crayfish amongst the reefs of mackerel further out.

Another aspect of the Bamaga experiment has been the mixing of Islanders and Aborigines in the hope that the latter

47, 48. Two faces of Bamaga: Geoffrey Waia, son of the Saibai chairman, performs an island dance; an an Aborigine. Photographs by courtesy of P. Berends.

will be influenced by the former. The process is something akin to that which took place on the Torres Strait Islands with the influx of South Sea Islanders, and has developed similar difficulties. Islanders have gravitated to the top positions available, have better housing, better facilities and better jobs than their Aboriginal counterparts. A comparison of thriving Bamaga, which is almost completely Islander, with apathetic, derelict Umagico illustrates this contrast.

The Islanders treat Aborigines with condescension, often verging on contempt, and it is an open question whether the Aborigines would be better or worse off without them for, whilst relations are generally cordial, trouble can easily blow up. In 1975 an Islander died during a fight with Aborigines from Umagico. Islanders took their revenge on the whole Umagico community, breaking doors, walls and windows till the village resembled a disaster area. Twelve months later the shattered houses were still being repaired and gaping holes covered to give dwellings a patchwork appearance.

Taken together with the common problems of unemployment, truancy and alcoholism, it is little wonder that morale in this particular community is at a low ebb.

In view of the natural assets of the northern peninsula — a large resident labour force, abundant freshwater (pumped from the Jardine River), good fishing and a reserve of some 45,000 hectares — the potential for success is still there. It may be that migrants from the Islands are going through a period of adjustment that will, in the end, wed them to this land and its possibilities. Only now are the first Bamaga-born Islanders reaching adulthood. Perhaps this generation will see a change.

One of the original stated intentions of the reserve was to create "a defence unit for the far north". The T.S.L.I. had acquitted itself well and it was anticipated that defence establishments at the Cape would provide impetus for local development. Today this concept is insupportable. Certainly there is a need for defence force bases in northern Cape York Peninsula but these must certainly go to Weipa, where technical, social and administrative facilities exist for coping with them.

However, whatever the future of the Bamaga reserve, it is expected to get larger while the other reserves on the peninsula shrink or disappear. The process of rationalization of reserves which has been operating for the last twenty years may be seen to be continuing. Mapoon is gone, Weipa reserve has become a poor suburb of Weipa, and in 1978 legislation was brought before the Queensland Parliament with the intention of resuming the Aurukun Reserve in favour of a mining company. When the elected Aurukun council opposed the move the state government casually dissolved the council and the reserve. The Aurukun people now reside in a shire with a local government council which comes under the authority of the Queensland minister for local government. Since Aborigines on Mornington Island had supported the Aurukun community in the dispute they were dealt with in the same fashion.

This humiliating episode revealed the Australian government's powerlessness in this area. Senator Neville Bonner, the only Aborigine ever elected to federal parliament and a Queenslander himself, returned from a visit to the northern communities angry at federal inaction. He subsequently became the butt of savage ridicule from state government politicians.

The Aurukun episode clearly shows that as long as black aspirations clash with white intentions the future for Cape York Peninsula Aborigines is anything but secure.

14

Papuans

In June 1975 a Queensland politician complained in the state Legislative Assembly about illegal Papuan immigrants entering Queensland by way of the north Queensland fisheries. The Department of Labour in P.N.G. immediately replied in a public statement that no Papuans were engaged in fishing industries in Queensland, suggesting that all those so engaged were Torres Strait Islanders. It is difficult to know if the government of P.N.G. is really so ignorant of the situation (which is hard to believe) or if it is simply continuing an un-official version of Murray's policy of reluctant approval. Perhaps the Department of Labour is hesitant to end such a readily available source of income in an area which has achieved negligible economic progress since the start of the century. Indeed a number of villages in Papua depend almost entirely on money derived from employment in the strait.

At Christmas the luggers take the Papuan members of their crews back to their villages — mainly they are from Sigabada and the Pahoturi River area but sometimes from the Binaturi or even the Oriomo River further east or Buzi to the west. At any time in the days before Christmas two or three luggers may be anchored outside Mabadawan. Dinghies travel some distance up the river to Togo and Ngau discharging the crews as they go. The returning men are greeted joyously for most have been away for nearly a year and pearling is still dangerous. Also they return with as much as $1,000 saved after twelve months. This

represents an enormous sum in Papua (where even urban
workers are lucky to gross K1,500 annually) and, of course, it
will be the families which will benefit.

Much of the money earned by Papuans never leaves Australia
but is merely transferred to branches of the Island Industries
Board on northern islands of the Torres Strait. When a fellow
from Mabadawan wants some pocket money he sails across to
Saibai and presents his D.A.I.A. passbook to be paid. Probably
he will spend his cash at the I.I.B. store on Saibai, for the only
other store along this coast is at Sigabada and it cannot compete
for variety or quality with goods available on the Queensland
side. A thousand dollars will buy a lot of things for a family
which has had no money before. It is not surprising then that
when the luggers return recruiting early in the new year there is
no shortage of volunteers.

In the late 1970s the crews of most luggers consisted largely of
recruited Papuan labour working under conditions or wages
which Islanders, for one reason or another, no longer found
attractive. Recruiting in the Eastern Islands ceased a decade ago.
Although Badu and Boigu still contribute men, youngsters in
the other Western Islands show little interest in such employment. Pearling is not a healthy industry but it would not be
possible at all without Papuan labour. In this context it seems
the Queensland government has been prepared to turn a blind
eye to keep the industry going. Many lugger captains nonetheless have resorted to crayfishing which is far more profitable.
Yet even here, luggers with crews of six to a dozen men are
basically inefficient when compared to European operations
which normally employ only two or three men to a boat.
However the lugger captains alone cannot be blamed for the use
of Papuan labour. It is accepted practice for any boat around the
islands which is having trouble getting a crew, to pass over un-
announced to the Papuan coast where men are readily found —
and at cheaper rates.

Labour recruitment is a springboard for illegal immigrants.
Crews get paid off on Thursday Island and, impressed by the
bright lights, decide to stay. They may obtain employment with
certain businesses — once again at lower wages and under
conditions that an Islander would not tolerate.

As an illustration of just how easy it is for a Papuan to enter
Queensland, take the case of a Kiwai primary school teacher on

Daru who decided to visit obscure relatives on Erub during his Christmas holidays. It should be remembered that relationships may be claimed on a tenuous basis derived from a fairly liberal interpretation of a family tree or even from a legend or story linking one people with another. A "sister" could refer to a female third cousin, no relation whatsoever or a real sister. A "daughter" may be a niece, a real daughter or almost any female younger than the speaker. In these circumstances European concepts of family relationships count for very little and are totally unable to accommodate the elaborations of Melanesian society. So it is that a fellow on Daru may claim an "uncle" on Iama or Saibai or Erub.

The Kiwai teacher went to Erub for his holidays, was attracted by the wages being offered and obtained a place on the Q.G.V. *Melbidir*, the flagship so to speak of the D.A.I.A. fleet in the Torres Strait. At the completion of his holidays he returned to his teaching position on Daru — but many of his countrymen would not have returned, especially in view of the chronic job shortage in P.N.G.

Complicating the situation are the traditional trade links between the islands and Papua so that contact occurs constantly. Canoes sail down to Iama or Erub, Mabuiag or even as far south as Badu, trading mats, sago, cassowary feathers and bird of paradise plumes. The Islanders pay for these items with Australian money or food such as flour or tinned meat. Many Papuans know Western Island language, contact is always cordial and intermarriage occurred in the past. Furthermore the Islanders feel genuinely sorry for their poorer cousins and will not mind if on occasions Papuans take jobs, while they themselves remain on unemployment benefits. So many Papuans are found scattered around the islands.

Islanders from Erub, Mer, Ugar, Saibai and Boigu travel to Daru to purchase stores at lower prices than in Queensland. One fellow from Boigu in 1975 established himself in the lucrative illicit grog traffic. On trips once a month he loaded his dinghy to the waterline with cartons of beer and flagons of wine. On the far Western Islands he sold stubbies of beer for a dollar each (having bought them for thirty cents) and a flagon of wine for fifteen dollars. There are canteens on each island but when the canteen runs out or is closed, which frequently happens, then prices escalate to these black market levels.

However travel is often dangerous, for the waters along this coast are perpetually brown. Silt washed down from the Papuan mountains across a wide flood plain, empties from the Fly and a hundred other estuaries into the northern Torres Strait. Rocks, reefs and shallow patches — all of which can be read without difficulty by the colour variations further south — disappear in a welter of muddy waves. During the southeast season the un-protected coast is battered by swells breaking hundreds of yards to seaward and often concealed in the foam are huge water-logged tree trunks riding just below the surface. Closer to shore other hazards await, for this is the barramundi coast. Along the coast fishermen erect nylon barramundi nets up to fifty metres long, tied to stakes below the water line.

Large Papuan sailing canoes are frequently seen travelling to Daru or far down the southern horizon looking for crayfish on the Wapa Reef, or dugong off the eastern end of Saibai.

The hundreds of Papuans in the Torres Strait are not a problem at the moment but in the future it is inevitable that difficulties must arise. In September 1975 a group of Papuans had a rowdy Independence Day party on the verandah of a hotel on Thursday Island. As anticipated the evening degenerated into brawling between Papuans and Islanders.

However, more serious is the impact which cheap Papuan labour has made on an already depressed labour situation. Most Torres Strait Islanders are unskilled, and Papuan immigration forces them to compete with Papuans. The result is that labour is the cheapest in Australia with many people having to remain unemployed or accept wages of $40 to $50 a week (in 1976). Also the unscrupulous exploitation of eager Papuans has permitted otherwise uneconomic industries to function, with benefits for only a few individuals and organizations.

Today Daru in independent P.N.G. is little changed from colonial Daru, except that the whites have gone. The population has grown to about five thousand, many of whom live in crowded bush material houses in the "corners" — each corner representing a mother village somewhere on the mainland. The population growth required more land for housing so that much accommodation is now built on drained swamps. In places, houses need drains a metre wide and a metre deep on four sides feeding into larger channels running beside the main thorough-fares, merely to stay above the water. These drains are crossed by numerous wooden bridges and offer a considerable inconvenience to movement, especially at night after a few drinks. The drains are also the breeding ground of clouds of mosquitoes, so that malaria is common and treated casually, attack by attack, as though it were a headache.

There is still no development, with little more to do than drink or play football, although football has lost some of its appeal since the famous 1973 football riot when excited spectators kicked a Papuan player to death on the field and chased a European player through the corners, with every intention of doing the same to him if they caught him. The tennis court is an overgrown relic of the colonial past.

The disagreement among the white community on which Murray commented and which slowed development in the past, is present today among the elected black leaders. In fact to see democracy so obviously malfunctioning, from a European point of view, is quite startling. Rumours of corruption and malpractice are the subject of constant gossip and are so pervasive and widespread that they are commonly believed to be true.

Europeans are at first appalled by the situation but soon become hardened and cynical. From the Papuan point of view it represents a confusing blend of old and new. Whilst leadership has tended to devolve on a younger, educated elite, some traditional leaders have also had their positions ratified by election to local government offices. A man representing a certain group has a responsibility to serve that group, and in a narrower sense his own family, and is totally unconscious of the principles which might guide a European councillor in similar circumstances. It is inevitable that these men of limited education and experience have conflicts of interest and that their ineptitude must hamper real development.

It is difficult to assess the benefits which have accrued to the people of west Papua since D'Albertis shot his way up the Fly River. Many Papuans now use plastic rice bags sewn together as sails. Most have an item of clothing to wear if they go to Daru. Some go to high school but then have trouble getting a job anywhere in P.N.G., let alone Daru.

An Australian patrol officer from Morehead used to say "We've spoiled these people", pointing out that as soon as a coastal family had saved sufficient money they bought an outboard motor, which just as promptly broke down through

49. Woman with a gardening basket at Waidoro village near the Pahoturi River not far from Saibai. The people are subsistence farmers on land, which is low and wet with rich soil. Photograph by courtesy of the University of Papua New Guinea.

misuse and lack of maintenance. The same patrol officer questioned the wisdom of installing freezers in isolated villages as they could not be kept functioning. Why not show Papuans how to dry and smoke fish? Why not introduce buffaloes as draught animals? Why not grow rice as is done in Irian Jaya?

The future of this area is a giant question mark. There can be no government expansion until there is a stronger private sector to support it. Copper in quantity has been discovered on the Upper Alice River among the Star Mountains. Originally Kennecott had conducted surveys of the area from 1967 onwards. The results indicated that substantial amounts of copper could be found about Ok Tedi but Kennecott were unable to reach agreement with the P.N.G. government over details for its exploitation. In October 1976 a B.H.P.-led consortium launched a feasability study with a view to mining, having already decided to allow the P.N.G. government a 20 per cent interest in the project if it goes ahead.

The obstacles are formidable. Among isolated, rainforest covered mountains up to 2,500 metres high the consortium plans the construction of a hydro-electric dam, crushing sites, an open-cut mine and all its facilities including accommodation for hundreds of men. Kiunga, a thousand kilometres from the sea will become a bulk handling depot for transporting ore by barge down the Fly River.

However, the exploitation of this copper might prove a mixed blessing to the people of the Western Province. There would be more money available for development and probably hundreds of well-paid jobs (by P.N.G. standards) but exploitation would fracture local society as has occurred at Bougainville. The consequences along the Fly could be the most far-reaching and potentially disastrous since D'Albertis's time.

The other major resource is fish. At times a canoe with an ice box will sail south to Wapa Reef, catch some crayfish and try to get back to Daru before the crayfish spoil. The villages near Daru lay barramundi nets in all directions during the barramundi season. Over the season of four to six months a fisherman can make two thousand dollars or more. But only during the season and only close to a freezer. Large fishing vessels with freezers are required with professional crews, yet these boats are owned by whites and the whites are leaving. The government discourages white enterprise whilst nationalist politicians often take a more direct method and simply tell the European to leave — though not officially.

So over the last few years Thursday Island has seen a sad straggle of exiled whites drift across the Torres Strait. Some are elderly and many have Papuan or New Guinean wives and children. For those who have spent their lives in P.N.G. there is no point in going any further south to an alien environment.

In 1972 there were 67,000 people living in the Western Province. In some areas people are still living in a confused limbo between the stone and the steel ages. Probably one of the most remote, backward areas in P.N.G. is the Nomad Sub Province; isolated among the mountains three hundred kilometres north of Daru, it is troubled by murderers and cannibals even today.

One aspect of the controversy surrounding Queensland's northern border that was much neglected was the presence of a third party — Indonesia. Boigu, part of Queensland, is actually closer to Irian Jaya than it is to mainland Australia. At a point about a hundred and sixty kilometres to the northwest of

Thursday Island the borders of three nations (P.N.G., Australia and Indonesia) meet. Generally however Indonesia remained silent in respect to the Queensland border question, because there has been enough trouble along its common border with P.N.G.

Although efforts have been made to establish cordial relations between Jakarta and Port Moresby, some Papua New Guineans continue to distrust Indonesia and, in view of the seizure of West New Guinea in 1963 and East Timor in 1975, regard its presence as threatening. However Indonesia's apparent aggressiveness is connected closely with the original national revolution which followed World War II. The nationalist government in Java claimed to have displaced the Dutch throughout all of the Netherlands East Indies including West New Guinea. The Dutch attempted to separate West New Guinea and the Papuans who lived there from the Malay revolution to the west. But this proved impossible.

Malay traders had been interacting with Papuans around the coast of New Guinea for over three centuries. Furthermore during the long struggle for independence hundreds of Indonesian political prisoners had been detained in Dutch prison camps in New Guinea. Among them were many who later ruled Indonesia with Sukarno. Hatta, who was vice-president of the Indonesian Republic from 1945 to 1956, was held in a camp on the Digul River for some years by the Dutch. Thus West New Guinea to many Indonesians became associated with Dutch oppression, and for them its seizure was justified on traditional and nationalistic grounds but the action was taken without regard for the Papuan people who lived there.

Many sophisticated Papuans had been led by the Dutch to expect movement towards independence as in P.N.G. Naturally these people resented Indonesian designs and expressed their resentment — unsuccessfully. With the controversial "Act of Free Choice" in 1963 West New Guinea was officially incorporated into the Republic of Indonesia, but before this Indonesian troops were seen beating Papuan separatists with bicycle chains.

Since that time some development has undeniably taken place. One example is the Arafura Sea prawn fishery around the Aru Islands. Japanese companies first made surveys and started joint ventures in 1969 from Serong on the south coast of Irian

Jaya. The initial catch of 504 tonnes has since increased to greater than 35,000 tonnes annually. But there is another side to the coin. Indigenous development such as has occurred in the Western Province of P.N.G. is unknown.

When three Australian school teachers from Daru travelled by motor bike to Merauke in Irian Jaya, they found the contrast quite startling, especially the absence of Papuans in the town. There were rice paddies, water buffaloes, Javanese school teachers and Indonesian soldiers doubling up the street but Papuans lived on the fringes or in the bush. Dissatisfaction with Indonesian administration is illustrated by the movement of Papuans from Irian Jaya into P.N.G.

Fishermen tell of boatloads of people fleeing east and refugees from Irian Jaya may be found scattered along the coast of Papua today. Some of the better educated, though initially handicapped by their lack of knowledge of English, are fortunate to have obtained jobs with the P.N.G. administration. It is ironic that the present day Tugeri, in this time of unrest, have sought sanctuary amongst their traditional enemies in the east.

Initially the Indonesians hunted these fugitives down, sometimes firing on Australian patrols they encountered. In 1968 two Papuan carriers working with such a patrol were shot dead twenty kilometres inside P.N.G. by Indonesian soldiers. Since that time however, despite persistent rumours in the Western Province of further shootings, no serious trouble is known to have occurred.

The situation has now eased somewhat. Traditional border crossings for the purposes of tending gardens and so on are generally viewed with leniency by the Indonesian administration, though Indonesian troops have visited Papuan villages inside P.N.G. distributing leaflets urging Irianese refugees to return home.

This is very different from the situation which prevails in northeast Irian Jaya, adjoining the West Sepik Province of P.N.G., and the Central Highland of Irian Jaya. Here some eighteen hundred Papuan insurgents of the O.P.M. (Organisasi Papua Merdeka) battle Indonesian regulars, seeking aid among supporters in P.N.G. when hard pressed. The situation is fraught with danger. In May 1977 a Papua New Guinean was claimed to have been killed by Indonesian troops within P.N.G.

Two months later an R.A.A.F. helicopter, engaged in a mapping project with Indonesian forces, crashed killing an Australian officer and severely injuring three Australians and an Indonesian officer. O.P.M. leaders claim the aircraft was shot down by their guerillas and warned that any aircraft involved in similar activities would also be fired upon. Within days an Australian army light aircraft was holed by small arms fire. O.P.M. insists, with some justification, that Australia is aiding the Indonesians in genocide.

Early 1979 saw the arrest in Madang of Yacob Prai, the O.P.M. leader and several of his supporters. Though officially said to have been seeking medical assistance, Prai was apparently involved in negotiations with an arms dealer. It remains to be seen what effect his arrest will have on the resistance movement. Prai has since been granted asylum in Sweden.

On the south coast of Irian Jaya, adjoining the Western Province, O.P.M. activity appears limited to subversion and isolated instances of sabotage. Reciprocal familiarization visits conducted on a regular basis between Merauke and Daru have helped to prevent difficulties arising. In fact the relationship between Irian Jaya and the Western Province seems far more cordial than that which Queensland enjoys with Daru.

This is not just a result of the recent Torres Strait border dispute but also emphasizes the clash of cultures which occurs here. Indonesia, as a developing nation in tropical Asia, has much of practical value which is readily applicable to the physical and economic environment of southwestern Papua. Queensland by comparison could make little constructive contribution except in the field of saltwater fishing. The expensive confusion at Bamaga is symptomatic of Queensland's ineptitude in the development of tropical areas by indigenous peoples.

Nevertheless it can only be hoped that in the future development of Irian Jaya the indigenous Papuan peoples will be the ones who finally benefit. It must also be hoped that the violent civil disturbances in Irian Jaya do not spread to its southeast corner where people of the northwest Torres Strait will be affected, although there are indications that this may already be happening.

15

The Islands Today

*Sydney Pa New South Wales Border**

Ngitha nguimun kunia wananoo
Ina B.R.I.S. bane, Brisbane
Ngitha cross manu wara Dthaudthai border
Kutthai gau, bab tau, too kui pau ngu lai gna
Kai ngul pa, Iagar, yawor
Innubi guiga mee luggia ngeh gar poothis
Kai ngul pa armartheh Blue Mountains
Sydney pa New South Wales au border
Wara dar gar mu Dthaudthai pa eh.

When the war ended in 1945 it seemed impossible to many
Torres Strait Islanders that they could return to live on the
islands as they had done before the war. Enlistment and their
performance in the T.S.L.I. had boosted their self-confidence,

* The translation is:
  You have left us behind.
  This is Brisbane.
  You have crossed the border to another mainland.
  My youngest (in the family), sister and cousin are journeying,
  Going down, I am sorrowful, good bye.
  Going down near to the Blue Mountains,
  To Sydney over the New South Wales border,
  The other side of the mainland.

This song in Western Island language is representative of modern language
songs. Gone are traditional subjects such as fishing and legends. The stress
on travel and parting is appropriate, for Islanders on the mainland are very
mobile and, typically, do not keep in touch.

whilst the friendliness and assistance proffered by the average white Australian soldier was something which most had not previously experienced.

The Torres Strait Islanders Act of 1939 had allowed for considerable authority to be wielded by the Island councils, but the new policy of "assimilation", which arose after the war, tempted ambitious Islanders away from their homes to the glittering cities of the south.

In 1951 Hasluck, at that time minister for territories, called a meeting of federal and state ministers responsible for Aboriginal affairs. The conference adopted a policy of "assimilation", later defined as assisting indigenous Australians to attain "the same manner of living as other Australians and live as members of a single Australian community..." This obviously could not be done while Islanders persisted with their distinctive lifestyle on the islands.

The "model" village was constructed at Tamwoy on Thursday Island, still separate and still a reserve, but the results of this move were dramatic and irreversible. Many ex-T.S.L.I. men settled on Thursday Island, some at Tamwoy, but others at a settlement around the eastern end of the island named T.S.L.I. Before the war, Islanders had not been permitted to live on the island but now, for the first time, Torres Strait Islanders resident there were absorbed into the Island Industries Board slipway workforce. The Island Industries Board is a modern, enlarged version of the earlier Papuan Industries Ltd. It has a retail monopoly on the islands of the Torres Strait and northern peninsula reserves and maintains a shell store (pearl and trochus) on Thursday Island. Other Islanders found work with the D.N.A. or in private industry.

Some Islanders were attracted to Thursday Island by the facilities available, such as hospital care. A minority were seduced by the availability of alcohol, although legally they could not drink. In the dark outside hotels waited knots of thirsty blacks, and sometimes a drunken white was assaulted and relieved of his drinks. Island girls were given alcohol by white men, though the utmost discretion was required, and it is even rumoured that one bakery produced a "bottle loaf", ten times the normal price, which included a bottle of cheap wine with the bread. Drinking of "metho" increased as Islanders lived outside their own strictly regulated communities. Old sheds and derelict buildings at the front of Thursday Island in what had been Yokohama and Malaytown were converted into accommodation for the steady stream of migrants from the Outer Islands.

On Thursday Island some Islanders lived much the same as they had on the islands — few furnishings, no electricity, water collected in buckets, and wood stoves. Even the houses at Tamwoy had no reticulated water within the houses (and still do not). They were tiny and easily overcrowded and constructed of fibro which needed continual maintenance.

Some Islanders realized this was not the new life promised through assimilation. The more confident began moving south, obtaining jobs with the railway, as cane cutters and labourers. Those who had difficulty adapting returned to the islands, but their stories of the south and the luxuries to be found there merely increased the desire of others to see this life.

As pearling died there was added impetus to migrate and hundreds of unemployed men left the Torres Strait. Yet the dazzling history of pearling blinded many people to the social decay which was the industry's only inheritance. During this time many visitors arriving on the tour ship *Waiben* were intoxicated by the atmosphere of pearls — the adventure and intrigue which their imaginations had manufactured. Unfortunately, as long as the public's vision was clouded by such romanticism the stark realities of the situation, which demanded urgent attention, were obscured.

Significant Island communities grew in Cairns, Townsville, Mackay and Brisbane, though other groups are scattered throughout the rest of Queensland and Australia. Wherever employment, social conditions and other elements are suitable, Islanders have settled in hundreds, dozens, couples or singly, often becoming totally absorbed in their new environment — most never seeing their islands again and lost to their people. Communication is a day to day matter and Islanders do not usually write letters.

In 1971 there were 96 Islanders in Tasmania, 773 in New South Wales, 715 in Victoria, 159 in South Australia, 278 in Western Australia, and 128 in the Northern Territory. After a few years in the south there is little likelihood that they will return to the Torres Strait with its poor housing, chronic unemployment, low wages, extravagant prices, restrictive atmosphere and limited future. By 1971, of 9,664 Torres Strait Islanders in Australia, only 4,510 lived in the Torres Strait (including Bamaga), and only 7,508 in Queensland.

It is important to note the relevance of the assimilation policy to the recent Torres Strait border dispute. Before 1940 the border could probably have been moved south without much reaction by the Islanders, but in the 1970s, with the greater part of the race living throughout southern Australia and with those on the Islands looking keenly to white Australian salaries, luxuries and expectations — as they have been led to do over the last thirty years — they strongly resisted any border change.

In some ways, the process of migration selects the most adaptable individuals for life in the south — those who are better educated, or speak English a little better, or have had wider job experience. But it is not true to say that all those remaining on the islands are not courageous enough to explore the south or have failed in the south. Some men genuinely prefer Island life and work hard at it — hunting, fishing, gardening — but they are a dying breed, and the atmosphere may vary tremendously from island to island. Too often the people of the village are sitting under trees during the day, eating rice, biscuits and tea, talking and waiting for their pension cheques. The migration of more than half their race has left its mark. Among the Islanders of the Torres Strait as a whole women outnumber men by 19 per cent, but on Thursday Island women outnumber their men by a staggering 25 per cent. Those absent are also predominantly younger men — the very people necessary for the proper functioning of Island society, since most middle-aged men have retired.

In 1965 Aborigines and Islanders were legally permitted to drink, though not on reserves. It is now more than ten years since that time but the adjustment period needed for such a radical step has not yet run its course. Many of the 1,600 Islanders living about Thursday Island exist in an erratic world of beer and taxis.

Thursday Island has from a dozen to twenty taxis on the road at any one time for a population of about 2,300 — without a doubt the highest proportion of taxis to population in Australia.

Taxi driving is a gruelling job, made all the more arduous because it is a form of employment which brings a European driver into contact with one of the Islanders' major traits — the

50, 51. The colonial-style customs house on Thursday Island, recalling a time
when the island was the northern gateway to Australia. In contrast are the
traditional houses, constructed of rough timber and intricate patterns of
woven coconut leaves, on one of the sand cays of the Central Islands.
Photograph 51 by courtesy of J. Manasero.

lackadaisical observance of time and economics. Some families spend up to 20 per cent of their weekly income on taxi rides, and the taxis run more or less according to Island fashion, most of the passengers and a large proportion of the drivers being Islanders.

Sometimes a driver can earn a fortune in one night. At Christmas, Islanders return home from all over Australia where they have been working during the year, saving up money for a month-long spree. One driver was hired by a group of fellows who had just returned from the Japanese pearl culture station at Kuri Bay in Western Australia. They wanted an all night "ride". A "ride" on Thursday Island is a form of entertainment involving a number of passengers, a taxi, its driver and other odds and ends including tape recorders and stubbies. The taxi moves around the island at 25 k.p.h. stopping off at the various scenic spots. The occupants of the taxi may throw greetings, abuse or bottles at the people they pass. There are no meters and the driver charges according to time elapsed, distance travelled and inconvenience suffered. As the driver announced the passing of each hour one of his passengers would push another twenty-dollar note into his pocket. By morning his pocket was bulging with notes.

Frequently the workers returning from the south or the west dispose of their accumulated savings in a few weeks, spending the bulk of it on relatives who may come to meet them on Thursday Island for this very purpose. This is where Island traditions clash most strongly with the new ways of the European. Young people working hard and perhaps earning good wages by standards on the islands (where anything over $100 a fortnight is looked upon as favourable) are often expected to contribute a greater proportion of their money to family members, and do so without obvious resentment usually. This arrangement combined with generous pensions, encourages middle-aged men and women to retire into houses provided by the government and adopt a series of children who, through familial obligation, will be required to support them in their old age. This is a logical development from traditional practices in the extended family, designed to ensure that elderly people always have youngsters responsible for their welfare. This structure of obligations is gradually and inevitably disintegrating under the weight of European education, attitudes and material culture, yet despite a decline it maintains a strong hold over Islanders in an Island environment.

The effect of the custom on responsible saving and home management by the young could be summed up this way: "If you have some money then spend it today, for tomorrow you may have to give it away!" It is little wonder that young Islanders living and working in the south, where a greater variety of goods and services is available at lower prices, show reluctance sometimes in returning to the Torres Strait, where this constant drain on their incomes continually drags them to the edge of poverty.

It would be a different matter if there were a strong basis of subsistence production and the cash economy was merely a fringe benefit, but in many cases subsistence crops have disappeared. Some Island communities are in danger of becoming totally parasitic societies.

The collapse of pearling has left Island males virtually without employment. Although almost three hundred vessels were licensed to fish prawns in the Gulf of Carpentaria during the 1977 season, only a handful of Islanders will obtain employment in this industry. Partly this is because few boats actually trawl for prawns in the strait or to the northwest about Irian Jaya. For the majority of vessels working in the gulf, Weipa, Normanton and Kurumba are more convenient ports of call. Nevertheless most boats make a point of calling at Thursday Island at least twice in the season, even if it is only at the start and finish.

There are three wharves on Port Kennedy. Starting at the western end of Thursday Island, these are the Engineers Jetty, Main Wharf and Navy Wharf. The Main Wharf, which was recently rebuilt, has been the scene of much drama and violence. Several old drunks over the years have mysteriously fallen off late at night and been drowned. Ten years ago a European armed with a rifle shot a young Islander in the leg on the wharf. The limb was later amputated at the knee. The Islander involved, now in his mid twenties, stumps about the hotels today with a wooden leg. One prawner, a witness in a rape trial, was found hanged at the wharf some years ago, on the very morning on which he was supposed to fly out for the hearing in Cairns. Assaults and brawls are common late at night. On a night in 1972 three Europeans had their jaws broken in savage skirmishing that spread along the wharf and even spilled onto the decks of the prawn boats.

Much of this trouble revolves around "wharf rats" (young

Island women sometimes in their early teens) and "dragons' (middle-aged hags), who haunt the wharves searching for drinks and a good time.

The prawners tend to be older men of wide experience — tough, sunbronzed and cynical. It is alarming to watch them seduce with apparent ease Island girls in their mid teens, some of whom during the day attend the high school. These girls of seventeen and eighteen sometimes accompany the boats as cooks-cum-concubines into the gulf or down the coast to Cairns. They are often sexually aggressive but prostitution as such is rare. There appears to be some underlying psychological motive beneath the casual exterior and devil-may-care attitude. Traditionally Island society is strictly male dominated but over the years unscrupulous women have discovered that sex is man's Achilles' heel — a way of evening the score. Past relations with married men or important personages may be used as a form of moral blackmail. A pompous or overbearing man is readily embarrassed by public exposure of his seduction and inability to resist temptation, the status of the shrewd woman responsible rising correspondingly. As Europeans came to dominate the islands so they became the target of these seductions. There is great rivalry between competitors as they seek to tempt a white "superior", and afterwards as they vie for notoriety in revealing his lapse. Sometimes alleged behaviour of this sort is mere fabrication. Certain government officials are widely claimed in Island circles to be involved though it is difficult to believe that all the excesses attributed to them are true.

A European teacher on an Outer Island, justifiably or not, acquired something of a reputation in this respect. Islanders, after listening to the story of another of his supposed affairs, observed contemptuously "nuther kind whiteman" or "whiteman for nothing". This denigration probably acts as a kind of safety valve for a depressed society which is unable to score at any other level and also probably explains why no similar blame falls upon the woman involved. In fact quite the opposite frequently occurs and she is lionized by her fellows since she was sufficiently desirable to tempt the European in the first place. However these scheming *femme fatales* are the exception rather than the norm.

A brash minority of women, loitering about bars and wharves on Thursday Island, sometimes convey to visitors the impression of unbridled promiscuity. Such an assumption demeans the bulk of Island women who are the backbone of Island society and who struggle to raise families, often enlarged by adopted children, in trying circumstances. On some islands the women are required to do much of the gardening and fishing and to cut trees down in the swamp or scrub for fire wood, as well as their normal household duties which are performed without the convenience of fridges, vacuum cleaners, washing machines or electric stoves. The absence of many of the men throws an even greater strain on these women.

Those Island girls who persevere at school may complete their grade ten year, then attend special business college courses conducted for them in Cairns and Brisbane. If after their twelve-month course they return to the Torres Strait, and many do not, they are thrust into offices full of European males, for curiously the educational process which allows them to become typists and secretaries does not prepare Island males for clerical or administrative positions. It should be remembered though that Island females vastly outnumber Island males, especially in the crucial age group around twenty, and that many Island males in this group are unemployed anyway and have difficulty competing with young Europeans. Inevitably these girls are drawn into a clique where males are white and females coloured, this being a fairly normal situation at a "mixed" party on Thursday Island. As a consequence an extraordinary number of Island women are married to, or living with, European men, and illegitimate halfcaste births have reached tragic proportions.

Young Island males meanwhile are found out of work or lingering in hopeless D.A.I.A. jobs. Some mixed race men have completed apprenticeships and gained masters' tickets for various categories of small ships, but Torres Strait Islanders have had little success in these fields. There are no Island tradesmen in the Torres Strait.

A similar story concerns tertiary studies. A woman from the Hammond Island mission was awarded a bachelor of science from the University of P.N.G. in Port Moresby and in 1979 George Passi, a teacher from Mer, was awarded a bachelor of arts from the University of Queensland. In the 90 years since the Papuan Institute began on Mer and the 13 years since secondary education became available on Thursday Island these are the only resident Islanders to complete tertiary courses. A special course is conducted for Islanders at teachers colleges in Brisbane, but these courses are necessarily aimed at lower secondary level as many Island primary school teachers have never attended high school.

This sorry record is an indictment of the whole inadequate educational system which is allowed to exist in the Torres Strait. It is ordained that any contact between the Outer Islands and the rest of the world — be it educational, medical or social — can occur only through D.A.I.A. agencies. With the exclusion of those at Thursday Island and Bamaga, all teachers in the area come under the D.A.I.A., including a number of European advisory staff. Undertrained and underpaid, these Island teachers send half-educated students to the secondary schools at Thursday Island and Bamaga, where the teaching staffs are entirely European and, of course, the students generally under-achieve and therefore fail to receive satisfactory employment when they leave school.

In June 1975 the Schools Commission presented its report to the federal government. Included in the report were recommendations from an Aboriginal consultative group which included two Island representatives. One comment is particularly appropriate: "We recommend to the Queensland Government that it consider transferring schools in the Torres Strait Islands from the administration of the Queensland Department of Aboriginal and Islanders Advancement to the Queensland Department of Education as quickly as possible". The report also recommended that a three-year high school with boarding facilities be established on one of the central Torres Strait Islands. From its inception the Bamaga high school scheme was seen by Islanders for what it is — another factor in the struggle by the white administration to encourage migration to Cape York. Demands by Island communities since well before 1975 for a secondary school in the islands have been consistently ignored.

Yet this is not the whole story. Around 1970 Island students in the schools were applying themselves and achieving more. Today's students lack motivation and consistently under-achieve. Even though paid by the federal government to attend school, students frequently stay away. At the high school on Thursday Island in 1976, for example, the daily truancy rate was up to twenty per cent for Island students.

The right to drink alcohol, the right to vote and the right to travel anywhere in Australia seeking employment all seem to have shown Islanders a path to another better world. European-style formal education was going to be the key which opened the gate to that world, but it has now been tried and found wanting.

A child born on the islands and growing to maturity will find himself a member of an extended family. Often children are adopted and raised by other than their natural parents, though it matters little in this context since there will be so many adults associated directly or indirectly with their upbringing. He will experience little externally imposed discipline (by European standards) and consequently little stress, providing he observes the customs of a strongly patriarchal society (where the women and children generally sit down to eat only after the men have eaten). Normal household tasks will be performed as a matter of course (chopping firewood, collecting water, running errands) and any child shirking these responsibilities may find himself in trouble. But apart from these basic functions, the individual child will be subject to few pressures. Many boys never learn Island dancing. They may never have indicated an interest in it and are therefore not forced to participate. Similarly others may show an enthusiasm and peculiar aptitude for dugong hunting. One who does not will not be pressed, but those who are successful hunters will share their meat across the whole extended family.

Generally the effect is that each individual appears to select a role which best suits himself and pursues that role for the benefit of the group. Even those unusual individuals who finally specialize in nothing are good-naturedly accepted (in most cases) by the others and often thereby seem to fulfil their own special role in society — frequently that of a buffoon or one who does nothing.

European-style education — emphasizing competition between individuals and generally insisting on a universal and comprehensive education in which everyone participates — sharply contradicts the general trend of customary Island society. Naturally the interaction of these black traditional and white academic values will influence and eventually change both the Island society and the European educational system.

Even in those cases though where a student has succeeded academically it is generally a case where the youth has once again selected a role for which he is suited and, if this enables him to receive higher wages, then this money will be spread across the extended family in the customary manner, though probably not in any systematic fashion.

Today it appears that it is not just education which has been tested and found wanting. Disillusionment is settling over broad sectors of the Island community, leading to further calls for government aid. Apart from supplying pensions and service jobs, airstrips are constructed, large prefabricated aluminium houses are built and expensive hospital boats are provided (which are frequently out of commission due to maintenance problems). Large grants are awarded to Island co-operatives with little else in mind than the creation of employment.

Despite this deluge of money, Island populations continue to fall (most islands have permanent populations of between one and two hundred) and, excepting Badu, no Island is involved in commercial production (except for minor cottage industries). This is not to say that they have no potential. Two Europeans on a nine-metre boat in one month of hard work, almost within sight of Erub, took $14,000 worth of mackerel, yet the Erubians sold no fish and absorb government grants of up to a quarter of a million dollars. This is the pattern throughout the Islands.

Despite such expenditure, there are massive health problems. In February 1977 a six-month-old child died of meningitis whilst being brought from Erub to the hospital on Thursday Island. It was established that the cause of the child's death was the lack of injectable penicillin at the D.A.I.A. clinic on Erub. The hospital superintendent at Thursday Island complained that he had made repeated approaches over a number of years to have the supply of drugs to the Island clinics supervised by qualified pharmacists within the Department of Health, only to be rebuffed each time. The superintendent also criticized the D.A.I.A. for using personnel totally untrained and unqualified in clinical medicine or medical administration.

Compounding the problem is the fact that disease is widespread throughout the islands. V.D. is out of control, sugar diabetes and high blood pressure are rife, and T.B., though much reduced since the 1950s, is still present. Occasionally, ugly cases of leprosy occur whilst the incessant migration of Papuans causes malaria scares every couple of years. As a result the average life expectancy of a Torres Strait Islander in the Torres

Strait in the 1970s was below fifty years of age, compared to an average life expectancy of over seventy for other Australians.

Despite the liberalization of some things, such as the sale of liquor through wet canteens on reserves, the D.A.I.A. has successfully retained educational, medical and employment control of reserve communities. But the most sweeping and intimidating of its powers is the right to approve or disapprove of a person entering a reserve Island. As whites are never permitted to live on the islands, unless they work for the D.A.I.A., then the many Island women and men who have married whites may never again live on the Island of their birth. They and their children are exiled for life, and may only visit occasionally, renewing contact with a world they love but one that will die. Their halfcaste children must be brought up in a European society.

Perhaps the only encouraging sign in this otherwise fairly depressing picture is the strength of indigenous languages. P. Sutton of the Australian Institute of Aboriginal Studies reported in 1975 that the Western Island language had a "speaker population" of about two thousand. This means that of all surviving indigenous languages in Australia the Western Island language has the second largest number of speakers, after the Western Desert language which has a speaker population of three to four thousand. A speaker population of seven hundred for the Eastern Island language is also claimed — but this seems unlikely. Many people use this language, including a good number of Europeans, but only a limited number of elderly people still utilize it as a language. The remainder speak broken English which is the normal medium of communications between peoples of the three island groups (Western, Central and Eastern). It is accepted, even today when inter-island communication is so simple, that each island may have its own unique variation of the main group language with the emphasis on construction, pronunciation or both. An example is the severe gutteral pronunciation of some Boigu people which is unmistakeable amongst all other Torres Strait dialects. Another example is found in the shorter construction of many Badu words. For example, "quick" is *kasigei* on Badu and *kasaiginga* on Saibai.

However, despite the continual use of these languages, it is conceded that in general the older, more complex word structures (place names for example) are being superseded by convenient shorter terms. Many youngsters admit frankly that they are unable to pronounce these old words. But this deterioration is balanced to some extent by the vitality with which new words are constantly being adopted, used and, where necessary, discarded.

On one occasion in 1973 while conversing with Islanders from Mer, I invented a word as an exclamation of dismay and shock — a very useful type of expression. It was favourably received and the memorable day arrived eight weeks later when another Meriam, ignorant of the word's origin and in all sincerity, tried to explain to me the meaning of the "Island word" which I had invented. Yet because the word lacked the qualities necessary for its wider adoption, within another two months it was no longer in use, and quickly disappeared.

This adaptability has permitted traditional languages to survive one hundred years of white domination, but with migration and detribalization, a more systematic effort is required if these languages are to survive a further century. Up until several years ago it was a punishable offence for Island students to speak their own language whilst within the grounds of the Thursday Island state school.

The 1970s have seen many changes, but what seemed to be the dawning of a new age for the Torres Strait Islanders could also be their twilight as a distinct race within Australia. This may be inevitable, given the present situation, but there are alternatives, though they require the support of a committed, cohesive Torres Strait Island community. Such widespread support appears to be lacking at the moment, although the border dispute did rally Island leaders, and the people they represent, into something of a politically active body.

Culture clash and conflict are of course only one part of the picture. They are generally hidden from white visitors by the gregarious nature, genuine hospitality and generosity of the Islanders. Few newcomers fail to be impressed by these qualities. Europeans visiting Torres Strait communities in an official capacity are liable to be treated with a deference and respect which can be embarassing. Informally however the hospitality is very real and touching. An Islander in a hotel, whom you met for the first time half an hour before, will call you *hala* or *sisi* (broken English for brother and sister) and buy you a six-pack of stubbies as he leaves. A casual acquaintance may suggest that he would be honoured by your attendance at a wedding feast or tombstone opening.

The cemetery at Thursday Island begins on a flat at the north of the island, gradually rising above a gully, with a rough, rock-strewn road winding precariously upwards. On the crests to each side of the road the more august members of the European community have been buried. On the eastern side stands an imposing grey monument which marks the last resting place of Sir John Douglas once Premier of Queensland, Special Commissioner to British New Guinea and Thursday Island Resident. Here also lie a European murdered at Badu in 1878 and a row of victims from the 1890 *Quetta* disaster. Further down there is a straggle of less auspicious personalities — men and women in their early twenties who died at pearling stations on Muralug in the 1880s and batches of poor children, some from visiting ships, mourned by grieving parents. There are two brown stone memorials to dead officers and men of the garrison artillery with clutches of rusting artillery shells about the bases.

On the western slopes of the gully, peeping through long, matted grass, are the tombstones of some of the old white families of the strait and a police constable killed in the line of duty during the early part of this century.

Beside the road in the gully bottom are a hundred South Sea graves. Although most epitaphs are in South Sea languages, the South Sea Islanders were Christian and so gained a place in the upper cemetery.

At the gully's lower entrance Moslems were buried (and continue to be today) and further down are forests of concrete Japanese grave posts. Hundreds of Japanese lie here with character epitaphs running down the posts and often a frangipani tree growing from the midst of a grave. Originally some finely carved wooden posts had been erected but few have survived the grass fires that periodically sweep through the area. Since the war the graves of Torres Strait Islanders have dotted the ground along the main road to the west of the old Japanese section.

In many respects these graves are the only lasting and visible reminders of the various peoples who contributed so much to the history of the Torres Straits. Their influence though is still echoed in the contemporary culture of the islands.

At a feast I have seen elderly Islanders stand to sing Japanese songs learned whilst working on luggers forty years ago. South Sea Island melodies and dances predominate. Some South Sea songs have been handed down from generation to generation over a century, changing in the process. Others are taken from recordings of Fijian or Samoan contemporary music. But this is not restricted to the Islands, for there is striking pan-culturalism across the whole region. The most astonishing example I saw of this was in Rabaul where my wife from Saibai, a man from Kupaire (northeast of the Pahoturi River mouth in P.N.G.) and another from Kerema (in P.N.G. hundreds of kilometres east of Saibai) performed together without rehearsal the "Kookaburra" dance — a simple but popular Torres Strait form. The tune and actions from each area were almost identical. Influences are absorbed by a group and transmitted to other groups creating a lifestyle which is an amalgamation of many features.

Some ancient customs persist. On Saibai the dance of the Aitthalgal before the *adthibuia* is remembered and played out before packed audiences on Thursday Island during the Saibai dancers' annual visit to the island. On Mer the extensive networks of stone fish traps (*sai*) are maintained with difficulty. However the young do not identify with this world and increasingly have assumed the appearance and habits of Afro-American culture as it has filtered through to the Torres Strait. This imported black image may likewise be incorporated into the composite Island lifestyle, along with all the other influences, or maybe it will help to finally obliterate what remains of genuine Island culture.

Islanders have a great confidence in themselves and they exert enormous energy in activities which interest them. But where this confidence and energy will take them no one seems to know, least of all the Islanders themselves.

Sources

Introduction

Blainey, G. *Triumph of the Nomads.* Melbourne: Macmillan, 1975.

Brierly, O.W. "Journals of the H.M.S. Rattlesnake 1848-49". Manuscript. Mitchell Library, Sydney.

Haddon, A. *Head Hunters: Black, White and Brown.* London: Methuen, 1900.

Idriess, I. *Drums of Mer.* Sydney: Angus and Robertson, 1933.

Lawrie, M. *Myths and Legends of Torres Strait.* Brisbane: University of Queensland Press, 1970.

Reports of the Cambridge Anthropological Expedition to Torres Strait. 6 vols. Cambridge, 1901-35.

Souter, G. *New Guinea: The Last Unknown* Sydney: Angus and Robertson, 1963.

Walker, D., ed. *Bridge and Barrier: The Natural and Cultural History of Torres Strait.* Canberra: Australian National University Press, 1972.

Williams, R.E. *Papuans of the Trans-Fly.* Oxford: Clarendon Press, 1936.

1. The First Whitemen

Bateson, C. *Australian Shipwrecks, Vol. 1. 1622-1850.* Sydney: A.H. and A.W. Reed, 1972.

Bayton, J. *Cross Over Carpentaria.* Brisbane: Smith and Paterson, 1965.

Blainey, G. *Triumph of the Nomads.* Melbourne: Macmillan, 1975.

Captain Cook's Journal. Libraries Board of South Australia, 1968.

Dunbabin, T. *Sailing the World's Edge.* London: Newnes, 1931.

Feekin, E. and G., and Spate, O. *The Discovery and Exploration of Australia.* Melbourne: Nelson, 1970.

Gill, W. Wyatt. "Three Visits to New Guinea". Royal Geographical Society of London, Vol. 44, 1874.

Haddon A. *Head Hunters: Black, White and Brown.*

Hilder, B. "The Voyage of Torres". Forthcoming (in 1980) from University of
    Queensland Press.
Idriess, I. *Coral Sea Calling.* Sydney: Angus and Robertson, 1957.
————. *The Wild White Man of Badu.* Sydney: Angus and Robertson, 1950.
Ingleton, G.C. *True Patriots All.* Sydney: Angus and Robertson, 1952.
Jukes, J.B. *Narrative of the Surveying Voyage of the H.M.S. Fly.* London: Boone,
    1847.
Mackaness, G. *The Life of the Vice-Admiral William Bligh.* Sydney: Angus and
    Robertson, 1931.
Queensland Heritage, Vol. 3, No. 1, November 1974.
Reports of the Cambridge Anthropological Expedition to Torres Strait.
Souter, G. *New Guinea: The Last Unknown.*

2. *Cape York Peninsula: Explorers and Developers*

Bateson, C. *Australian Shipwrecks, vol. 1, 1622-1850.*
Bayton, J. *Cross Over Carpentaria.*
Beale, E. *Kennedy of Cape York.* Adelaide: Rigby, 1970.
Blainley, G. *Triumph of the Nomads.*
Captain Cook's Journal.
Cummins and Campbell's Monthly Magazine, November 1952.
Douglas, J. *Past and Present of Thursday Island and Torres Strait.* Brisbane:
    Gutridge Press, 1900.
Dunbabin, T. *Sailing the World's Edge.*
Farnfield, J. *Frontiersman.* Oxford University Press, 1968
Franklin, M. *Black and White Australians.* Melbourne: Heinemann, 1976.
Feekin E. and G., and Spate, O. *The Discovery and Exploration of Australia.*
Holthouse, H. *River of Gold* Sydney: Angus and Robertson, 1967.
Idriess, I. *Coral Sea Calling.*
"Lectures in North Queensland History". James Cook University, 1974.
Jinks, B., Biskup, P., and Nelson, H., eds. *Readings in New Guinea History.*
    Sydney: Angus and Robertson, 1973.
Marshall, A. *These Were My Tribesmen.* Adelaide: Rigby, 1972.
National Trust of Queensland Journal, April 1977.
Reports of the Cambridge Anthropological Expedition to Torres Strait.
Reynolds, H. *Aborigines and Settlers* Melbourne: Cassell, 1972.
Roberts, J., ed. *The Mapoon Story by the Mapoon People.* International
    Development Action, 1975.
Royal Historical Society of Queensland Journal, December 1949.
Walker, D., ed. *Bridge and Barrier.*

3. *The Coming of the Light*

Bayton, J. *Cross Over Carpentaria.*
Douglas, J. *Past and Present of Thursday Island and Torres Strait.*
Haddon, A. *Head Hunters: Black, White and Brown.*
Holthouse, H. *Cannibal Cargoes* Adelaide: Rigby, 1969.
"Lectures in North Queensland History".
Reports of the Cambridge Anthropological Expedition to Torres Strait.

4. The New Guinea Coast

Bayton, J. *Cross Over Carpentaria.*
Biskup, P., Jinks, B., and Nelson, H. *A Short History of New Guinea.* Sydney: Angus and Robertson, 1968.
Cilento, Sir Raphael, and Lack, Clem. *Triumph in the Tropics.* Brisbane: Smith and Paterson, 1959.
Feekin, E. and G., and Spate, O. *The Discovery and Exploration of Australia.*
Haddon, A. *Head Hunters: Black, White and Brown.*
Hides, J. *Papuan Wonderland.* Glasgow: Blackie and Sons, 1936.
Hudson, W.J., ed. *Australia and New Guinea.* Sydney University Press, 1971.
Jinks B., Biskup, P., and Nelson, H., eds. *Readings in New Guinea History.*
Jukes, J.B. *Narrative of the Surveying Voyage of the H.M.S. Fly.*
Lett, L. *Sir Hubert Murray of Papua.* Collins, 1949.
Pearl, C. *Morrison of Peking.* Sydney: Angus and Robertson, 1967.
Reports of the Cambridge Anthropological Expedition to Torres Strait.
Souter, G. *New Guinea: The Last Unknown.*
Williams, R.E. *Papuans of the Trans-Fly.*
World Review, University of Queensland Press, March 1974.

5. Thursday Island: The Beginning

Australia: The First Hundred Years. (Facsimile.) Sydney: Ure Smith, 1974.
Bayton, J. *Cross Over Carpentaria.*
Burchill, E. *Thursday Island Nurse.* Adelaide: Rigby, 1972.
Cilento, Sir Raphael, and Lack, Clem. *Triumph in the Tropics.*
Cummins and Campbell's Monthly Magazine, November 1952.
Douglas, J. *Past and Present of Thursday Island and Torres Strait.*
Farnfield, J. *Frontiersman.*
Haddon, A. *Head Hunters: Black, White and Brown.*
National Trust of Queensland Journal, April 1977.
Queensand Geographical Journal, 40-41st Sessions, 1924-26.
Pearl, C. *Morrison of Peking.*
Royal Historical Society of Queensland Journal, December 1949.

6. Government Control

Bayton, J. *Cross Over Carpentaria.*
Bolton, G.C. *A Thousand Miles Away.* Canberra: Australian National University Press, 1972.
The Geographical Magazine, January 1940.
Holthouse, H. *Cannibal Cargoes.*
Jones, D. *Hurricane Lamps and Blue Umbrellas.* Cairns: G.K. Bolton, 1973.
"Lectures in Nort Queensland History".
Long, J.P.M. *Aboriginal Settlements.* Canberra: Australian National University Press, 1970.
Pearl, C. *Morrison of Peking.*
Reports of the Cambridge Anthropological Expedition to Torres Strait.
Reynolds, H. *Aborigines and Settlers.*

Stevens, F.S., ed. *Racism: The Australian Experience,* Vol. 2. Sydney: Australia and New Zealand Book Company, 1972.
Thomas, J. *Jubilee of Thursday Island.* 1927.

7. *World War II*

Bamaga High School Magazine, 1974.
Gwynn-Jones, T. *True Australian Air Stories.* Adelaide: Rigby, 1977.
Lockwood, D. *Australia's Pearl Harbour.* Adelaide: Rigby, 1973.
Marshall, A. *These Were my Tribesmen.*

8. *The Border Problem*

Australian Foreign Affairs Record, Dept. of Foreign Affairs. Vol. 47, no. 9, September 1976; and vol. 48, no. 2, February 1977.
Bennett, I. *The Great Barrier Reef.* Melbourne: Lansdowne, 1971.
Jinks, B., Biskup, P., and Nelson, H., eds. *Readings in New Guinea History.*
Nelson, H. *Papua New Guinea: Black Unity or Black Chaos.* Penguin, 1972.
New Guinea and Australia, the Pacific and South-East Asia, Quarterly. Vol. 8, April 1973.
World Review, March 1974.

9. *The Sea*

Australia: The First Hundred Years.
Lawrie, M. *Myths and Legends of Torres Strait.*
Reports of the Cambridge Anthropological Expedition to Torres Strait.
Willey, K. *Crocodile Hunt.* Brisbane: Jacaranda Press, 1966.

10. *Magic and Death*

Reports of the Cambridge Anthropological Expedition to Torres Strait.
Walker, D. *Bridge and Barrier.*

11. *Pearling*

Bayton, J. *Cross Over Carpentaria.*
Burchill, E. *Thursday Island Nurse.*
Cilento, Sir Raphael, and Lack, Clem. *Triumph in the Tropics.*
Coppleson, V. *Killer Sharks.* Sydney: Angus and Robertson, 1968.
Hall, V. *Outback Policeman.* Adelaide: Rigby, 1970.
Holthouse, H. *Cyclone.* Adelaide: Rigby, 1971.
Idriess, I. *Coral Sea Calling.*
Marshall, A. *These Were My Tribesmen.*

Pearl, C. *Morrison of Peking.*
Queensland Heritage. Vol. 2 no. 10, May 1974.
Roughley, T.C. *Fish and Fisheries of Australia.* Sydney: Angus and Robertson, 1951.
───── *Wonders of the Great Barrier Reef.* Sydney: Angus and Robertson, 1936.
Royal Historical Society of Queensland Journal, December 1949.
Thomson, J. *Jubilee of Thursday Island.*
The Torres Strait Islanders. Australian National University Press, 1974.
Walkabout. Vol. 23, October 1957.

12. *Portrait of Three Islands*

Bateson, C. *Australian Shipwrecks, vol. 1. 1622-1850.*
Bayton, J. *Cross Over Carpentaria.*
Blainey, G. *Triumph of the Nomads.*
Brierly, O.W. "Journals of the H.M.S. Rattlesnake 1848-49".
Burchill, E. *Thursday Island Nurse.*
Dunbabin, T. *Sailing the World's Edge.*
Gill, W. Wyatt. "Three Visits to New Guinea".
Lawrie, M. *Myths and Legends of Torres Strait.*
MacGillivray, J. *Narrative of the Voyage of the H.M.S. Rattlesnake.* London: Boone, 1852.
Reports of the Cambridge Anthropological Expedition to Torres Strait.
Royal Historical Society Society of Queensland Journal, December 1949.
Walkabout, 1 January, 1939.
Walker, D., ed. *Bridge and Barrier.*

13 *Missions and Reserves of Cape York Peninsula*

Bayton, J. *Cross Over Carpentaria.*
Long, J.P.M. *Aboriginal Settlements.*
Marshall, A. *These Were My Tribesmen.*
Roberts, J., ed. *The Mapoon Story by the Mapoon People.*
Stevens, F.S., ed. *Racism: The Australian Experience.*
The Torres Strait Islanders.

14. *Papuans*

Australian Outlook. Australian Institute of International Affairs. Vol. 31, no. 1, April 1977.
B.H.P. Journal, 2.76.
Jinks, B., Biskup, P., and Nelson, H., eds. *Readings in New Guinea History.*
Nelson, H., *Papua New Guinea: Black Unity or Black Chaos.*
Souter, G. *New Guinea: The Last Unknown.*

15. *The Islands Today*

Aboriginal News. Dept. of Aboriginal Affairs. Vol. 2, no. 1, June 1975.
The Torres Strait Islanders.
The Torres Strait Islanders Regulation of 1972. Queensland Government
   Gazette, 2 December 1972.

Glossary

A Guide to words from different language groups, mainly denoted as follows:

(W) — Western Island Language

(E) — Eastern Island Language

(B) — Broken English

adthibuia — the mystical, glowing rock of the Aitthalgal (W)
Aitthalgal — the people of Aitth (W)
Aitthaukadalaugudalgal — the crocodile god people of Aitth (W)
augud — god (W)
Badulgal — the people of Badu (W)
barb — father or uncle (W)
barbuk — to sit cross-legged (E)
beizam — shark (E)
Beizamle — the shark god people (E)
bisi — sago or cassava (W)
boo — trumpet shell (W)
burum — pig (W)
carpu (or *kapu*) — good (W)
Dauanalgal — the people of Dauan (W)
Deaudepat — an extensive valley running the length of Mer (E)
Dthaudthai — mainland New Guinea (W)
Dthaudthalgal — the people of the New Guinea mainland or Papuans (W)
dtheibau — a vine leaf (W)
Dtheibauaugudalgal — the leaf god people (W)
dthungal — dugong (W)

gabba gabbal — war clubs (W)

Gamoolgal — tribal grouping representing the combined peoples of Badu and Mabuiag (W)

gapu — sucker fish (W)

Gudang — Aboriginal tribal grouping near Cape York

Jadhaigana — Aboriginal tribal grouping south of Escape River

kadal — crocodile (W)

Kadalaugudalgal — the crocodile god people (W)

Kauralgal — the original tribal inhabitants of Muralug (W)

Kauwagal — Aborigines (W)

kedi — garland of vine (W)

Keraki — language/ethnic grouping west of the Fly River in P.N.G.

Kiwai — language/ethnic grouping in Fly River delta and extending west to the Binaturi River

kuibarb — big uncle (W)

Kulkalgal — the original tribal inhabitants of Nahgi (W)

kunu — small, black swamp fish (W)

Kupamal — Kiwai Islanders (W)

kussa — river (W)

kusu — coconut-shell water containers (W)

lamar — ghost or whiteman (E)

lava-lava — a calico sheet wrapped around the lower body (B)

lug — place, house, island (W)

maidle — sorcerers (E)

maidthalgal — sorcerers (W)

Malo Bomai — predominant cult of the Torres Strait centred on Mer (E)

marap — a word meaning bamboo at Saibai today (W)

marappi — word for bamboo recorded at Muralug by Brierly in 1849 (W)

marap(pi) soogooba — bamboo tobacco pipe (W)

markai — ghost or whiteman (W)

Meriam (Miriam) — language or person of Mer

meta — house (E)

Moalgal — the original tribal inhabitants of Moa (W)

Muroi-ig — ancient spirit people on Saibai who often assume the form of snakes (W)

Nagilgal — the people of Nahgi (W)

nara — body odour and spirit among Mapoon people

ngookie — water (W)

ngookie marap(pi) — bamboo water containers (W)

num — turtle (E)

oomai — dog (W)

Oomaiaugudalgal — the dog god people (W)

parma — red clay (W)

poud — recorded by Lewis at Mer in 1836 and interpreted as an expression of friendship (E)

pouri pouri — sorcery (B)

powdah — reported by Jacky Jacky in 1848 among Aborigines near

Escape River and interpreted by Kennedy as an expression of friendship

Saibaialgal — the people of Saibai (W)

samu — cassowary (W)

Samuaugudalgal — the cassowary god people (W)

sarzi — fish poison which is dissolved in water (W)

soogooba — tobacco (W)

Suki — a tribal grouping on the lower Fly River

Tjungundji — Aboriginal tribal grouping near Port Musgrave

toolick; or *toree*—a word meaning iron recorded by Lewis at Mer in 1836 (E)

toorick — a word meaning iron at Saibai today (W)

tthabu — snake (W)

Tthabuaugudalgal — the snake god people (W)

Tugeri — language/ethnic grouping west of the Bensback River extending into Irian Jaya

upis — bamboo beheading knife (W)

wakaus — coconut fibre belts (W)

wakasu — coconut oil (W)

waru — turtle (W)

Wera Kauwag — Island Aborigine, specifically the Kauralgal (W)

whap — harpoon for spearing turtle and dugong (W)

yegalli — coconut fibre rope (W)

zogole — priesthood (E)

Zogo meta — holy house (E)

Index